Contact: Cameron Lundgren

info@beautifulbook.us

Print: 979-8-9872699-0-9 eBook: 979-8-218-08548-3

First edition

Cover Design by Books and Moods

Beautiful

A memoir of romance and self-destruction, how one bullet destroyed two lives

Cameron Lundgren

C Lundgren Publishing

For my sons —
There is always light at the end of the tunnel.

Contents

Author's Note

Lots of care went into the validity of the information presented in this memoir. However, in addition to government documents and text conversations, I've also relied on my memories. Any dialogue herein has been recreated as I remember it, and some events have been compressed and some are nonsequential for the sake of the storyline. I recognize that some people's memories and lived experiences of the events described in this book are different from my own. If I've erred anywhere, please forgive me. For reasons related to privacy, all names of real people have been changed, except for Shaina, Glen, Chevy, Jason, and me.

Images and Figures:

- There are supporting images online. These images are located in the Beautiful Memoir Instagram account: https://www.instagram.com/beautiful_memoir/

- Figures referenced within the book can also be found on the Instagram site.

Preface

Suicide leaves loved ones with a heartbreaking, all-consuming question:

Could I have done something different to change the outcome?

The bad memories, the truths never shared, and the unresolved fights plague us. The unanswered questions drive us insane. Suicidal thoughts plant a seed in the earth, growing and stretching and taking hold of us, and those of us left behind. It becomes a suffocating vine that inflicts sadness, hopelessness and emptiness until there seems to be no way out with all hope lost. But I have found, firsthand, that beyond the emptiness there is hope; hope found through love, friendship, family, success, and spirituality. Once we find our hope, we can find peace.

Shaina and I had something special. I like to think we were connected before this lifetime. I also like to think we had a purpose. Maybe it was to tell this story, in the hopes of saving someone who's also considering suicide. I know her purpose was to shed love and shine light onto others, as evidenced by anyone who met her. She was approachable, she was adored, she was bubbly, she was kind. She was loved.

I questioned myself many times while writing this book: what I should leave in, what I should leave out, what I think people would be able to handle. A few friends even asked what Shaina would approve of. I spent many nights on my knees looking for an answer to that question. I feel in my heart she wanted the story told in whole, and in the end, I left it all there — a deep, dark journey of love, depression, drug use, romance, and addiction.

Though this story is about many things, I feel the purpose of this story is to shed a light on suicide, both before and after trauma—the part of life we can't see—don't believe in—while we're in the trenches of pain. It's also the story of a recovering addict learning to rebuild his life after the suicide of his girlfriend whose death he was wrongfully accused of. A death *I* was wrongfully accused of. A trauma I still feel deeply, and a life I'm still rebuilding.

Shaina's and my relationship was filled with so many special moments that I was fortunate enough to capture on camera. While this book includes images of police reports, I compiled personal photos, text conversations, evidence, X- Rays, and additional items related to the chapters and have shared them on an Instagram account specifically for this book.

As you read, please feel free to access the Beautiful Memori Instagram account and follow me @Beautiful_Memoir.

Dial 988, to reach the National Suicide Prevention and Mental Health Crises Hotline. They can help.

Chapter 1

NIGHTMARE

June 25, 2019, 10:04 p.m.

"**W**hat in the hell just happened?"

As I move through the house, cleaning up our taco spread from the party, I'm trying to channel my frustrations from our fight into productive energy.

As I pass by the front office window, I see Claire and Avery, two of Shaina's girlfriends, sitting in Avery's car seemingly listening to music in my driveway. My stomach flips at the sight of Claire, thinking this woman must have a thing for me. *Is she trying to break us up?* as I recall the earth shattering news she had let slip to me only moments earlier. I was happy she was out of my house. I inhale, trying to calm my rising anger. I just have to talk to Shaina, sort this out.

Padding up the stairs to the master bedroom, I know this conversation won't go over well; every cell in my body wants to believe Claire's news isn't true, to pretend everything is okay so Shaina and I can kiss and make up. Besides, I screwed up tonight, too, by opening my big mouth, what a shit show we were tonight. I'm desperate to put the night behind us.

As I turn the knob on the bedroom door, I find that it's locked.

Well, that's a new one. She's never locked herself in the bedroom before. "Shaina, you can't lock me out of my own house—I'll call the cops!" I scream as I bang my fist against the door. Silence. As if I was the only one home; strange I wondered.

I wait a few moments, then head down to the attached garage to grab a small screwdriver, one I've used several times to fix broken screens on my mobile phones or to jab the keyholes of the finicky doors that would often lock me out of my old house. The screwdriver was just small enough to poke its way through the small hole to unlock a door—the problem is, this is a new house. I recently sold my home in Cedar Hills at Shaina's suggestion because she didn't feel my former one was "ours" since I had lived there with my ex of twelve years.

My anger brewing, I rush back—stumbling every few steps from the liquor—I approach the master bedroom door, screwdriver in hand. My fist pounds on the door once more. "Shaina, open the door or I'm going to call the cops!"

More silence.

I cram the tool into the keyhole, and to my disappointment, the rod isn't long enough to reach the mechanism that unlocks the door. Frustrated, drunk, and tired, without a shred of energy left for all this nonsense, I decide to give up momentarily and move to the adjacent bathroom in the hallway. Throwing the tool on the sink counter in frustration on my way to the toilet, I unzip my pants en route, getting ready to pee. My head jerks up when I hear the bedroom door finally open.

Shaina walks over to stand just outside of the bathroom door and faces me. I move my lips to speak, but my heart drops when my eyes flicker to the nickel-plated CZ 9mm handgun in her right hand, raising it to her head.

"Shaina, NO—" My plea is cut short by the jolting sound of the gun firing. Any trace of emotion on her face, any hint as to why she pulled the trigger, disappears as she drops to the ground landing on her back, legs crippling as every muscle in her body gives out.

Two seconds feels like a lifetime.

Am I hallucinating? This is supposed to be the moment where I wake up in a pool of sweat with Shaina lying next to me, beautifully sound asleep, her head propped on my chest. *It was just a nightmare,* I'm supposed to say. But something quickly shakes me back to the present moment—there's something dripping down my leg. I frantically pull up my shorts, soaking them with urine in the process and scramble for my phone in my back pocket.

Why am I struggling to remember my password? With shaky hands, I dial.

"911, what's your emergency?"

My head is spinning. I feel sick. "My girlfriend just shot herself in the head."

I hear the words come out of my mouth, but it doesn't sound like my voice. My thoughts are all jumbled and all I can think about is wanting to reverse time, to take back our fight that night, to hold her and kiss her forehead and tell her life will be okay.

"Is she breathing?" The emergency responder's voice snaps me back to the reality surrounding me and my adrenaline kicks into gear. I can still save her.

As I kneel over Shaina, I check for any signs of life. Blood is gushing out of her head, while a slow drool of blood leaks out the corner of her mouth. "No, she's no—" in that same instant Shaina gasps, blood gushing out of her mouth and she begins choking on it.

"Where is she bleeding?"

"Blood is . . . everywhere," I hear myself saying, "it's coming out the sides of her head and her mouth."

The responder calmly asks, "Sir, do you have a piece of cloth nearby?"

Confused and frantic, I search the bloodstained carpet, whipping my head around in a frenzy, looking for something, *anything,* until I realize, and say, "I can use my shirt."

"Can you wrap it around her head to stop the bleeding?"

But I'm already ahead of her, carefully wrapping my shirt around Shaina's head. "Shaina, stay with me, baby. If you can hear me, please stay with me, Beautiful," I plead over and over and over . . .

"Sir, I need you to stay with me." The responder knows she's losing me to panic, I can tell by the strain in her voice. "I need you to perform CPR with me on my count of one, two, three, and four."

Fuck. What? Count how many times? "Do you mean compressions on four?" I ask, hysteria rising in my voice and clouding my judgment.

"No—compressions on each count," she clarifies.

I'm begging my brain to focus. "Okay, I'm ready." The responder begins her count. I begin pushing into Shaina's chest, hoping she can hear my pleas. "Please, baby, stay with me . . ." I quietly muster.

With every compression, more blood gushes out of her mouth and she again starts to choke it up, her body convulsing on my hallway floor. I'm not sure if she's fighting to stay alive, or if I'm keeping her alive with the compressions. Her gagging makes my stomach lurch forward and I scream into the phone, "Where is the ambulance? She's dying!"

"They're on their way, sir, I need you to keep doing CPR." Her voice is calm, and I know she's trying to keep *me* calm. She sounds like a drill sergeant barking orders at me. Levelheaded. The voice of someone whose girlfriend isn't gurgling blood. "Sir," she presses, "is the front door unlocked?"

My heart drops. I have a compulsive habit of checking the doors every night to make sure they're locked; tonight was no different. Of course, the door isn't unlocked.

"No, the front door is locked."

"I need you to go unlock the door so the paramedics can get in."

It feels physically painful to leave Shaina lying here, but I lay down the phone and jump down both sets of stairs in my two-level home, skipping as many steps as I can. I unlock the door then jump just as quickly back up the two flights of stairs to get back to Shaina. I pick up my phone to let the responder know the door is open, then lay it back down on the ground and put it on speaker phone.

"I'm ready to start again," I bark, counting out loud now without any help from the responder. "One, two, three, four and one, two, three, four and one, two, three—where is the ambulance!" I scream as tears begin to well up. "Where is the fucking ambulance!" my voice croaks, but I continue the chest compressions. The responder doesn't answer my question, but instead continues to count with me.

With each passing moment I'm beginning to lose hope, and I'm breaking quickly. Then I cry. "Why, Shaina, why would you do this? Why? Why? Why? Why?" I'm wailing into oblivion. "Why. Why. Why. Why?"

The robotic responder once again interrupts my spiraling thoughts. "Sir, I need you to stay with me."

I hear the door open downstairs. "Police!" A man's voice booms inside the house. "May we come up?"

"I'm upstairs! Please come, she needs help now!" I squawk.

When they reach the top of the stairs, I collapse into a pile on the floor. Shaina is still gasping and choking on her own blood. I can barely see through blurry eyes. I beg the cops, "Please save her, we were supposed to get married . . ." as I continue bawling my eyes out. "God, take me—take me, not her. Let her live, please. You can take me, but not her. Please, God, I beg you . . ."

Two officers offer me their hands to help me up from the floor as I continue to plead and sob. "Sir, we understand you called this in as a suicide," one of them says, "but someone has been shot so we need to take you into custody."

My mind is numb and overwhelmed at once. "I understand," I say weakly. I cooperate and comply. Just as I turn and place my hands behind my back, the paramedics shuffle up the stairs and take over. Shaina's head is lying in a pool of blood, still shaking and choking, her body reaching for every breath. But I can see she is no longer here. Not aware of the officers, the paramedics. Me. I watched her soul leave her body the instant the gun went off; life left her body as if an angel had swooped down to save her from the pain of the bullet.

I pray silently. I beg for God to save her. Take me, but save her . . . please, she had so much more life to live.

As I'm led outside, I again see Claire and Avery, who strangely still had not left my house. My stomach flips again remembering the secret Claire had shared with me earlier. Cops surround the two girls next to their vehicle, conversing with other officers in muffled tones I can't comprehend. Their attention quickly focuses on me; they stare as I'm guided to the police car. Not even an hour ago, Shaina and I had just got in a fight in front of everyone. The reality of the cold metal cuffs around my wrists fills me with dread.

They're going to think I killed her.

There are supplemental images online.
"Read Me First" https://www.instagram.com/stories/highlights/182
99751898039364/

Chapter 2

MIRROR LAKE

BEFORE THE NIGHTMARE – AUGUST 2018

One early Wednesday morning, I was cleaning my basement when my phone buzzed. A new notification displayed "You have a message on Plenty of Fish." Cringing at what new broken harlot I'm about to talk to and fighting the thousands of men likely flooding her inbox, my instinct was to continue sweeping when suspiciously I clicked the notification.

I had sworn off the app at least three times in the three years since my divorce. At the time, though, I considered Plenty of Fish to be the least serious app—the one where you'd find a girl most likely to be your rebound, and she'd be happy to wear that title. Normally I would swipe the notification away, but in the middle of my work-from-home day, I was hungry for the distraction.

My prototypical woman appeared before my eyes: long black hair, athletic build, beautiful smile, and eyes that could kill. But what had me was her legs. I gaped at her picture for a few seconds before returning her message. Suddenly, my day had just perked up.

Initially, I complimented her legs—I'm a leg man, admittedly. We flirted and messaged for hours. It got so bad that I quit working in my basement and ended up in my bedroom, pacing back and forth with my hands glued to my phone, asking her question after question. This woman had me hooked. I wanted to know *everything* about her. It seemed we had so much in common, and she admitted she loved older men. Point for Cameron.

In my former relationships, my confidence was seen as a negative quality. I'm not sure if my past partners were insecure of how social or easygoing I was—I'm sure part of my confidence was seen as arrogance, as much as I'd hate to admit it—but whatever it was, Shaina seemed to welcome it rather than perceive it as a threat. My ego was on fire.

After a couple frustrating attempts at meeting up I was near being over this woman, but the hunter inside of me wanted that next step. We were still in contact, I told myself. Maybe the third time would be the charm. She hit me with a fresh text.

> **Shaina:** Hey, I'm going camping at Mirror Lake this weekend with my family, would love it if you came. We'll be leaving soon.

I was in it now, no questions asked. She was playing the long game and my ego needed to succeed. I had to finally meet her. Based on her pictures, she was the most beautiful woman I'd ever seen—driving a few more hours to meet her wasn't the end of the world.

> **Cameron:** Are there camping spots to rent? Can I bring my trailer?

Shaina: No, but we have two spots. You can park your truck across from our campsite and sleep in the bed of your truck.

Without thinking, I called into work and explained I was taking the weekend early and would not be in. I went straight home, packed my camping gear and headed out, before remembering to ask:

Cameron: What are you guys driving?
Shaina: Gray Dodge gasser and a white trailer.

During the two-and-a-half-hour drive, I could not think of anything but her, so I tried, to no avail, to preoccupy myself with music. She had manipulated me to become the ultimate challenge and I wanted to see her so badly. When I pulled into the campground, I discovered there was no service, and I was happy I had asked what car to look for. We were way up in the High Uintas Wilderness; I might have been living as a city boy, but I was raised by a cowboy who loved the mountains. I knew better than to drive to that elevation and not ask questions first.

Though my family grew up in the suburbs of Utah, our home had been approved to house horses, and we had anywhere from three to six of them at any point during my childhood. Cats and dogs roamed our property, too. Dad taught me hard work through pulling weeds and tiling the garden, cleaning up after the horses and pets and mowing the lawn. My favorite family pastime, though, was camping in the mountains. I felt right at home here, about to meet the world's most stunning woman.

I drove through campground after campground—I must have circled the three loops twice each. Shaking my head, I muttered, "If this woman ghosts me one more time, I might lose my shit up here."

Finally, coming to a turnoff I had missed earlier, I drove slowly drove down to be greeted by a half-ton Dodge in front of a white trailer. I pulled in my newly washed GMC Denali and parked out front, but no one was around.

I decided to go knock on the camper door. Someone was stumbling around inside, and it took a minute for them to come to the door. Then my heart nearly stopped when the door creaked open.

"Wow." She beamed, eyes wide and giving a playful smirk. "I didn't think you'd come."

In front of me stood a woman stripped to her natural beauty: no makeup on, no high heels, yet still five foot nine (compared to my six foot one), no short skirt and no low-cut shirt revealing any cleavage. If my jaw was capable of disconnecting, it would have dropped to the ground. To my gratification, she had on Daisy Duke shorts that showcased her sexy legs and a black tank top, hair slightly messy. She was a vision.

I caught myself staring and then stumbled to speak. "My God, I didn't expect someone so beautiful . . . glad I made the trip." She laughed and turned a little pink.

"Funny you should say that. That's my name."

"I couldn't agree more," I said, nearly drooling.

"No, I mean my name is Shaina, but in Hebrew it means *beautiful.*"

"Well, your parents must've known you were going to be gorgeous." She blushed again. I tried to get my bearings. "Have you fished yet?" I asked.

"Have not." She was eyeing me with a look that said she was testing my patience, like she was trying to keep my confidence in check despite the perverted schoolboy bubbling to the top.

"Well," I said, "get your boots on, I'll grab the gear and beer."

We packed two poles with gear and a cooler full of Coronas, then headed out to the water through some small trees, avoiding people as we walked. We set up quickly at a secluded spot on the shore and made small talk while casting our lines. I was happy to finally get some face time with this woman; The more I looked at her, the more I had to resist kissing her sexy face. I could tell she was happy to meet me finally, too, and I could tell she was into me. I was feeling, *the tables had turned, I was in control now, I knew I had her.* I couldn't help myself when I walked right up to her, put both hands around her neck and pulled her in for a kiss.

Not just a kiss though. I wanted to make it a *real* kiss, to make sure I would want to kiss that mouth forever. And I was right; in that moment our kiss felt like a lifetime. "Sorry, Beautiful, I couldn't resist." I was enjoying teasing her, watching her grin as we pulled apart.

"I'm glad you did," she said, smiling up at me before pulling me back in for another kiss. Suddenly, a pole dropped, pulling our attention from each other's lips.

"We have something!" I exclaimed. "You want to do the honors and reel it in?" I handed the pole to her. She reeled it in about halfway until the fish got loose, disappearing back into the water. I quickly lost interest in fishing—I wanted to reel Shaina in. We ditched our poles and gear and went on a walk around the lake. It was quiet, romantic. I grabbed her hand and she quietly giggled.

She asked, "You're not scared of anything, are you?"

"Could be a little scared of how much I like you." I admitted as much, giving a cheeky shrug.

She turned to me. I was taken aback by her flirtatious smile. "Why's that?"

"I'm not sure I've seen a more breathtaking woman in my life." Seeing that blush in her face again made my heart flutter. We continued talking while we slowly traipsed around the lake, acting like two children in love, like we had known each other for ages. When I saw someone approach us, I stopped them and asked if they would take our picture with the lake behind us.

Just then we watched a beautiful purple and turquoise butterfly float down onto her shoulder as it perched elegantly holding its wings wide.

"Ouch!" Shaina screamed. "It bit me!" swatting it away.

"I didn't know butterflies could bite?" I exclaimed, confused as well.

"Me neither." I grabbed her hand, and we continued down the trail.

By the time we got back to camp, it was time for dinner. I knew I had to impress her parents, so I prepared chicken and beef fajitas using the grill in my truck. The night passed quickly as we hung around the fire, drinking. I could tell Shaina's mom was wary of me, holding back a little from the conversation. Shaina had told me she'd recently left an abusive relationship, and her mom felt she was moving on too quickly. I think she wanted her daughter to be on her own—be strong on her own—before jumping to the next guy. Her sister, brother-in-law, and stepdad welcomed me, though, and we stayed up laughing and chatting until her mom called it a night.

As her mother got up to go to bed, her stepdad following suit, she asked, "Shaina, where are you sleeping?"

Without missing a beat, she replied, "With Cameron."

Now it was my turn to blush. "Uh, no that's really not necessary, I'll sleep alone." I quickly responded, my eyes darting between Shaina and her mom.

"Shaina, you should sleep in our trailer," she snipped.

Shaina snipped back. "Mom, I'm a grown-ass woman. I can sleep with whoever I want." Then she shot me a devilish smile, and I tried not to grin. With her parents defeated, her mom shot me a look as if to say, "You're being watched." She turned and walked into the trailer.

I couldn't help but be impressed, and I certainly couldn't deny my excitement. "Well," I said, "I guess we should make where we lie tonight. Under the stars?"

"Can't wait," she said, and grabbed my hand to pull me out of my chair.

I moved my truck to the adjacent campsite, which ended up working out because it incidentally left us some alone time. Without my trailer, I had packed my cab with as much as I could to make my truck bed comfortable enough to sleep in: an airbed, five pillows, a foam topper, and enough blankets to keep an army warm. The only thing I forgot to pack was liquor. I suggested to Shaina we sneak back to her parents' site to take a few more shots of their Fireball, and we quietly ran over there like two mischievous kids in the dark.

After a couple quick swigs from the bottle, we made it back to my truck. I pulled down the tailgate. As I turned to Shaina, she stared at me with greedy eyes like a cobra ready to strike. Holding her hands behind her back, she tilted her hips toward me. Then in an instant, she sprung at me, jumping slightly to my height, and pecked me on the lips.

The rush it gave me, despite only a day together, began to give me hope she was the one. She stayed close to my face, looking up at me. "I like you, Cameron." I grabbed her hips and lifted her onto the tailgate.

"Be careful, Beautiful, I might love you." Leaning forward, we pressed into each other and made out like a scene from *The Young and the Restless.*

That night, we did not sleep. We must have talked, laughed, and had sex, and then talked, laughed, and had sex again and again until daylight came. It felt so right and so natural, even if it was too soon. At one point, we overheard a woman in a tent at the next site over say, "Sure wish you'd still do that to me." Shaina and I belly laughed until we finally found sleep.

Chapter 3

CONCRETE WALLS

AFTER THE NIGHTMARE – June 25, 2019, 10:49 p.m.

I was placed in the back of a cop car, trying to understand what the hell was happening, trying to hold on to my emotions, wishing I could reach far enough back and rewind time just an hour back so I could bring her back. The scene kept replaying in my head like an old movie: Shaina outside the bedroom door, her hand moving to her head, the scream coming out of my mouth . . .

I caught a glimpse of Claire and Avery being escorted to the back seats of different police cars likely due to drinking and driving, each of us being detained, it seemed, while the cops worked out the scene. And then I caught a glimpse of long dark hair, hanging off the side of a stretcher. Shaina was being lifted into an ambulance I caught a glimpse of hope, maybe she'll be saved

I sat there for four hours, having gone over my statement a few times with an officer. He was bald and overweight, and I think he was looking at me with . . . pity in his eyes? He read me my Miranda rights, then said something about conflicting reports on the direction of the bullet, but I barely registered his sentence through the fog in my brain. Then he left.

Conflicting reports? What was he implying?

By then, the tears had run dry; I was left with nothing but an overwhelming void of sadness. Thinking back to that scene, my body tried to muster up more tears, my body searching for something wet to fill the pain, but all I could do was choke on emptiness. The ambulance had driven off over two hours ago. What was I waiting there for? I slunk down in my seat and laid my head back, hoping I could wake up from this nightmare.

Maybe I was dreaming . . . maybe, it was actually six in the morning; Maybe I was fast asleep having the worst dream of my life. I'd wake up, turn on the coffee pot and make Shaina's iced coffee in my best Starbucks barista attempt, then I'd start her car, so the engine is warm since she's leaving early this morning and—

A knock on the police car window pulled me from my fantasy. The officer opened the door, the same one who cuffed me and took my statement, and sat in the driver's seat, pivoting his body to face me.

"Please tell me she's alive, tell me she's okay," I pleaded.

"She's alive, but"—he paused as if choosing his next words carefully—"it doesn't look good." His voice sounded sympathetic. My body somehow managed to find more tears, and I felt as though they'd soaked the seat beneath me.

The officer cleared his throat. "Can you tell me the direction the gun went off?"

"She put the gun to her head and pulled the trigger." I was trying to stay calm, but I didn't like the direction this was headed. "What are you asking me?"

"There's some confusion on the direction of the bullet. What was the direction of the gunshot?"

My brow furrowed. "She used her right hand, so right to left. How could it be anything else?"

The officer remained calm, like the emergency responder on the phone. How was everyone so calm? "We're being told the direction of the bullet was back to front, and right to left."

Still confused, wrapping my brain around the news, I probed. "Like . . . on an angle?" I considered the question. Shaina could have held the gun at an angle, I had no idea. It had all happened so quickly. "I guess it's possible it could have gone off on a slight angle."

There was a long, painful pause, as if the earth stood still. Surely this was a dream; was the officer saying what I think he was saying?

Without flinching, the officer announced, "We're going to take you down to the station for questioning."

Everything became too real all too quickly. The buckets of tears and emotions now faded; I went into survival mode. As we drove to the police station, I was in total disbelief—from Shaina's body lying bloodied on the floor, to being carted away to jail like a guilty man. *How did a night take such a drastic change for the worst*, I thought. I decided to calm myself down by talking to the officers. They all seemed somber, like they believed my statement but had to follow protocol due to this lie about the bullet trajectory, wherever that story came from.

"Suicide had to have been tough to witness. We see a lot of that in law enforcement," one of them said. They asked me repeatedly whether my handcuffs were too tight, or if I was comfortable. They didn't treat me like a murderer; they treated me like I had just lost someone I loved. In kind, I was never disrespectful or rude—my father had taught me better, no matter how I was treated. Dad was an old-fashioned cowboy with good character and values. He's the reason I address people as "yes, ma'am" and "yes, sir" to this day. This was going to clear up soon enough anyway, and I'd be able to go home. I nearly gagged at the thought. Home without Shaina. My mind flashed to my upstairs floor, which was now a crime scene, soaked in blood.

When we reached the station, I was placed in a four-by-six room, sitting in what felt like a desk from elementary school, my hands cuffed to the top of the desk. It was close to four in the morning, and I was drained, steeped in shock. I sat there for one hour, maybe two—time was hard to gauge; I could still feel the liquor through my veins from the party.

A few times I almost nodded off, but the hard, cold table would bounce my head back up each time. A new officer came into the room to interrogate me, followed by another man I hadn't seen yet. Robert, I learned—the lead detective on the case. He wore a hat, was tall and looked like he'd just returned from a far-off country fighting war. He looked at me like he was trying to ascertain my guilt.

"We've been informed Shaina has died from her injuries," Robert said. "We would like to hear your story one more time."

The news that Shaina had died wasn't exactly surprising given how everyone had been talking to me, but it didn't make the sting any less painful.

"I want to speak to an attorney," I said. I had seen enough crime shows to know when to ask for a lawyer, and this was definitely one of those times. Now I was fighting for my innocence and had Rambo in check for the time being.

Placed in the holding tank shortly after, my mind racing, I decided I needed to call someone, let them know what happened and where I was. In the tank, there was a red corded phone surrounded by colorful characters all loitering around waiting to make calls. Whose number do I know? Who can I call? It had been easy to remember numbers when I was younger, before I solely relied on my cell phone. Plus, I had learned from my previous stay in jail over a decade prior that not all cell phones are set up to receive calls from jail—and you can't even leave a voice mail. Of course, my mom's phone kept going to voice mail. I dialed my friend and coworker Carter's number; to my surprise, he answered.

Half-asleep he greeted me. "Hello?"

"Carter, it's Cameron. You're not going to believe what happened last night, but I'm in jail . . . Shaina killed herself."

"What did you just say?" That jolted him, sounding much more awake.

I started to choke on my words. "Yeah, man . . . I guess somehow they think I did it. Listen, man, I won't be in to work this morning, but I need you to cover for me. I'll be in tomorrow." I hung up oblivious to the seriousness of what was happening.

Someone was confused. I'd be released on a misunderstanding before I'd be booked in. Life would go on tomorrow…life without Shaina, but at least I'd be able to properly begin to grieve. I'd see my family and her family, and we'd all lean on each other. I desperately needed to be near someone who knew Shaina, to talk about what had happened; for someone to tell me it was real.

A few hours went by, and breakfast came at six o'clock: grits, toast, an orange, and box milk, but I couldn't eat a thing. I couldn't even look at it without wanting to throw up. Nine hours had elapsed since Shaina shot herself. I walked back to the concrete cell corner, the concrete walls closing in suffocating me, and laid down, wishing I could just go to sleep. An old homeless woman next to me was talking to herself when three young kids, probably in their early twenties, were checked in, laughing loudly about how they ran from the cops while on acid. I laid there for hours on the concrete shelf; it felt as if the concrete was bone on bone. And then, despite everything I had believed, and despite everything that was true, I wasn't released.

They booked me.

I had done it before, in my hell raising early twenties, but it didn't make it any less degrading. After removing my clothes, bending over as the officer put on his plastic gloves, I was sprayed with hot water for what I could only assume was for sanitization purposes. Changing into my orange pants and top, I was given some pillow as thin as a laptop, which wasn't nearly adequate, sheets, and some hygiene supplies. I was then led to a pod with six other men, each of them with their head held low like they were walking to their death. All the other cellmates quickly came to their windows and stared with cold eyes to size up their new companions as we marched past, like we were the cold steak on the grill with hungry eyes.

I learned our pod was on lockdown for another day because a fight had broken out the day before. Our pod had a main area with a few rickety picnic tables etched with chess boards and some plastic-lined couches. Outside the main room, six to twelve men at any given time would pace around, talking, trying to pass the time. Then there was a concrete cube for exercising—maybe forty by forty feet—where inmates could be checked in or out like sheep led into a new pasture. The walls were lined with two levels of about fifteen cells, each holding two people. My first night in jail, my cellmate and I talked for hours. He was a nerdy-looking guy sporting a bowl cut, but his speech indicated that he had grown up on the streets. I poured my heart out to him and told him everything about the night before.

"Whatever you do, don't speak a word of this to anyone," he said. "You're in here for some things that, if you're not careful, most of these guys will use to get out. They'll become lying informants to their benefit." I didn't say another word terrified I'd be used as a pawn in their game.

There was a TV in the main area, and I expected to see my face on the news, but there was a bigger murder story that overshadowed Shaina's death—some guy killed a girl at the local University of Utah and burned her body in a trash can. After hearing my cellmate's warning, I was lucky none of the other inmates would see my face flashing on TV. My mother told me in a call, "that was your saving grace."

Utah jail is not like the jail shows you watch set in Chicago; it was neither scary nor was it comfortable. In Utah, a suspect brought into county jail can only be held for seventy-two hours for questioning; then, the prosecutor managing the case must decide whether to press charges. What I hadn't realized is that in rare instances, the Salt Lake County Attorney's Office can request an extension on the seventy-two-hour hold. I guess I was one of the unfortunate rare instances.

Every time we were let out of our pods, I would run to the PO—patrolling officer—station and ask an officer, "Have they set bail?" But the response was always the same.

"They have not officially charged you yet. It still shows 'discharge of a weapon in the direction of a person,' but no formal charges." Those words sank deep and hit hard. All I wanted was freedom to make this right.

Four days and nights had gone by. My biggest worry became missing Shaina's funeral. She'd told me repeatedly that one of her deepest fears was that no one would show up to her funeral, and I would always reassure her she was loved. I was in total denial of what was going on outside those concrete walls; I just waited for them to call my name.

"Lundgren, pack your stuff." I begged in my mind.

But it never came.

Two years prior to all this happening, I had been married for thirteen years. For ten of those years, I had worked in payroll sales, a job I never should have had after fighting past a felony of drug possession early in my twenties. The position had been set up by a friend through my wife's and my church.

I remember the day I was hired. Because I had previous experience in phone sales from my early twenties—a job I had making six figures a year by the age of twenty-one before my felony—they had offered me a salary plus commission position. A week went by after the interview, and I'd thought I was in the clear. I had been stringing together odd jobs paying below minimum wage for the year I was clean following my short stint in jail. Finally, I would land a job—a real job, making real money—and help provide for my family.

Then the bomb came. The owner of this small family-run business came to me and said, "Cameron, we need you to get a urine test, and we're going to pull a background check." And with that, all my hopes were dashed. I remember going home that night to my wife, my head held low, telling her the news—that I had failed, that I was a loser, every man's worst nightmare. I created a scenario where we'd moved out of Utah to a poverty-stricken area of Albuquerque, New Mexico, and share an old Tahoe, live off ramen and rice, barely making ends meet. If it had not been for my father-in-law's generous financial assistance, we would have been on the streets.

I got on my knees that night and begged God to soften the owner's heart and to give me a chance, but I knew I needed to be proactive. By the grace of God, this opportunity had landed in my lap. I wasn't going to let it get away that easily. That next day, I called the owner and asked if I could talk to him; he agreed. When in his office, I almost chickened out. The owner was older—probably in his mid-fifties—and had the persona of a "no nonsense" guy, straight out of *The Godfather*. I was sure he'd laugh me out of his office.

I went for it, after all, I had nothing to lose. "When you pull my background check, you're going to find some bad things. But I want you to know I'm not a bad person, and if you give me a chance, you won't regret it."

I worked for that company for five years and fought my way to the top in the career chain. The income from my job doubled, and with my wife's job as a paralegal, our incomes generated enough money to more than support our family. I felt I had finally made it.

During my marriage, my wife and I lived a Christian life, going to church every Sunday. I had married at twenty-six, my wild early twenties a thing of the past. My father-in-law would often tell me that if we kept God in our hearts and in our lives, we were a cord of three strands that could not be broken—a quote from the Bible. My wife and I bought a house, and my wife got pregnant—we had no choice but to grow up. Then came our second kid, and family life overruled everything.

My oldest son had been the sweetest boy, and I would often question how he came from me, even though he was my spitting image. I hadn't possessed his sweetness at that age; in fact, I'd been somewhat of a terror.

One of our favorite hangouts was the local arcade. Every ticket he would win, he would smile and pass it to his little brother so he could have any prize he wanted. I remember thinking, I would have never in my life done that as a child for my brothers. It had been feast-or-famine during my childhood.

Our youngest son, however, was much wilder—much more like me. When he was a baby just learning to crawl, my wife and I had woken to find him outside of his crib, in the kitchen with the dishwasher door open, playing with the cleaned knives. He was the daredevil to our eldest's more cautious personality.

I remember the day we learned of his diagnosis. Leading up to that day, my wife and I had known something was different with him. He was fearless no doubt when I caught him in the clean dishwasher playing with knives early in the morning before anyone woke up, a story that will never get old.

By the age of three, he was mostly nonverbal, and taking him to the store or anywhere in public was chaos. He would kick and fight like he wanted to rip our heads off, refusing to get into his toddler seat. By the time we'd manage to get him settled in the car, my wife and I would fight like cats and dogs due to the frustration. We would take him to the local carnival, and he would not understand the concept of a line, kicking and screaming because he just wanted to go on the ride — now —as if he were the only one waiting. As young parents without the tools or research we'd needed, we couldn't help but feel embarrassed.

And then he was diagnosed with Autism. I didn't know much about Autism, and my thoughts swirled with the worries that most parents have when they're told their child is neurodivergent. I remember the day I was told, I sobbed like my son had died. I was worried he'd never find love, or a career, or live a normal life. But we learned quickly through our daredevil that nothing could be further from the truth.

My wife and I eventually fell out of love. That, or I just couldn't be the partner she needed anymore. I had thrown myself into my career and the sales life was mentally exhausting; all my emotional energy was spent at work, and when I'd come home at night, I had little left for her. Toward the end of our marriage, I envied my single friends and yearned for the party life again, to have little responsibilities of my future. My wife had been an introvert during our relationship, while I had been the more social type, and our differences meshed well for a while until I began to selfishly feel suffocated.

Without realizing, my life had become a routine: wake up, go to work, make dinner, help the kids with homework, clean up the house, lie down, make love, repeat. It had grown to feel mundane in comparison to my friends who would spend their time traveling, going to concerts, and enjoying spontaneous activities with their partners.

After the divorce, my ex and I split custody sixty-forty, respectively, which gave me the freedom to do . . . well, whatever I wanted. My behavior became a bit extreme after years of sheltered family living. I started dating women who were free-spirited, women who loved to party. Women like Shaina—the Bonnie to my Clyde.

I had a roommate back before I was married who was constantly trying to get me to invest in whatever his latest "lucrative" idea was. After the divorce, I bought into one of his ideas—I purchased a dump truck that he would drive. Using my sales finesse, I called around for work and landed a multimillion-dollar contract for a state freeway expansion, competing against some of the top Utah dump truck companies. One dump truck turned into two, then three; I was a new, successful entrepreneur with just two years of business under my belt by the time I was dating Shaina.

Looking back after the divorce, I think I had started to miss the "simple life." The life I had quickly written off as being tired and boring. The short thrills were just that—fleeting—and I longed for a more meaningful existence. The simple life definitely would have kept me from getting to the place I'm in now.

I had spoken to my mom and dad on the phone, but aside from my friend Chevy, I didn't call other family or friends my first week in jail. I just thought at some point the cops would realize the mistake and let me go.

On the fifth day, I called my mom and was surprised to hear she'd talked to my ex. "She told me without hesitation, 'Cam didn't do this, I know it. He's not that stupid. Cameron is a very smart guy, and he would never do something so stupid.'" I missed her.

Toward the end of the first week, I was in my cell reading an old, torn up, coverless copy of *Blade Runner* given to me by my cellmate when the PO came over the intercom:

"Lundgren, you have a visitor."

The solid steel door unlocked, echoing through the concrete walls as if saying, "you are no longer in control of your life."

I had not had a visitor yet and was told I could not for seven days, so I was a little confused. As I walked by the PO desk, I asked him who it was.

He barely glanced up at me. "It's an attorney."

That was weird. I hadn't called one yet, thinking I'd just be let out due to a mistake. As I entered the steel cell box about the size of a small shower, separated by plexiglass, I saw a man in his early thirties with a dark complexion and black hair. When I picked up the phone, he started the conversation.

"Cameron, my name is Glen Thomas, and I was sent here by your friend, Matt. He thought you could use some help. Have you spoken to any other attorneys?"

"No, I was kind of hoping I didn't need one," I said in confusion.

Glen stared at me stone faced before responding. "You're being suspected of murder, Cameron, and it doesn't look good. Do you want to tell me what happened?"

Everything became very, very real. Once again holding back tears, I relived that night and explained what happened with as much detail as I could. Glen looked a little shocked by my story, but he later told me he would not represent someone he felt was guilty, and not once did I ever get the feeling he felt otherwise about me.

"So, I'm confused," I said, thinking back to my conversations with the police officer in his patrol car. "How was the gun shot reported as back to front?"

Glen's voice was steady. "The radiologist reported the bullet traveling from the back of her skull to the front, from the back right to the front left."

Report of shooting and initial radiologist finding

I nodded slowly. "That's what the arresting officer told me. I thought maybe the gun went off on an angle or something, I didn't think he meant I pulled the trigger. I mean, it was clearly right to left. Not from behind."

Glen scribbled notes in a pad of paper and told me he'd look into it, then left shortly after for my house to get my debit card to pull a ten-thousand-dollar retainer.

I called my mom to tell her I'd secured a lawyer; it seemed to be the first bit of good news since I had been arrested. She told me she had looked up Shaina's obituary online earlier that day. Her funeral was tomorrow. As I laid down to sleep that night, all I could think about was how I was going to miss it, how I was going to miss the funeral I promised I would never miss.

I spent the day pacing the open area, upset I wouldn't be there for her funeral. I grew even more upset when checking the clock, I knew it had passed. I thought about what I would have said about her if I could have been there, rehearsing my speech in my head as I was held by these concrete walls. That night, I spent hours crying in bed, hoping my sleeping cellmate wouldn't hear me.

The next week, Glen was trying to arrange with the district attorney and the prosecutor for me to pay to expedite evidence including pulling DNA off the weapon, to cover the costs of extracting the data from mine and Shaina's cell phones and hiring an investigative team to research the case. I told him he had my full consent to spend whatever he needed to and left it at that.

Glen went to work. As my savings began to drain, spending now more than I'd ever even spent on a car, frustrated, I also started to feel a little more optimistic, especially when compared to the other inmates I spoke with.

One in particular said he was there for murdering a cop; While out driving with a friend—the driver— engaged in a high-speed chase with the police. Once their car was cornered, the driver reversed, running over an officer, killing him; The officers shot and killed the driver. As the only living accessory to the crime, the passenger picked up the murder charge. He had already been waiting a year for evidence to go through the system, and I felt very fortunate to be in a place to afford the luxury of moving evidence at my pace. I was also not naive enough to believe everything I heard inside was true.

Two weeks had passed since I was initially booked, an eleven-day extension from my original seventy-two-hour hold. And still, they had not formally pressed charges. While in jail, I worked on liquidating my assets, which led me to selling all dump trucks but one, and property. I wanted to make sure that if a million-dollar bail came, I could get out and set this all straight. I had been calling a bail bondsperson daily, but without charges, there was nothing they could do.

Every time we were let out of our cells, I would rush to the phones. My mom and dad had placed a few hundred on my "jail" account, so I had hours of call time, which made me a popular guy in the cell.

I fought hard to hold back tears to avoid showing any weakness in front of the other inmates, often trying to get to the phone farthest away, so I could face away from all of them as I choked up talking to family and friends. Each call I made was so emotional and each call further solidified my distance between myself and the outside world.

As I was reading in my cell, halfway through my seventh book in fourteen days, the PO called my name again.

"Lundgren, you have a visitor."

Glen, who had been stopping by almost daily, was back. We made our way to a private room to discuss the case, then picked up the phones on either side of the plexiglass.

"I have an idea. It's a bit of a risk, but I want to get your thoughts," he said.

I nodded and he continued. "I've reached out to a company that performs lie detector tests."

Although we were working with prosecution to try to expedite the DNA tests, Glen and I were told it could still take up to a month to get any results back.

"This isn't your standard lie detector test. It tests your pupils to detect if you're lying—"

"Let's do it," I cut in.

"Hold on, hear me out." Glen cut back in. "The guy that does it is an ex–police officer in the department you were under investigation in, and he knows many of the detectives on this case. If you pass, he can speak to them directly and it may get you out of here. But here's what you need to know—these things aren't perfect, and this could really hurt your case if you don't pass with flying colors." He paused and looked at me nervously. "I want to know your thoughts."

I didn't need a moment to answer. This was my shot at clearing my name, and I wasn't about to wait through any more weeks in jail for forensics to process.

"Let's do it, Glen," I said. "If these things work like they should, I have absolutely nothing to hide and I want to do it."

As confident as I had been in my answer earlier that day, my mind now raced as I laid in bed, thinking of all the things that could go wrong. What if I was too nervous and it falsely picked up my answer as a lie? What if my pupils told a different story than what had happened? I swallowed hard and tried to get some sleep.

Several days passed, and they extended my hold for the third time. I was beyond frustrated. I called Glen that morning and he was as confused as I. Why hadn't they pressed charges? Without charges, I couldn't post bail. I was stuck, and I wanted to get the hell out of there and see my family. Glen explained he would be there that afternoon for the lie detector test.

I was called into a secure room, another box made of three concrete walls and a plexiglass window that I imagined could contain even the strongest man from breaking it with his fists or a chair. My insides were blended up into soup.

As the ex-cop set up the lie detector equipment, I asked all sorts of questions, but I was mainly concerned about how the test was administered. It was explained that I'd be taken through a set of questions, questions you were supposed to be honest about and then some you were supposed to intentionally lie about. The machine would monitor your pupils and detect the slightest movements in them, indicating a lie. First, we had to configure the test to record when my pupils would be showing a lie and the truth.

The examiner set me up with questions I had to lie about. "Have you ever broken a traffic law?"

He asked me to answer dishonestly, and the machine logged my pupils while I was lying. "No."

Then came questions I had to be honest about. "Is your name Cameron?"

"Yes."

The machine logged my pupils while I was telling the truth. Easy enough.

Then came the real questions. He assured me that if I was lying, there was no physical way to pass the test. Once again, I re-lived that night with Shaina, holding back the tears as they welled up in my eyes. The questions were always the same but phrased differently.

"Did you pull the trigger on the gun that killed Shaina?"

"Did you shoot Shaina?"

"Did you fire a gun that shot Shaina?"

Beginning to get upset with what felt like accusation, with no doubt in my mind, every time I answered with a firm, "no."

Afterward, I was led back to my cell for another lockdown—a couple inmates had gotten into a fight over food, which was common. The next day we weren't allowed any time out of our cell. I paced back and forth, anxious about my results and needing to expel my impatient energy. Every time the PO would come by, I would ask, "Are we being let out?"

The answer was always, "We don't know."

Minutes ticked by like hours until morning became day, then day became night. Suddenly I understood what it felt like to be an inmate with years on their life.

Just when I was about to give up, steel doors unlocked all thirty pods at once, sounding a heavy thud like a firing squad.

"You have thirty minutes only," rumbled the PO over the intercom.

I raced to the phone, but I wasn't fast enough to beat the dozens of other inmates who had equally been locked behind bars all day. While awaiting my turn, I decided to walk around the pod so that I could run in the second someone got off the phone; but each time an inmate would finish, another guy would beat me to it.

My eyes burned into the clock, which was quickly reaching our thirty-minute mark. Each inmate took their time on their call, talking to their wives, girlfriends, or family as long as they could. My frustration mounted. It wasn't worth getting into a fight over, but the clock wound down. The PO sent us back to our rooms.

It was the longest night of my life. I laid on my half-inch thick mat and stared at the darkness of the pod trying to take my mind off the lie detector results. The last thing I remember was glancing at the clock at five-thirty, only to be woken up at six o'clock for breakfast. The bright overhead lights kicked in as my eyelids peeled open after only a few minutes of sleep.

The PO's familiar voice crackled to life over the intercom pulling my eyelids apart. "Breakfast. Line up."

Trudging along in line, I grabbed my tray of puke, which had surprisingly started to taste good at that point. I immediately gave it away so I could speak to the PO rather than eat breakfast.

I stood in line at the PO station waiting patiently for the other inmates to finish requests for razors to shave—which are immediately seized after use; questions about court and bail; asking to be let into the rec room; asking about their account balances.

Finally, when I reached the front desk, I asked, "May I use the phone? I have an urgent call with my attorney." I was fully expecting to get shut down.

"Yes, you may, Mr. Lundgren."

Calls were not normally allowed during breakfast time, aside from the occasional inmates I would see asking to use them with approval. I wondered if the PO knew something I didn't. Bolting for the phones, I first tried Glen, but he didn't answer. Shielding my body in front of the phone so the PO couldn't see me make another call, I discreetly dialed my mom.

"Cameron, did you hear?" My mom's booming voice nearly knocked me over. "You passed the test; your scores were off the charts! Glen told me that you passed with 'high accuracy' in honesty!"

I couldn't hold back the tears but tried to shield them from the other inmates. This would finally set me free, I thought.

We continued to stay in lockdown that entire day and I waited, and waited, and waited for my name to be called. Yet, as nighttime drew close, I was prepared for another sleepless night in my cage.

We were let out for our normal schedule the next day—a Monday—and I threw myself into two books, barely digesting the story I was reading. I must have driven Glen nuts calling every time we were allowed to use the phones, but he hadn't heard anything about me being released, despite my test results. It was now a waiting game.

Nighttime came again and we were checked into our rooms. Other inmates had previously told me that inmates are only released at certain times of the day, and that last time was coming awfully close. Just as I had given up hope for the second night in a row, the PO's voice came over the intercom.

"Lundgren, roll up. You're going home."

Chapter 4

FEELS PERFECT

BEFORE THE NIGHTMARE – August 2018

We spent two nights up at Mirror Lake, two nights that felt like a dream. I was already starting to fall in love with Shaina. She even decided not to go home with her parents but came straight home with me to my house in Cedar Hills.

On the drive home, we stopped at a little café in the closest town; the waitress came up to us taking our order, "you love birds ready to order?" We could not take our eyes off each other, and both of us had severe motor-mouth, talking about anything and everything we wanted to.

Shaina told me she had been a go-go dancer at electronic dance music, or EDM, festivals.

"Don't you mean a rave?" I asked.

She laughed like I had just told the world's funniest joke. "You're old!" She teased, still giggling. "Das Energi is coming up this weekend. It's an EDM festival in Salt Lake City—we should go."

I had my kids every other weekend and I had them the weekend of Das Energi.

"Sorry, babe, I've got my kids then, and I don't miss my time with them." Sharing that intimate detail made me realize I didn't actually know that much about her. "Do you have kids?"

"I had a girl early in life." Her body deflated a little as she spoke. "But we decided to give her up for adoption to have a better life."

Shit. I hadn't intended to make her sad or uncomfortable. Not sure how to respond, I said, "Well, you can have another." I wasn't sure if that's what she wanted me to say, so I offered, "And I'm sure the baby you gave up would want to know her mom at some point, right?"

She smiled a little, then changed the subject. "I don't think I asked how old you were?"

"I'm thirty-nine," I confessed, rolling my eyes. To be honest, I was a little scared of her reaction. Not only did I have kids, but Shaina and I also shared a thirteen-year age difference.

But she just smiled again. That big, beautiful smile I had already fallen in love with.

"That's perfect." She smirked, eyes glinting. "I like older men." Relief flooded through me. "So," she continued, "do you want more kids?"

I had an eleven-year-old and a fifteen-year-old at the time, but I had always wanted a third—a daughter. Except I had hated the baby years; I much preferred when my kids were old enough to throw the ball around or go to the park. Some parents dreaded the teen years, but the baby years had always seemed the hardest for me.

"I'd love a daughter," I replied. "I want to spoil the shit out of her."

We both laughed as the waitress approached our table with the bill. I paid, and we made our way back to the truck.

We didn't get home until late Sunday night, but I was too excited to sleep just yet, so I gave her a tour of my home and all my toys. As we pulled into my garage, my commuter car and my fully modified Polaris RZR—with dark red and black candy paint—were illuminated by the garage lights. My brain immediately went to all of the future activities Shaina and I could do together. And if our future was anything like Mirror Lake, it was going to be fun.

"One of my ex-boyfriends owned a shop that builds those." She pointed to the Polaris.

"Well, he'd have made a fortune if he built mine. But I did it all myself," I said smugly. "Let's go inside."

We began our tour at the kitchen, then my office, then out back to see the backyard with my gazebo-covered hot tub, overlooking the golf course. I was trying to impress her with everything I had, hoping she felt as excited as I did. I could spend every day with her for the rest of my life, she felt perfect.

"What's downstairs?" she asked, breaking my fantasy.

"I'm still finishing the basement. Want to see what I want to do?" She grabbed my hand to pull me along. Maybe she was as excited as I was.

In the basement, I showed her where I was going to put a theater room, a bedroom, and a bathroom. We approached the corner of the room, and I grabbed her from behind.

"And here," I explained, "is where I plan to put our sex room."

I felt her butt rub against my frontside, and I continued, "I'm going to make a sex bench and a wall for toys, like whips and handcuffs. I want to build a hidden bookshelf to hide the room from my kids. But..." I paused to kiss her neck, "over there is where I'm going to tie you up against the wall and please you."

She tilted her head back and whispered, "Are you going to tie me up tonight, handsome?"

I stopped my assault on her neck. "We'll see." Teasing her, I led her upstairs.

I had spent my three years post-divorce dating all sorts of women; learning what turns them on, what makes them hot. And what I found out is that most women love one thing: confidence. Many of the women I'd been with had told me that men in their past had been intimidated by toys in the bedroom, but I found that toys only emphasized physical intimacy, and what many women would use in private was only made that much better when used as a couple.

As I led Shaina up the stairs to the main floor and to my makeshift liquor cabinet—my kitchen cupboards—she immediately noted my collection of whiskey and grabbed for the Fireball. Figured—we both seemed to love Fireball. That could be a problem, I thought.

We shared a few drinks before heading upstairs to the master bedroom, where Shaina made a stop into the hallway guest bathroom to check her hair. Even still without makeup from camping, that woman was a dream. She spun around to stand in the doorway, wearing a sly grin.

"So," she said, tilting her head as if asking me an important question. "Where are your whips, handcuffs, and ropes, then?"

I casually walked up to her. "We're going to buy them together. I don't share whips and handcuffs." She leaned into me, her lips grazing my ear, her breath hitching. "Fuck, you're hot." With a slight tug on her long, black hair, I pulled her head back, exposing her neck. "Lucky for you, I always have my ropes."

I licked from the base of her neck, trailing toward her chin, then slowly let her head come back down.

Her hand grabbed the bulge in my pants, and she whispered into my ear, "Be careful. I might love you more."

She moved from the bathroom entryway to the entryway of the master bedroom and then slowly pulled her pants down, giving me a show. She struggled a bit to peel them off her strong, thick legs, which caused her butt to sway from side to side. Seeing those naked, sexy, long legs made me freeze in place. My eyes locked on her hips, then followed down the length of her body as she slowly pulled each foot from her pants.

Shaina turned, blowing me a kiss over the shoulder and giving me a much-anticipated look of her butt. "I'll be in the bed. Bring your ropes, Boy Scout."

The thoughts of all the ties I could put her in, the sexiness of *shibari* on her body, had my head in a tailspin. All I could think about was tying her hands to the bedposts and making her uncontrollably orgasm over and over and over again.

I made a dash to my master closet, stumbling, and started tearing it apart in search of the red and black ropes I had bought just weeks earlier.

"I'm read-eey," she called. "Are you, ah, coming?" She teased me from the bed, giggling at her sexual innuendo. My closet in shambles, I finally secured the rope, still in its original packaging. I tore open the package, fumbling to untangle it as I reached the end of the bed.

Shaina was already exactly how I wanted her, lying with her back against all my pillows, her legs propped up and spread long and wide toward the bed posts. She held out her arms toward me indicating she was giving me power over her, waiting to be tied up.

Rushing to the side of the bed, I ripped off my shirt first tying one wrist with the red rope into a handcuff tie.

"I like your choice of color," she cooed, winking at me as I secured her bound wrist to the bedpost. I stayed quiet and went around to the other side and secured her second wrist with the black rope.

I moved to stand at the edge of the bed, Shaina displayed before me like prey accepting its fate. "What do you want?" I asked, my voice steady and commanding.

She looked at my crotch. "That."

"We'll see." I taunted her as I pulled off my pants. Climbing on the end of the bed, I approached her like a lion about to devour its prey. My head dropped down and starting at her feet I began a slow, methodical torment licking her from toe to knee, from knee to hip, slipping just past her vagina but grazing her skin just enough to draw excitement.

Her hands struggled as I pleased her, confirming her satisfaction. Moaning, she bucked her pelvis up to meet me, but I didn't give in. I continued licking up toward her belly button, her breaths getting more ragged, grabbing my attention. She was giving me non-verbal clues to find her spots. As her breaths grew even deeper, my tongue found them.

Then slowly, my tongue made its way up to the middle of her chest, circling both nipples, wet and erect, and biting them gently. Shaina was gasping and struggling beneath me. I slowly, carefully mounted her, the tip of my cock just barely inside her. My tongue lingering on her ear, I whispered, "Are you ready to cum now?"

"I have a secret to tell you," she whispered back. "No man has ever made me cum. I've always faked them . . . my orgasms, I mean."

At first, I thought it couldn't be possible. But the look on her face told me it was true. I put on a playful grin and lowered my voice. "If you ever fake an orgasm with me like last night again," I growled into her ear, "you'll have to find another man."

"Yes, sir," she whimpered. The thought of her obedience had me hot.

"Tonight, it's not my cock that will make you cum." I slipped my tongue into her ear, and she pulled away, her whole body shivering uncontrollably. "Tsk-tsk. I might have to learn a rope tie to secure your head."

Gently pulling away from her, I navigated my tongue back down to her waist; I eased my finger inside of her as my tongue made its way there too.

I began to massage her with my tongue when she said, "Slower."

My eyes look up catching hers and I decreased my pace and smiled; she was in ecstasy. So was I.

The next forty-five minutes she spent coaching me, training me, guiding me while she was bound. When she orgasmed, her hips thrust back and forth, but I kept my tongue wrapped around her clitoris.

Her body finally slows, yet her breathing was still uneven. Without a word, I gently unbound her hands and positioned myself so that I cuddled her from behind.

We lay like that for a while. She still hadn't fallen asleep or attempted to move.

I could sense something was on her mind, but I didn't want to disturb her quiet. I wondered what was going through her brain, my cock still pressed hard against her butt, but it wasn't my turn.

I held her close until I eventually dozed off.

***

The weekend of the Das Energi festival, I was supposed to have my kids—I'd planned to take them to the arcade—but a few days prior, I got a text from my ex asking if she could have them for two weekends in a row because her brother was in town. I agreed.

As soon as Shaina came home from work, I shared the news. "You've got me for Das this weekend, babe."

She squealed and ran toward me, wrapping her arms around me. "You're going to have so much fun, old man!" she exclaimed, planting a big kiss on my mouth.

Shaina had not left my house since we arrived from Mirror Lake, except for one quick stop at her mother's to grab work clothes the Friday of the festival. She had left early for work that morning and planned to get ready for the concert at her mom's, and we'd meet at the festival. However, that first night got rained out, so I headed back alone to my place for an early night.

Saturday morning, I immediately messaged Shaina on Snapchat. God, I hated Snapchat, but it's what Shaina and this younger generation was using so I supposed I'd better keep up.

> **Cameron:** Hey, so I'm taking this super-hot chick with me to Das, and you wouldn't like her 'cause I'm falling in love with her.
> **Shaina:** Could her name be Beautiful? I'll kick her ass!
> **Cameron:** Sorry, babe, her name is Shaina. I'll tell her she needs to keep her hands to herself.
> **Shaina:** Nah, you should tell her to take advantage of you.

She sends me a winking emoji and I realize I've been smiling to myself.

> **Shaina:** You just made my day, handsome. Whatcha going to wear?

Oh shit—what in the hell do I wear? What do *they* wear, people Shaina's age? I immediately thought of Spencer's, so I hopped in my car and drove to the mall. As I wandered the aisles, it became clear to me I had no idea what I was actually looking for.

Das seemed like a rave—despite being laughed at by Shaina for using the outdated word—so I bought as much neon gear as I could find: a neon mask, neon glow suspenders, the whole nine yards. I went straight home, put it all on, and took a picture in the mirror and sent it to her. Less than a second goes by and she responds:

> **Shaina:** You're old, but that's super cute.

Feeling defeated and *old*—and my ego a bit bruised—I decided to wear my tried and true black fitted shirt that showed off my muscles, and some ripped up black jeans with boots and a black hat.

Shaina: Hey, my friend Sarah wants to come with us. Her cousin, Mandy, can drive, but she's going to stay home because she's on probation and she can pick us up afterward. Can she use your commuter car?

I was happy to offer my spare car in exchange for a designated driver.

Cameron: Of course, should I pick you up?
Shaina: Yeah baby! But one more thing—they have mushrooms and want to go to your house afterward for some fun. You down?

Of course, I was down, I loved mushrooms. Even more so, I love taking mushrooms with someone I love; it's a euphoric experience I can never quite put into words.

Cameron: Hell yeah! Let's do this, babe.

As I pulled up to her mom's house, Shaina sauntered to my car, and I knew I was going to love all the concerts she'd take me to. She came out in these black, skin-tight Daisy Duke shorts—her legs on full display—and a top with the Deadmau5 logo which looked like Mickey Mouse on her chest. I fell head over heels all over again . . . I couldn't have conjured up a more perfect image of her in my head if I tried.

She bounded into the passenger seat with all the excitement of a five-year-old going to Disneyland.

"Hey, babe!" She looked me up and down, a small frown marking her face. "Why'd you change? I loved the look you sent me!"

"You told me I looked old," I said, mimicking her frown.

"Well, you still look old," she snickered, "but you're very handsome." Her full smile returned. "I can't wait to do this with you." She leaned over to give me a kiss, but stopped before pulling away to add, "Going to get naughty with me tonight after?"

"That depends . . . going to give me your wrists?" I threw it in reverse and left for Sarah's.

During the drive, Shaina requested the song "Drunk All The Time" by Dillon Francis and she would point to me, wink, and blow a kiss each time the chorus came on. By the end, it may have been my new favorite song.

I pulled out a little secret weapon I had known about for years called horny goat weed, an herbal supplement of the *Epimedium* genus. At the suggestion of a friend, I had done a ton of research on its benefits for increasing libido and circulation. I initially used it for myself, and it had made my dick during sex feel like riding a unicorn in heaven. Later, I learned it works just as well for women too.

"I have a present for you, Beautiful."

"What is it?" She giggled.

"Do you trust me?" I poured out three pills into my palm and offered them to her. "Take these now. I also want you to take this every day we're together; the more consistent you are, the better it works."

Without even hesitating or asking a single follow-up question, she obediently popped them into her mouth and chased them down with her Mountain Dew Baja Blast from Taco Bell.

We picked up Sarah and Mandy, briefly introduced ourselves, and were on our way, Mandy at the wheel. As promised, Mandy pulled out a bag of mushrooms. "Look what I got!" she teased, smirking as she swung the little baggie back and forth.

Not to be outdone, I pulled out a few pills of Molly and smiled back.

Once Mandy dropped us off, we dropped the Molly and headed for the line. Shaina and Sarah had friends that worked security, so they were able to get in quickly—as the guards' friends and as beautiful women. That meant I was stuck waiting in the hour-long line while the two of them were undoubtedly partying already. To make matters worse, my high was starting to kick in, and I was getting antsy being by myself. A couple of times, the security guards told the crowd the show was going to be canceled due to rain. Great, I thought. All this for nothing.

My phone pinged, which gave me a quick sense of relief thinking Shaina and Sarah had somehow worked a miracle to get me inside.

Shaina: We're in and up at the bar, when you get in text me.

Guess not. I sighed heavily.

Cameron: OK just waiting in this big ass line.

Eventually, the line started moving fast, and once I was in, I was on a mission to find my woman. Pushing and fighting my way past people to the upper bar felt like a marathon, I finally found her, and she greeted me by jumping on me and hugging me until I about choked. We went straight to the bar for shots of Fireball. And more Fireball, and more, and more. At that rate, it didn't take too long for us to be drunk, which hit concurrently with the Molly. Every time we moved through the crowd, Shaina grabbed my hand with a death grip so as not to lose me. Then it was back to the bar, then back into the crowd. This happened four or five times, and my frustrations grew—we had spent most of the night plowing through the crowd rather than watching the show, and I wanted Shaina to know that I had listened to and learned all of her favorite songs.

Still, I took comfort in Shaina never wanting to let go of my hand. Just then I got a text from my friend Everett, who had spent a considerable amount of money to snag a VIP table as close to main stage as you could be. Bingo. I turned to Sarah and Shaina and yelled over the music, "So my friend has a VIP table with bar service—all you can drink—and it's right up next to the stage." The two women looked up at me like I was a god, and I didn't know whether to feel prideful or to laugh. The benefits of an old man, I thought.

As we approached the bouncers at the VIP section, they turned me away just as I caught a glimpse of Everett behind the ropes. I yelled out his name and, fortunately, he heard me.

"Let him in," he said to the bouncers, motioning to me. Everett and I had gone to high school together, but we didn't actually become friends until post-divorce as part of my business venture.

"Let's consider this a business write-off," I quipped as the men pulled back the rope and let us in, and Everett laughed. Shaina and Sarah were staring at each other, mouths agape, like we had just been cleared to meet the president of the United States.

The show finished with Deadmau5, and we watched as close as you could as I held Shaina tight from behind. Every movement of our bodies touching was ecstasy; the mixture of the music, the booze, the Molly, and the atmosphere coalescing into the most perfect moment, and I knew I'd never want this moment to end. I couldn't remember a time I had felt this happy, or this in sync with another person. Shaina was giving me back my youth; she was taking me as I was. I finally had her in my arms, the endless walking through the crowd stopped—I finally had her where I wanted her.

Once the set finished and we pushed past the crowds to the parking lot, we found Mandy in my car. "Dude, I love this car!" she told me as we climbed in.

I had to agree—it was fun to drive. We had over an hour drive to my house in Cedar Hills, so Sarah and Mandy decided to eat the long-awaited mushrooms halfway there. I'm not going to lie, I was afraid for my life for a moment, but I knew that we had enough time to make it to my house before the effects of the mushrooms kicked in. Shaina and I followed suit, placing the mushrooms into each other's mouths.

We made it to my house safely. By the time we walked inside and turned on the lights, the red-painted walls glowed to life, every accent color in each room glimmering and pulsating. The mushrooms were in full effect.

Shaina and I had branched off solo and we were laughing hysterically at each other, making all sorts of stupid jokes. I pointed at Shaina and announced, "You're Silly Two." She howled with laughter.

"Who's Silly One?"

I gave her a serious, drug-induced, all-knowing look.

"Oh!" she yelped, "You're Silly One!" She doubled over again with laughter before looking at me and amended, "I just let you *think* you're the silliest, Cameron." Then she blew me a kiss.

Shaina walked over to my whiteboard where I'd jot down grocery necessities, and with my black marker wrote: Cameron needs a wifey. The effects of the drugs and the love I had already felt for this woman intensified. One day, I would make this woman my wife.

I had just gotten the PlayStation VR a year prior and thought there was no better time to test it out than now. I had previously downloaded a virtual reality video of Kygo's song "Carry Me," not knowing Kygo was Shaina's favorite EDM artist. As I placed the VR set on her head and started the video, she exclaimed, "I love Kygo! He's on my bucket list to see at least once before I die." *Noted,* I thought.

She was in pure bliss. The big, childlike smile reached from one side of her face to the other, and with her VR mask obstructing her view, I slipped in a kiss. Then I crept up behind her and pulled her tight into me, both of us swaying as her butt rubbed back and forth against me, watching the show.

When she finally pulled the mask off, she turned around and did her infamous jump kiss, the one she had given me the first time I met her at Mirror Lake. I always tried my best not to flinch, but she always managed to pull off the perfect kiss, planting dead center on my lips.

With Sarah and Mandy in the guest room, Shaina and I jumped into my bed where I pulled up Adam & Eve on my laptop. We ordered all sorts of sexy toys together including lingerie, vibrators, cock rings, a sex swing, more ropes, handcuffs, and at Shaina's request, a strap-on. Confused, I asked, "What are you going to do with that?"

"I don't know," she giggled, "guess we'll find out," then leaned over to give me a kiss. "I love you."

My heart had left my body. "I love you too," I vowed.

Her happy face quickly disappeared, and her tone became irritable. "Cameron do not ever say the word *too*. It's insincere. It's not an action, but a reaction." She crossed her arms over her chest. "Would I ever say *ditto* when you say you love me? I would never. So please never use the word *too* after saying you love me. Please?"

I was momentarily caught off guard. I had never thought of it that way, nor did I think someone could have such a strong opinion about such a tiny word. But it was one of the cutest rants I'd heard, and if Shaina discouraged it, then I would obey. "I love you, Shaina Beautiful." I saw that huge smile once more.

Chapter 5

NOWHERE TO HIDE

AFTER THE NIGHTMARE – July 15, 2019

It was late Sunday when I was released, and I hadn't had the chance to call any of my family to tell them I'd be free. *Would someone be outside waiting to pick me up?* The sting of the cold corridors chilled my bones. I made my way to processing, my fist tight around the pillowcase that held the plastic bags of ramen noodles I bought with commissary shuffling around that I didn't want to leave behind. When I reached the release station, several inmates had already changed out of their orange clothes.

"You won't let me make one more call, so I don't have to walk home in the dark?" One of them argued with an officer.

I had gotten used to the firing of the steel doors unlocking as an officer directed me, "Lundgren, A1, to change your clothes" pointing to a solid metal door.

Inside at a window reminding me of ordering fast food, my stomach growls. An officer slides clothes through the small opening and slams the window shut. Realizing I wasn't going to get my clothes back from that night when it all began, I knock on the window. Apparently, I had no choice but to wear someone's abandoned clothes.

"Can I please get something that fits better? I'm a size 34 waist. Or even a belt?"

"Deal with it." The window slams shut.

McDonald's, I thought, *cheeseburger meal with fries.* I sure hope someone is going to be here for me. As I waited to be signed out it felt I had no more meat between my tailbone and the concrete shelf I sat on. Then my name was finally called by a corrections officer. The first thing presented to me was a document used in domestic violence cases when a suspect is not permitted to return to the home of the crime scene until the courts decide they can. He told me to sign it.

I cocked my head. "But this is *my* house. Shaina was only staying there with me."

"I don't make the rules, I just enforce them," he responded. "Take it up with your attorney, your single call is over there, your phone will remain with the detectives."

As I stalked off to the nearest phone, the officer called me back. "Oh, I almost forgot—your attorney left this envelope."

I opened it, and to my surprise, Glen had left me fifty dollars, my saving grace from potentially spending the night on the streets if no one answered my call. Can't forget to give that man a huge hug in case I need this.

I walked over to the phone to make my single call, wondering who the hell would be up at this time of night. I decided my best chance was my mother. The phone rang, and rang, and rang, then voice mail . . . shit. I turned to the officer. "Can I make one more, please?"

"Nope, you got to go," he replied a little too quickly. I would have pushed harder had I not seen him shut down four others before me. Disappointed and frustrated, I turned to leave.

I held up my shorts ten sizes too large as I pushed through the doors leading outside. Pitch-black darkness down a concrete ramp to a desolate road. I walked down the sidewalk for about a quarter mile until I reached a gas station, where I realized I could use a payphone. I searched the perimeter of the store before realizing payphones were irrelevant nowadays, so I stepped inside to ask the store clerk. "May I use your phone?"

He looked me up and down and began laughing. "Do you have any idea how many times I'm asked that a day? Everyone that gets released from jail comes here. No!"

Feeling defeated, I walked out the doors back into the dark of the night, startled by the sight of—thankfully—another newly released inmate who had just called a cab for himself and offered to give me a ride.

I told him my address and he said he was being dropped off right near my house in Midvale. Only, I couldn't go to my house . . . Looking down at the cash from Glen, I only had enough to get halfway to my mom's house in Lehi, another ten miles away, after the guy was dropped off at his destination. We climbed into the cab and an idea sparked in my head.

"Could I please use your cell phone?" I asked the cab driver. "I'll give you ten dollars."

The driver agreed and handed me his phone. I called my friend Everett, who lived near my house.

"Who's this?"

"Everett, it's Cameron. I was just released from jail, and they told me I can't go home. Can I stay at your place tonight?"

Without hesitation, Everett warned, "You can't come here, dog, people want to kill you. I'm surprised you made it out of the parking lot." And with that, he hung up the phone.

People want to kill me? What the hell had happened since that night?

Terror seeped in over me and survival mode kicked in. This was clearly a suicide. And now, I had no choice but to go to my house—the house I had been banned from entering—and nowhere to sleep. I would have to go to my home at this point, but I was defenseless. If Everett was right, would people be there waiting for me? Was I safe? But I had no choice—it was either sleep there or sleep at the park, because I was not going to make it to my mom's.

I handed the driver the rest of my cash and had him drop me off a few blocks from my home, praying my spare key was where I had left it outside. It was eerily quiet, and the darkness of the night only egged on my paranoia; every car that drove past me felt like they were looking for me. I kept my head down, my hoodie covering my head as much as it could.

I snuck into the backyard, glancing at every dark corner carefully. The key was there! I crept to the front door, opened the lock, and went inside. I stopped myself as soon as I entered, taken aback by what I swore was the smell of Shaina's perfume. And then I was overcome with a second feeling: I hadn't secured the house. The last person inside was probably someone in law enforcement, and who knew if they'd locked up after they last left. *What if Everett was right? What if someone was inside, waiting for me?* Surely, I couldn't turn on a light to check for intruders—if someone had been keeping an eye on the house, it would be a dead giveaway to my arrival.

I snuck up to my bedroom in the darkness, running into walls and even stubbing my toe on the stairs, letting out an involuntary "Damnit!" I took all the blankets and pillows off my bed and placed them in the walk-in closet and closed the door, making my best makeshift bed. If someone were in the house, or tried to come in, the last place they'd look was the closet.

I tried to fall asleep, but the hours ticked by, and my mind never silenced. Even the smallest peep terrified me. My mind raced and each minute that passed I began to become more terrified for my safety. My guns had been confiscated by the police and I had no protection. I rolled over for the hundredth time. Clearly, I wasn't going to get any shuteye. I made the decision to go to my mom's.

Grabbing the essentials—a change of clothes and a toothbrush—I tiptoed down to my garage. I thought I might take my truck, but I doubted it would be stealthy, so I decided to take my car. It was unsuspecting, and I would be able to make a quicker exit. I started the car and opened the garage, not waiting for the garage door to open all the way before backing out and speeding down the street as fast as my Jetta would take me. With every turn, I watched for cars in the rearview mirror, waiting for someone to follow me so they could pull up beside me and spray my car with bullet holes. *Was Everett messing with me?*

When I pulled up to my mom's, the time was four in the morning, and it took a few solid knocks before the door opened.

"Cameron!" My mom's sleepy eyes opened wide at the sight of me. "When did they release you?"

I couldn't hold the tears back, and I threw myself into her arms and cried. "Mom, I didn't do it."

"I know, son, I know."

We talked for a few hours despite my exhaustion. She confirmed what Everett had said. People were angry; They even had to shut down my Facebook account because so many people in the community were posting threats to my public profile.

I began to feel the heat in my skin warm in frustration. I had no idea why I was even held for her murder—I watched her shoot herself in the head right in front of me, for God's sake. I was first robbed of my opportunity to mourn her, and now, it seemed, I had to convince everyone of my innocence.

That next morning, my brothers, Joe and Logan, came and took me camping for a few days to get my mind off things, strategically picking somewhere with no wireless connection. We loaded up the camper and all our toys and headed off to the Little Sahara Sand Dunes for a few days. We spent the time around the campfire, discussing happier times; their goal was to distract me for a while, and they had accomplished it. Until we got back.

We came home late from camping, and I woke up the next morning on my mom's couch. I wasn't worried about going to work, or about paying my mortgage—or any other bills for that matter. I woke up on a mission. First, I needed to get my phone back and start calling people so I could set this all straight. I called my attorney from my mom's phone.

"Glen, when can I get my phone?"

"I don't think you'll get your phone for a few weeks, but I'll request it."

First my Facebook was under siege and now my phone was being held hostage for the foreseeable future.

"Also, we still need to hire an investigative team. How would you like to pay for that?" Glen asked.

"Charge my card."

I hung up and pulled out my laptop so I could log in to my Facebook account.

My mom, sitting across from me, told me to search for news footage. *Shaina, Cameron, shot.* I typed. I took a deep breath then clicked on the first video. A reporter was standing in front of my house.

"Cameron, who lives at the home behind me, called in the suicide of his girlfriend and was later suspect to have shot her in the back of the head—"

What the . . . *fuck* did she just say? My brain couldn't even place an emotion, but bewildered, confused, annoyed, and upset were all surging to and competing for the forefront.

I opened Messenger and was bombarded by an influx of messages—hundreds—from strangers and some of Shaina's friends that I had never met.

Some of the hundreds of Facebook Direct Messages read:

> **FB DM:** Next time, point the gun in your direction.
>
> **FB DM:** If you get out, I'll find you and kill you.
>
> **FB DM:** I hope you rot in hell for killing her.
>
> **FB DM:** Putting all my wishful thinking into the universe that karma bites you in the fucking ass. Piece of shit woman beater.

Woman beater? Seriously, what the hell was going on?

> **FB DM:** You are a weak man. You are a fucking bitch, Cameron, and I know right where you fucking live.
>
> **FB DM:** Me and my crew will be keeping an eye out for you, mother fucker, and if we see you, you'll pray you live.

There were even messages about how I was a piece of shit to do this to my kids.

My kids. My heart sank. The most innocent bystanders here; surely, my oldest son had seen some of this. I could only imagine what their friends had said at school, or what they had read online. How would I even begin talking to them—how does that conversation start? My mind racing and beginning to become overwhelmed with all that needed to be done.

As I started reading through Facebook posts, my name popped up everywhere. Apparently, people had been driving by my house to see if I was home. One of my neighbors posted, "If he comes here, I'll let everyone know." God. Everett was right. Should I be expecting a lynch mob on my doorstep? I don't think I could go home at this point.

I scrolled through more videos. Oh, right Valentine's Day. I thought back to that night, the incident in the truck. Shaina's mom posted the video Shaina made of her broken nose - an accident – but her mom accused me of beating her. It was another stupid argument. I didn't physically hurt her on purpose.

"My God," I said out loud. I looked up from the screen and stared at my mom. "My name, my reputation, everything about me is being dragged through the mud." I almost laughed at the implausible narrative unfolding before me. "And I have nutjobs wanting to kill me."

To top it off, a woman I'd never seen before had posted a picture of my alleged Bumble profile, claiming that I was currently active on the dating app since getting out of jail. "What a piece of shit," she wrote. "Two days out of jail looking for his next victim."

Her post had already been shared over three thousand times. This was insane. Of course, someone was snooping around my phone and opening up apps—the police! I shook my head, hoping I could will the madness to subside.

For every hundredth hate message, I'd spy a comment from one of my friends defending my honor. It slightly comforted me, knowing that despite the nightmare I had been heaved into, the majority of my friends had taken the time to support me. I was completely alone, but maybe I wasn't *so* alone. For each friend that posted on my behalf, they'd be attacked by countless Internet strangers. I messaged them each privately to thank them but told them they'd be better off to just stay quiet. It wasn't worth the barrage of insults tossed their way. Many of them replied, to my relief, telling me they knew me not as the person I was being accused of, but as someone that couldn't possibly have done it. The smallest glimmer of hope burned through my body.

The threats and posts went on for months afterward. Everyone had become an alleged expert on me overnight. Some were saying I was ex-military (I wasn't) and to stay away from me because I was trained to kill; some were saying I was a professional fighter (I wasn't), which was the root of my rage problems.

These rumors had been spread to thousands of people on social media, all accusing and all agreeing that I was, indeed, a monster. But could I really blame these people? If I put myself in their shoes and watched the news as it was reported—a boyfriend called in the suicide of his girlfriend, who died from a shot to the head, back to front and right to left—would I have thought he was guilty? And if I had believed he was guilty, I'm sure I would've wanted to kick that guy's ass too. What was confusing was the 'and.' *Were they suggesting two shots or a single trajectory?* It was all so confusing.

I spent the next two weeks at my friend Chevy's home a few cities away. Chevy was an old friend from my teenage years; we had been branded as "troublemakers" together back in our heyday. A real ladies' man, he's the kind of guy who knows everyone—the man with a million friends, whose favorite phrase happens to be "I love my friends!" that he often shouts at parties. It was easy to see why everyone loved him: Chevy is one of the most loyal people you'll meet, and his loyalty never wavered from me once after I was released from jail. He cooked me a rib eye steak dinner my first night with him.

As he pulled the two-inch steak from the smoker and placed it on a plate with asparagus, handing it to me, my eyes large with anticipation, I cut off a large piece and threw it into my mouth. I hadn't eaten food like this for four weeks. Barely chewing, it instantly went down my throat and got stuck.

My first thought was run out the back door and force it out, no one needed to know of my embarrassment. Throwing my gut on a nearby lawn chair and forcing it into my stomach while I kept choking, wasn't working. I went from scared to terrified quickly.

Throwing the door open, back into the house Chevy looks at me briefly confused, then figures it out. He immediately begins the Heimlich maneuver and in one solid motion the meat flies out of my mouth as I gasp for a deep breath. Once recovered I belt out laughing and we all crack up with Chevy exclaiming, "I love my friends!"

I brought no electronics with me, except my laptop to monitor the social media threats and news coverage. I would occasionally leave to go to the gas station, and even tried to go to the gym once, thinking some exercise might clear my head. The next day, I discovered people had taken pictures of me while I was out and about, even if it was only for that short time.

> **FB post**: I saw him at the gas station, what a monster. He's out free—I can't believe our legal system.

My face was all over social media and the news, everyone so upset I had killed my girlfriend and called it in as a suicide and now I was free, or so they thought.

I couldn't leave my house. I didn't have my phone. I was totally helpless while I waited around for my name to be cleared if it ever would be. My plan to take back my innocence was to post any evidence on my phone that would prove to people I hadn't killed Shaina—that she had been thinking of suicide long before the nightmare in June. I had many texts between Shaina and me that included her talking about being depressed. I also often recorded my calls for work and had an accidental recorded conversation of her begging me to take her to the University Neuropsychiatric Institute, or UNI, suicide watch one day while she was at work.

About a week after being released—with no sign of my phone being remanded to me soon—I bought a burner phone and restored it using the Cloud. I then started posting some of those conversations and responding to some of the hate posts. Not five minutes went by when my phone rang. It was Glen.

"Cameron! Do I need to remind you we're in an *ongoing* investigation?" he said emphatically.

He was right. I'd been so blinded by the need to clear my name I hadn't really been thinking of the legal ramifications to my actions. "I didn't think it through," I said sheepishly.

He continued. "I've asked my paralegal to keep an eye on your social media accounts and she came upon your post. Mark my words—if you even show a hint of yourself on social media, you'll be looking for another attorney."

I was a little shocked, but fully understood where Glen was coming from. "Yes, sir," I responded before adding, "One more thing. Will you ask the detectives when they'll give me my phone back, and if they're opening my old dating apps?" I hung up the phone.

I quickly removed the posts, frustrated that despite the evidence contrary to my supposed guilt, I still couldn't do anything to salvage my name. I might as well still be in jail.

I quickly learned I was not going to convince tens of thousands of people that had already made their minds up. After all, it looked as though I did it. I was a hostage; I could not leave the house and be seen in public. I was shut out from the world, watching as a bystander as my character was ripped apart and destroyed. The fight was more than I had anticipated since initially being released, more than I could comprehend.

My thoughts turned again to my kids, and I called my ex-wife Haley hoping I could have a piece of happiness back if I could visit them. Before being hauled off to jail, I had my kids with me every other week. My ex answered, sounding upset. "Cameron, what the hell?!"

"Listen, this is a huge misunderstanding, and it will be all cleared up soon."

She sighed. "Cameron, I know you better than to do something like this. You're way too smart to do something so stupid . . . I knew you didn't do it."

My hopes lifted a little at her confession. "I just want to see my kids." Tears started puddling up. "I want to see my boys."

"Cameron, your oldest doesn't want to talk to you. Please understand he's a teenager and has access to social media. I'll try and encourage him to talk to you, but as of now, he doesn't want to see you."

I could feel myself choking up—how could my pride and joy, my son, not want to see me? "What about—"

She interrupted before I could mention my youngest Bo. "We've kept all of this hidden from him, and you're welcome to see him, but you cannot talk about *any* of this to him."

And like the dark of the night ending and the light and the heat of the sun coming out for the first time, all my worries went away. At least I would be able to have a slice of happiness and be motivated to continue this fight. We hung up the phone, and I collapsed to my knees and wept asking "why me, how could you take Shaina from me and leave me like this."

Pulling up to the driveway of Haley's home I message "I'm here to pick up Bo" and waited there for thirty minutes before I became frustrated.

"I'm here! Send him out please!" I demand.

"Cameron the kids don't want to see you anymore."

My heart sunk, I began to get angry thinking *you can't keep them from me, legally I have rights.*

Picking up the phone I called the local police. "My kids are being kept from me by my ex-wife. I'm at her home trying to pick them up for my time with them."

The dispatcher responds. "We cannot remove a child unless they're being harmed, are they being harmed?"

"No, they are not, but I have a right to see them," I reply.

"I can report it and you can follow up with your attorney tomorrow, sir. Outside of that there's nothing we can do," she responds, as my anger subsides, while beginning to feel defeated with no hope.

I stayed parked in front of their home and cried, "Why Father, why is this happening? Why have I lost Shaina and now my kids? I've lost my freedom and everything good in my life, why? Why? Why?"

My ex quickly became embarrassed of my situation, constantly fending off questions and judgment from neighbors and coworkers. But I quickly calmed down and knew the circumstances weren't their fault, nor my ex's. I not only wanted to keep myself out of the limelight, but I also had to respect my sons' wishes. Throughout the divorce, I slowly began to neglect my sons, diving headfirst into my newfound freedom and spending every waking minute with Shaina. I was sure they formed resentment toward me for putting her before them; I couldn't say I blamed them. I had nearly lost it all.

Chapter 6

MUSIC FESTIVAL

BEFORE THE NIGHTMARE – Fall 2018

After Das Energi, concerts became a thing for Shaina and me, and I suspect we went to over a dozen concerts in our first four months to come, including Ozzy, Metallica, checked off a bucket list seeing Kygo, and more EDM shows than I can even remember. As a middle-aged man, I never thought it possible that I'd be listening to this kind of music or seeing live music so regularly, and I felt like a little kid again.

The weekend after Das, my friends Everett and Dan had VIP cabins for Reggae Rise Up—another weekend-long music festival—but it was too late for me to get a cabin and the tent sites were further away from both my friends and the stage. Everett and Dan said Shaina and I could stay in their enclosed trailer next to the cabins, so long as we didn't fear "roughing it." All we needed were tickets to get in.

I was told we could have a UTV at the festival, which is essentially a four wheeler that has bucket seats for up to five people. I loaded mine up and the two of us headed out in the truck. As we pulled into the festival grounds to unload it, we learned they weren't allowed in the tent camping area, but my friends must have known that because they brought along a banner that read SECURITY for the front windshield. Everett said they had just used a printer, but the sign looked legit; not one security guard batted an eye as Shaina, and I drove right through and parked next to the cabin.

After setting up shop, we drove the truck back to the main parking lot where Shaina saw her ex's Dodge truck and she laughed. "He always wanted a GMC Denali," she mused, then an idea lit up her face. "Can I drive past him?"

Rolling my eyes, I responded, "Of course, Beautiful."

She jumped in the driver's seat and looked like she was born to drive a truck, even though she looked so miniature from my stance outside the window. "Why do you look so short in a car, but so tall in real life?"

"I've got a short torso, silly. I'm all legs." *Well, that should've seemed obvious,* I thought. I hopped into the passenger's seat, and we cranked up the stereo, bumping the subs, as we drove by the Dodge. I'm not sure her ex even saw us, but it didn't matter—I loved her smile while driving that truck, and I loved helping her win her small battles.

After parking, we shuttled back to the cabin. Our friends had outdone themselves. They brought two portable hot tubs, a pool table, more string lights than on a house at Christmastime, and plenty of speakers for music. We immediately started pounding the Fireball. As things grew dark, I was tipsy, but my friend Brody and his girlfriend, Emily, challenged us to a game of pool. Brody started it off and with the next turn, I finished the game. Shaina admired me with a look in her eyes, I knew exactly what she was thinking.

The two of us wandered down a couple cabins where we bumped into a friend who offered us mushrooms. Shaina and I exchanged hesitant glances. "Well, we're going to need them, otherwise we'll fall asleep soon," she suggested. I couldn't think of a fair retort. We ate them and went back to the trailer—our home for the weekend—to make our bed before the drugs kicked in. Just as I finished fluffing my pillow, I looked at Shaina and we laughed hysterically. "You're the one who's 'Silly Two' tonight," she added. I conceded, giving her the glory for the night.

We made our way over to a tree with four walls of sheets hanging up and snuck inside to make out. Once she pulled away to catch her breath, she cautiously looked around at the sheets and whispered, "The walls . . . they're breathing." I wanted to take my black-haired angel then and there, but the sound of a commotion pulled us from our fort.

A brunette was hunched down crying. Shaina ran over to the girl to console her, picking her up and wrapping her arms around her back in a protective stance. I could see the girl's red, swollen cheek from where I stood. I confronted the guy standing at a close distance watching. "Dude, did you hit her?" *I was sure steam was blowing out of my ears.*

"No, she just fell down, dude!"

I yelled over to the girlfriend to ask what happened, but she just stammered, "Nothing," and turned away, continuing to be consoled by Shaina.

"If you touch her," I threatened through clenched teeth, "me and you will have problems." The guy put his hands up and backed away.

I walked up to Shaina and her new friend. "Are you okay?"

"He's just a dick when he gets drunk," she mumbled. I knew she was lying. Her bruised cheek said otherwise.

"If you feel unsafe for any reason, you come find us, okay?" The girl seemed more than happy to take me up on my offer.

"Can I hang out with you guys? I like you two."

The rest of the night we watched hundreds of people come through our camp in a blur as we sat on a log next to the pool table under the trees, cuddling our new friend. We ended up seeing maybe thirty minutes of the concert, but our bodies were toast and we called it an early night.

I woke up the next morning with a drumming in my skull. I rubbed my temples, moaning as I tried to sit up. "Fuck, my head is pounding," I mustered.

"I just want to die," Shaina groaned.

"Not on my watch, Beautiful." Then Shaina groggily formed her hand into the shape of a gun and pretended to shoot her head.

"Don't you do that; I love your brains. Don't you ever hurt them," I demanded, then I leaned over and kissed her forehead.

Shaina seemed kind of shocked by my comment and I didn't know what to make of it, but before I could decipher her expression, she pushed me on my back, ripped off my pants, and started riding me, never once taking her eyes off mine. We got changed and opened the door to my friend Jack sitting in the defective hot tub just outside the trailer. He was scrawny, covered in tattoos, and probably hadn't seen the inside of a shower in a few days—the quintessential stoner.

"Have fun, kiddos?" he asked casually, taking a hit on his joint. Shaina awkwardly laughed, grabbing my hand to head for the food trucks, but not before I turned back to give Jack a sly wink.

Someone at the festival approached us on our way over to snag some coffee and asked if we wanted any acid. I was totally caught off guard—I hadn't done acid since my early twenties. But I remembered liking it, and I thought it might cure my hangover, so I obliged. I hadn't really talked about my divorce with Shaina; she wasn't fully aware I was mid-midlife crisis for the last three years post-divorce, or the extent of my speed dating, partying, and sleeping with women to fill the void my ex-wife left. I definitely wasn't making the best decisions at the time and agreeing to drop acid was one of those poor decisions, but I was no stranger to drugs. I felt safe with myself.

"We're here to have fun aren't we?" I looked at Shaina and gave her a small shrug.

"Why not?" Shaina said.

She didn't seem to have the same reservations I did, though she wasn't going through a midlife crisis. She was young and allowed to party. The guy put two drops of acid on our tongues.

Shortly after, Shaina was clinging to me as we walked the festival grounds. "Cameron, please don't leave me," she insisted. "I get scared when I'm alone."

"Alone? Baby, I'm right here."

"I know, I'm sorry, it's just—I have abandonment issues and drugs really bring them out." Her clenched fingers around my arm confirmed this.

"I'm not going anywhere," I said as I held her close.

Two hours had gone by, and I felt nothing, which was very strange for acid. Chalking up the acid as a bust, we decided to go on a long UTV ride with Everett and his girlfriend up a tough trail at Snake Creek in Midway, Utah, which leads up to the backside of Brighton Ski Resort overlooking

Lake Mary. With my vehicles, I always live by the rule "when in doubt, throttle out," which I imagine made for some scary rides for my friends. But as we twisted back and forth down the trail, Shaina didn't flinch and it turned me on, she loved the intensity as I drove recklessly. I planned to surprise her as we summited.

It was a short hike to the tippy top from where we parked, maybe twenty feet or so, and as we climbed to the peak with a view that was something otherworldly. I asked Shaina if she would hike down to a nearby ledge where we could take a picture overlooking Lake Mary and gave my phone to Everett to take the shot. As we traversed down the steep ledge, Shaina gripping my hand tightly, we made it in front of a tree.

I took her hands and said, "Shaina, in the short time I've known you, you've stolen my heart and I want you to keep it. And I want to ask for yours, and I promise to keep it in a safe place at all times. Shaina, will you be my girlfriend?" That beautiful smile I came to love broached her face from ear to ear.

"Yes, baby! Yes!" She squeezed me so tight I could hardly breathe. She was mine!

One night while we were lying in bed, Shaina admitted, "I'm so tired of waitressing. I want to do more with my life, ya know?"

"Baby," I hesitated, "where do you work?" I felt a little foolish knowing she was a waitress but not knowing where exactly she worked.

"The Park Café in downtown Salt Lake City."

Shaina was notorious for not showing emotion, even in her most vulnerable times.

"You know what, babe," I started, "you're so amazing with people, why don't we start a business together and I can help you?"

Her face immediately lit up at my suggestion. She flipped to her stomach and perched her fists under her chin. "What are you thinking?"

My mind started racing. I had started a trucking company a few years earlier and was addicted to the success. Maybe she could do something similar, something she already knew how to do.

"Why don't we start a coffee truck?"

Shaina would often share with me all she knew about her repeat customers; it was in those moments I knew she was loved by more than just me. In fact, she told me about one specific couple that would come in monthly—an older couple in their retirement—and she'd tell how much she admired them for being together so long, and she'd ask them questions on how they did it.

Shaina began to glow. "I would love that," she said. "I see one across from my work all the time. It's close to a bus stop for students going to the University of Utah, and it *always* has a line."

My brain started clicking, working out the logistics, motivated by her enthusiasm. "Tell you what; you work on what we need, and I'll be the funding. I'll make you a sixty-percent partner, and together we'll build this for you."

That next morning, I woke up and made her coffee and started her car. The weather was starting to grow colder. I was not an early riser, but Shaina worked the breakfast shift and she mentioned to me she had always wanted a remote car starter because she hated getting in her cold car in the mornings. I noted that for a Christmas present idea.

She also talked about how much she loved going to Java Jo's for her daily coffee after her first shift break. Because Shaina was mostly staying at my house every night, I decided I would wake up every day at 5:30 a.m. and recreate her favorite coffee order. Granted, it was Keurig iced coffee, but I bought all the mixings. I began parking my commuter out front to make space to park her car in my attached garage, and I'd start her car every morning so it was warm for when she would leave.

She always came downstairs in the morning with a smile and gave me my adored jump kiss followed by an "I love you."

Every so often, I would say "I love you too" by mistake and receive a scolding; it always upset her, and I tried to be more careful with that "too" word.

On her drive to work, I would lie in bed—unable to sleep after getting up so early—scrolling on my phone looking for some meme or quote about love to send her and wait for her to respond. As soon as I heard from her, I would call her and ask her how her drive was going, talking nearly her entire drive to work. She would often complain that my house was too far from her job—a nearly hour-long drive—but she said she would do it for me. So, I wanted to do everything in my power to make it easier for her.

I would always buy her flowers. When they died, she'd arrive home to a fresh bouquet on my kitchen counter. One chilly morning, I decided to deliver flowers to her work. I grabbed a vase from my house, then stopped in at a local florist and bought two dozen roses. I decided to sweeten the deal by adding some of her favorites: Reese's, a pack of gum, and a handwritten note that spelled my love for her through ink.

As I pulled up to The Park Café, I saw the diner was still unopened, but even still, her car was nowhere to be found. Confused, I called the restaurant.

"Hi, I'd like to leave some flowers for Shaina before you open if you don't mind."

The gentleman on the other hand stuttered. "Uhh . . . what is her name again, sir?" Now it was my turn to sound confused.

"Shaina," I repeated.

"We don't have a Shaina here."

I hung up. I didn't understand why they wouldn't know her.

Cameron: Hey, you, I wanted to surprise you this morning at
your work but they're saying you don't work here.

I was still sitting in the parking lot. Twenty minutes went by with no response, the flowers on the passenger seat taunting me. Finally, I got a text back.

Shaina: Hey, babe. What do you mean?
Cameron: I'm here at your work trying to give you flowers.

I was starting to get mad . . . she wasn't answering my question, and she clearly wasn't in the parking lot with me.

Cameron: Where in the hell are you?
Shaina: I'll see you when I get off, I'm not there now.

I felt duped and embarrassed, and definitely betrayed. Why was she lying to me about where she was? I drove home in a fury, throwing the flowers in the trash when I got home.

Shaina really never fully moved in. Once a week on Mondays she would stop at her mother's and switch out her clothes for the week, often bringing a laundry basket of of them to hang up in my closet, which added another thirty minutes to her drive to my place.

We would normally text throughout the day, but I had not given her much attention that day due to my workload and my annoyance with her outright lie. Later that afternoon, she texted me.

Shaina: Hey, handsome, I need to tell you something when I get there. I'm heading to my mom's now and I'll be there as soon as I can.

She was taking longer than usual, which only fueled my anxiety.

A flash of headlights from the window announced her arrival in the driveway.

She walked inside and we met in the kitchen.

"Shaina, I wanted to surprise you this morning ... at work... with flowers ..." I trailed off waiting for her to fill in the gaps.

She looked down. "I lied to you, and I'm sorry." Her gaze fell on the roses in the trash can. "I love the flowers," she added.

I didn't speak, only waited for her to take the lead.

She took a big inhale. "I work at Village Inn," she confessed on the exhale. "I've worked there for seven years now and I'm not proud of it. I'm ashamed of my job, actually."

Village Inn is a chain diner; not the cute, local diner that The Park Café is, but a restaurant, nonetheless. I almost wanted to laugh. *This was her big secret?*

Every feeling of anger left my body. I walked up to her, placing my hands on her cheeks and pulling her face up to me from the ground.

"Shaina, baby, I don't care where you work. You're mine, and I want you to know I'm so proud of you for even working. It shows your true character to be strong and to survive, Beautiful."

She began to cry so I scrambled my brain for something more to comfort her. "I'll help you if it's something you don't want to do anymore. We can do the coffee truck if you want, remember? Just let me know what you want to be."

A single tear rolled down her cheek. "I want to be a nurse," she sniffed. I pulled her face in and kissed her.

"Then a nurse you'll be, Beautiful. I have a payroll client, a college that offers nursing school. I'll make an appointment right away with my contact."

"I have a friend at Salt Lake Community College—I think I'd like to go there so I'd know someone."

"Well then tomorrow I'll call them and see what they can do."

Almost instantly, she hit me with a jump kiss, almost breaking my teeth. "Cameron, I'm so ashamed, I've never told a boyfriend where I worked before. I always hid it."

Restless to see that smile again, I added, "Shaina, please listen to me. You're amazing, and you should never be ashamed of where you work."

She jumped up onto me, cradling me with her legs and wrapping her arms around my neck. "Take me upstairs, handsome," she whispered.

Before we dozed off, my phone buzzed with a text:

Texter: Cameron if you don't pay us maybe we'll just come see you

As my anger rose, I began to think of my innocent kids and their room on the front of the house next to the street.

"What's wrong?" Shaina asks.

"Just some guy working for me wanting to get paid before I do. I'm worried a little bit if he were to do something stupid, though. He usually comes to my home to pick up his checks." I say this cautiously not wanting to scare her off.

"Well, what are you going to do?" she asks.

"I'll be right back."

As I went down to my basement where I kept my safe of guns for hunting and protection, I grabbed my 9mm pistol, which was secured in a small safe by key and went back to the room.

"Babe, I need to ask if you, are okay if I keep this under my bed for protection? It's locked by key so no one in the house should be able to get to it." The key was on my keychain.

"Yes, that's fine, it's kind of hot how protective you are of us," she says, as I lay down.

She turns on my chest to give me a kiss. "Good night, handsome."

Chapter 7

HER SPIRIT

AFTER THE NIGHTMARE – August 2019

Two weeks had passed since I had been released, and I finally got my phone back from the police and was able to trash my cheap burner phone. I spent entire days watching news reports and hours and hours combing through Facebook. I'd take screen shots of threatening conversations and send names to the authorities, watching everyone run my name through the mud. I had never had this much hate projected onto me and wanted to confront each of them. There were lots of threats from people claiming they'd come find me.

I kept reporting to my attorney and asking for updates on the case; I must have called him a dozen times a day. At one point, probably realizing I was driving myself insane, he asked me, "Cameron, can you get out of town?

You're not giving me the time I need to focus on this case, and honestly, I think you're a hazard to yourself."

"I'm going crazy, Glen, but I can't say I disagree …"

"Oh, and one more thing," he interjected, "If you post anything to social media you will ruin this, and I'll remind you, you will have to hire another attorney."

I sighed. Glen reminded me to stay off social media often; I don't know if I found the frequency of his warnings annoying, or the fact that I needed the constant reminders.

"Cameron, do you understand?"

"Yes, Glen. I got it." I assured him the best I could.

After hanging up with Glen, I called my brother Joe, who answered the phone with an emotion I'd grown to know well over the weeks: pity.

"Hey, Cam, how are you holding up?" I had already spoken to my family many times by now, all of them hurting for me and standing in my corner.

"I'm not doing particularly good, man, "I said. My attorney wants me to leave town, but I need to go by my house first and grab some things. I'm sure you've seen all the threats on Facebook." It wasn't a question so much as a statement.

"Of course, I have."

I wasn't sure what to expect from him when I asked the next question. "I need to borrow a pistol from you . . . the police have all my weapons, and if someone wants to hurt or kill me, I at least want the chance to defend myself." Silence hung in the air for a few moments. I wasn't sure if Joe thought I had other intentions. Maybe, in hindsight, I was just trying to convince myself of the next part that came out my mouth. "You have my word: no matter what happens, I will not turn it on myself, Joe. You have to believe me, I just need to protect myself if need be."

"Of course. I trust you, Cam, and I love you. I know you must be scared outta your mind lately. Swing by my house?"

"Be there soon."

I met my brother, and we exchanged hugs and the pistol before I was quickly on my way back to my house. Once again, every car that passed me was a suspect in my eyes, paranoia clouding my every judgment. *Was I being followed?*

As I got off the exit, I took circuitous route to my house so that if someone *were* following me, my cockamamie path would convince them I was lost or not, in fact, Cameron Lundgren, Alleged Girlfriend Murderer. I circled my block four times before stopping a few houses down from mine, then hit my garage door opener and waited for it to open fully before speeding in and closing it behind me. I turned off the car and took a deep breath, anxious to exit my car and even more anxious to step foot in the house that had come to symbolize tragedy and, potentially, danger.

Picking up the pistol on the seat beside me, I threw the clip in and put a bullet in the chamber. As I placed my hand on the doorknob that led inside the house, I paused and took my shoes off so I could be quiet while pacing my home. My heart pounding, I slowly turned the knob of the garage door and inched inside the kitchen. I half expected my alarm to start the count-down to disarm. I wanted it to go off; if anyone was in there, the blaring sound would hopefully scare them away—but all I heard was silence.

Turns out, the silence was more eerie than the screeching of an alarm. The last time I had been home—really been home with the lights on—the place had been teeming with cops and paramedics. This soundless aftermath felt like a hoax, like a dream even. As I slowly made my way across the kitchen, I couldn't fend off the sadness of what happened the night she killed herself and tears started welling up once more.

It was as if nothing had changed. The Taco Tuesday taco bar was still laid out, empty beer bottles still splayed on the counter. A horrendous moment in time, memorialized right here in my kitchen.

But something was off. It only took a few moments to register what I was seeing. My kitchen table had a huge hole in it, that definitely hadn't been there the night of the party.

Moving to the living room, holding the gun out in front of me, ready to fire at any movement, I see my TV ... shattered.

My couches have been slashed by a razor blade. Gun still held high, I surveyed the rest of the room and focused on the wall to my left where my mirror was hung. The word MURDERER is sprayed in black paint.

My head reeling, I'm feeling gut-punched: People had broken into my house and trashed everything, graffitied my walls, ripped up all my furni-ture, which now looked like it had been dropped off a cliff. Upstairs, even my clothes have been spray painted. All of my belongings, ruined.

Shaking, wanting to fall to my knees and cry in defeat, I needed to pull it together and check the rest of the house. My alarm was disarmed—which I assumed as much when I walked into silence—*but am I alone?* I hoped no one would hear me padding through the house in my socks.

I kept my pistol in front of me, ready to fire, and gently crossed over to the door leading down to the basement. As I opened the door, the sound of a glass shard hitting the cold concrete of the basement floor nearly spooked me into pulling the trigger.

"Get the fuck out of my house! I have a gun and I will shoot!"

This is why I had asked Joe for the pistol, this is exactly what I was worried about—*was I about to have a standoff in my own house with an Internet vigilante?*

I tiptoed down the stairs when I hit the bottom. I shifted the pistol in every direction, searching for movement or any sound that was out of place.

I noticed a window had been broken with a few loose shards still hanging from the frame. I went back upstairs to trace my steps and be sure it was safe.

The house secured, I realized whoever was there had left in a hurry. I had little interest in seeing the police again, but I grabbed my phone anyway and dialed 911.

"911, what's your emergency?"

Confident I was now in my home alone, I responded, "My home has been broken into, and I need help as soon as possible."

As I walked through the lonely house, I took a video of the damage. The police arrived and logged the incident. While they were there, I couldn't help but think if they knew who I was or had recognized my address. *Did they think I was a monster too?* But they acted calm and professional as if I was any other person, and I thanked them as they left.

Once gone, I grabbed whatever I could that was not ruined and quickly packed it into a bag. I noticed all of Shaina's items were missing from the house. While in jail I had told Glen that I'd allow her parents to enter my home and retrieve her belongings. I guess I shouldn't have been surprised they had come to get everything, but it meant I was left with nothing to remember her by.

As I stuffed the last item of clothing into my duffel and turned to leave, I noticed Shaina's Crocs were still next to the bed. The same Crocs she would wear every day to work at Village Inn. They were badly worn and dotted with holes. Her family had picked up all of her things except the one thing she had worn the most. The one thing I saw her in every day as she kissed me goodbye, and I sent her off with my homemade coffee. I grabbed them and brought them with me.

At the instruction of Glen, I got out of town. Out of state to be exact. He was right; I was being a nuisance to him and the investigation and a menace to my own well-being. The days spent cooped up in my house, forcing myself to rewatch news clips and scroll through social media, was really playing with my sanity. "All work and no play makes Cameron a dull boy" began circulating in my head and I knew I had to leave, and I knew Vegas would be my best bet at forgetting every morsel of grief that had become my life.

The drive felt like days, and I must have turned the radio on and off a hundred times. Every time I turned it back on some song would be playing that reminded me of Shaina. "Girls Like You" by Maroon 5 was popular that early summer, and I always told her that song reminded me of us—of how we would always make up after our fights. Anytime we'd fight, we'd have incredible make-up sex; the sweetest piece of heaven I have ever experienced. I think we both were addicted to that physical intimacy, to keep us from dwelling on the breaking pieces in our relationship that would cause each fight. The sex always kept us coming back to each other, even when things were bad. It was our addiction.

I used the back of my arm to wipe away the tears that were now falling. As much as I needed to get away, the last thing I needed was this much time alone in my car to reflect on our memories. I felt like the day Shaina died, my whole body fractured. And now, day by day, those fragile pieces were falling. There was nothing to look forward to, nothing to get me to see the alleged light at the end of the tunnel. I didn't have Shaina, I didn't have my job, my friends for good reason didn't want to be seen with me in public, and I didn't have my kids. The investigation seemed to be stalling at an agonizing pace, and now I couldn't even talk to Glen. I was losing my will to fight.

I thought back to Joe and to the promise I had made him before I left. I had to push these negative thoughts out of my mind and stop ruminating. Things had to get better. They definitely couldn't get any worse.

I pulled up to the MGM Grand in Vegas with a new sense of conviction. It didn't look like the next couple months were going to get better, but at least I could make my weekend better. I checked into my room, turned on the TV, and fell asleep. I woke up around eight o'clock and though I could've easily spent the rest of the night in bed, wallowing in misery, I knew I had to keep my mind busy. I got dressed and headed down for some gambling, one of Shaina and I favorite things to do.

As I made my way to the table, there were two guys sitting next to each other, followed by two open seats and then one woman sitting alone. I couldn't help but smile: two people, both in Vegas alone. Maybe she was just as miserable as I was. I pulled up into the empty chair beside her and struck up a conversation. She was from California, tall with long dark brown hair, a dark complexion, and about my age. I couldn't lie—she was beautiful. Her hair and her height reminded me of Shaina, causing my heart to pang.

"Where are you from?"

"Utah, but I feel Vegas is where my heart lives." I laugh.

"I've been to Utah a few times; weather is nice until wintertime," she chuckles.

"I find the cold weather as a challenge, driving in the sun is boring."

"Well, you sound fun."

I was aware she was flirting with me, but I didn't have the same intentions.

We chatted about playing blackjack. She was friendly and had a beautiful smile. Most importantly, she had no idea who I was or what had led me to Vegas in the first place.

The dealers up card showed "7" and I had a pair of fours.

I doubled down as the table looks at me like I've lost my mind.

"You're fearless, aren't you?"

That sounded like something Shaina would say as my mind wandered to her. "Nothing gambled, nothing gained," I smugly say as I look down. My stack of thousands had dwindled to a few hundred. Quite honestly, I didn't even care—it felt good to talk to someone who didn't stare at me with either pity or hatred.

The dealer gives me a "10" and then shows an Ace and takes my chips.

I didn't want to end the conversation despite my losing streak, so I invited her to dinner with me and she accepted. We walked to the closest restaurant in the casino and sat down to eat, all the while still making pleasant conversation. The more I talked though, the more I felt those prickly emotions bubbling to the surface, and I found myself wanting to tell someone what had happened.

"So, what brings you down here?"

"Just needed to get away from life," deflecting the question and truthful answer as best as I could.

The more we talked, the more I could sense how kind she was, and how lonely she must have known I was. Dinner over, I paid the bill, but our impending departure sent me over the edge, my brain telling me this was my last chance to spill my guts out to this stranger. *Why did I need to do this?*

I could not hold back any longer and I broke out in full-blown ugly crying. She quickly put her hand over mine and asked, "What's wrong?"

I was crying so hard I couldn't muster a word. I'm sure she thought I was insane, and she would've been right. I'm sure this was her first experience having a stranger ask her out to dinner so he could have a meltdown in front of her.

"Where's your room? Maybe we should go talk?"

All I could manage was a nod in agreement, suddenly feeling a bit embarrassed. My room wasn't far off—just near the elevators—I managed a brief synopsis of what happened, only telling her "my girlfriend committed suicide."

She was sympathetic, and kept rubbing my back, but she got quiet when we approached my room door.

Sniffling, I pulled out the room key and placed it up against the handle, and the lock went green. As I began to open the door, she gently pushed in front of me to enter first. When I closed the door behind me, she turned around to face me. I noticed her face had become ashen and her eyes had grown wide, like she had literally seen a ghost.

"Cameron . . . I can't be here. I have to go."

She started to move toward the door as I stood there speechless, dried tears staining my cheeks. She placed her hand on the doorknob then paused, exhaled deeply, and turned to me. "Did your girlfriend have dark hair?"

Tears again swelled in my eyes.

"Yes," I choked out.

She was silent another moment longer then finally spoke. "Cameron, I've enjoyed my time with you, but I have to leave. I must tell you, I can see spirits." She paused. "I see this woman sitting on the bed and—well, she's crying, and she wants me to tell you she's sorry. She wants you to be happy—she wants you to be her 'Happy Cameron,' and she loves you."

I gaped at her, then looked toward the empty bed, not entirely sure what was happening, but a small shiver worked its way through my body. She opened the door then turned to look at me once more.

"I expect her spirit to be with you for a long time. She's attached to you, Cameron, at least until you're well. Take care of yourself, handsome." The door closed behind her.

I stayed put, blinking a few times, then nervously moved my head to scan the room. All I wanted to do was see Shaina's face, but there was nothing. Desperately, I called out to the room. "Shaina, I need you to show me you're here." I needed to see some small piece of evidence she was with me. Nothing. Out of desperation, I picked up my phone and typed out a new message to Shaina.

Cameron: Baby, are you here?

Nothing.

I sat down on the bed and stared at the spot where the woman had looked, where she said she saw Shaina crying. Tears continued rolling down my cheeks and I closed my eyes and quietly said, "It's okay, Beautiful. I'll be okay."

Though those words did little to comfort me, in fact, they made me weep harder.

"It gives me comfort to know you're still with me and I would give anything in this world to hold you again. To feel your touch, to kiss your lips, to kiss your forehead while you lay on my chest. Just one last time, and tell you everything will be okay, and it will, Shaina, it will. I love you." I grabbed the bottle of Fireball I had picked up in the lobby on the way up and chugged as much as I could pass down my throat.

I spent the night holding Shaina's Crocs as tight as I could, talking to them as if it were her and reminiscing on all the good times we had. Something about what that woman had said felt so real. I knew she was talking to Shaina's spirit, which meant she was still here with me and her Crocs. When I would laugh retelling one of our funny adventures, I envisioned her laughing with me. When I would cry, I would envision her crying with me. I fell asleep pretending she was lying on my chest.

My plan had been to fly out of Vegas to New Orleans and then maybe New York. I wanted to busy my mind with sightseeing. But after last night, I didn't feel safe with myself, so I packed my stuff into the car and headed back home. The trip had finished before it started.

On my drive home, I decided to call my payroll employer. After I hadn't showed up to work for the three weeks I was kept in jail, I hadn't even bothered to tell them I was out. The investigation hadn't seemed to be making any strides in the two weeks since I was released and virtually the entire state of Utah was gung-ho to believe I was guilty, so I thought, hey—this job isn't going to matter when they throw my ass back in jail.

But it had been nearly a month now since my release and still no charges had been pressed. It was probably time to see if I still had a job. As the phone rang, a small knot twisted in my stomach. My manager answered and I blurted out," Tom listen, I know you guys must be asking yourself what in the hell happened and honest to God I would never do something like that, so you know —"

Tom cut me off. "Cameron you're on a recorded line, be careful what you say. This puts us in a tough position, and you've been our top sales rep for years, I don't know where things stand with the owners, but I'll reach out to you as soon as I know something."

A few miles down the road, he called me back on his cell phone.

"Cameron, you can no longer work here. We've recorded it as job abandonment. I'm sorry."

I threw my phone on the floor, luckily not damaging it. "Just fucking great," I sputtered. Before Shaina's death, I made more than enough money to enjoy the finer things in life. Now, my businesses had stalled, and I had drained most of the money I liquidated on legal fees and an unlucky night in Vegas. My motivation to fight for life was slowly chipping away.

I began to slip deeper into a dark hole.

As I pulled back into town, I made the conscious decision not to be controlled by fear. I was supposed to be in Vegas for another few days before heading off on another trip and hadn't called my family to tell them my grand get-out-of-town plan had been cut short. No one knew I was coming back home.

I had been monitoring Facebook a little while I was in Vegas (not posting!). and there were still people posting that they were driving by my home, reporting things like "it didn't seem like anyone was there" and "no lights on at night." My plan was to be safe, case the home, and set it up like a fortress.

My home was a newer build and a good 4,000 square feet of quietness—when my boys weren't there.

I pulled into my garage in the same fashion as before: quick and stealth, taking the same steps to load the clip in my pistol and chamber a bullet. I had talked a big game in my head on the drive over, but now, being back, my heart started to thud against my chest.

I slowly opened the garage door to enter the kitchen—only this time the alarm was set, and I let the countdown begin until it began blaring. I repeated the process of checking every nook and cranny, gun at the ready to fire if needed. Luckily, the house appeared empty. I gradually lowered my weapon. As I finally laid down to rest on my couch—all sliced up from someone's thin razor-blade handiwork—I heard the doorbell and my heart dropped. *Had someone been tipped off that I was home?*

I scurried to my front living room windows to sneak a glance at the front porch, but the angle wasn't right, and peeping over the small windows at the top of the front door would undoubtedly blow my cover. I could check the security cameras, but I still hadn't reactivated them after the police's initial search of the house.

Whoever was at the door knocked again. They had to know I was home. I slowly opened the front door and peered around, making sure my hand was on the gun in my back pocket. To my surprise, I was greeted by a middle-aged woman with fiery red hair and a welcoming smile.

"Hi, Cameron?" she asked, smiling up at me. I hadn't gotten to know my neighbors well since moving into the neighborhood, so I couldn't be sure who she was and whether she was one of the Facebook neighbors threatening to alert everyone to my presence.

"Yea . . . yes."

"I live next door."

The sweet smell of baking hit my nose and I looked down to see her holding a plate of homemade banana bread.

"Cameron, my husband has been through some bad times, and we wanted to bring you this treat and let you know that sometimes bad things happen to good people. We're pulling for you."

She grinned up at me with a sympathetic look in her eye that confirmed she'd been through some sort of a struggle, too, but I didn't press her for details. Instead, my hand came off the gun that was placed in my holster hidden halfway behind the door. Tears started welling up again, but I pushed them down.

"Wow, I'm a little shocked," I managed to say. "After these weeks . . . I just—I thought it was me against the world."

She outstretched her arms to offer me the banana bread. "Cameron, you need to know there's a small, silent army out there rooting for you. Those people see through the lines and aren't fooled by what the media is saying. We can see there's more to this story. Please keep your head up, and if you need anything, please let us know."

I was about to start bawling, but I maintained my composure enough to take the bread from her hands.

"You have no idea how much that means to me," I choked out. "And thank you so much—I love banana bread. I'll eat every last piece."

She gave me a final smile then turned to amble down the walkway. As I started to close the door to be alone with my tears and my homemade dessert, she spun around as if she had forgotten something.

"Oh, one more thing—please be safe. My husband is former military, so we've kept a close eye on your home in case this more—" she bit her lip in search of a word "*immature* crowd threatening to hurt you actually turns dangerous."

"I can assure you I'm armed, and if anyone comes into my home, they'll wish they hadn't."

"Good. Take care of yourself," she added before turning on her heel once more, the door closing behind her.

As I stepped into the kitchen to place the banana bread on my counter, a glimmer of hope filled my heart and it felt like, for the first time, my head was above water. My world had been filled with so much hatred and hostility, and this neighbor brought a moment of peace; a small moment for me to feel that the entire world didn't want to kill me, and that there were people—strangers! —who felt the coverage of Shaina's death and my alleged involvement was suspicious.

It gave me time to pause and exhale, even if momentarily. My will to fight had dwindled, but if my neighbor was right and others believed I was innocent, maybe this nightmare had a happy ending. After all, it wasn't just this "small, silent army" on my side; the police had let me walk free with no charges. There was a chance I could clear my name.

Nevertheless, with no new updates from Glen and a larger, louder army of social media soldiers threatening to hurt me, I knew I couldn't let my guard down and be stupid after a little, vulnerable display of hope. So, I moved on to build my home fortress.

I grabbed the ladder in my garage and removed my wireless cameras from the exterior of the house. Later that day, another neighbor who had been threatening to keep tabs on me via Facebook posted that she saw me pulling down my security cameras in an attempt to "destroy evidence," despite the fact it had been a month since the police had seized any available evidence from my house, including security camera footage. I couldn't help but chuckle at the blatant stupidity of some people.

I opened my kitchen drawer and took out all my silverware, scattering it across the tile floor at all the entrances to my home; at least if an intruder came in the night, at the very least, I'd hear them. At the very most, they might break their neck. As I set up my booby traps, I started laughing, feeling like Macaulay Culkin in *Home Alone.* Laughing felt good. Today felt good, and I was beginning to feel like my old self again.

Nightfall was coming fast, and I needed to hurry before it became too dark outside that my interior lights would welcome a "visitor."

After I was done with the main floor, I went to the basement with a piece of cardboard to seal the window that had been broken by the previous couch-ruining, MURDERER spray-painting intruders. Then I retreated back up the stairs and grabbed one of my wireless cameras. Opening the affiliated app on my phone to check the settings, I was surprised to see it not only monitored motion, but sound. I set up a stool halfway up the stairs and placed the camera on top, positioning the lens toward the bottom of the stairs. To test it, I stood behind the camera and spat "punks" in my regular voice. The siren blared so loud I worried a neighbor would hear it, and I laughed while simultaneously letting out a scared "fuck!"

I continued to the main floor; six feet back from the front door I set up another stool and placed the camera so that it captured both the front door and around the corner to the hallway leading to the kitchen and the garage door. It was the perfect spot. Unless these assholes had a tall ladder to get onto the second story, they weren't going to get in. At least not anywhere on the first floor, without getting caught by the cameras.

The last thing I did was make sure all lights were off and doors were locked. The next step was going to be the hardest: I would have to go upstairs, back to where it all happened. I guardedly plodded up the split-level stairs and stopped at the midway landing to carefully place my last camera on the top step, facing forward down the stairs.

I had been in good spirits all day, finally feeling comfortable and safe in my own home.

I felt like playing music, so I opened my phone and turned on Pandora. Ever since the hotel, I felt like Shaina's spirit was following me, and I knew she'd like to listen along with me. The default station that popped up was Kygo, one of Shaina's favorites. I hit play.

The first song that came on was "Carry Me," and my body instantly sank into the floor. It was one of the first songs I held her to, as we watched the VR music video on our third night together. The memories flooding into my stream of consciousness became unbearable and breathing became far too difficult. I turned off the music.

As I finished to the top of the stairs—where I was no longer safe from painful memories—I saw, in the dim glint of the last daylight, blood at the top landing floor where I last saw her.

Her blood had soaked and hardened into the carpet. My limbs went numb, and my body dropped to the carpet, breathlessly crawling over to the stain. I laid there, weeping, whispering, "Shaina, why, Shaina, why" over and over.

After an hour, my tear ducts had become numb like the rest of my body. Still lying on the bloodstained carpet, I picked up my phone and flipped to the video of me proposing to her, and then her snowboarding for the first time, and then to us ice skating at the Peaks Ice Arena. I slowly scrolled through every beautiful image of her face, taking in every shape and curve and color.

For a moment I felt her next to me, then suddenly I felt this warm sensation on my forehead. It reminded me of every night when we cuddled in bed just before falling asleep. I'd whisper, "I love your brains" before kissing her on her forehead—she'd always told me she loved my forehead kisses because they made it easier for her to fall asleep.

As I lay on the floor, feeling that sensation of warmth on my head, I couldn't help but whisper, "Baby, I loved your brains. I cannot believe you did what you did, but I hope you're in a better place. I miss you." I fell asleep with my pistol next to my side.

Fire engines roar down the street. When I look down, I'm mounted on top of Shaina in the spot she lay after she shot herself. I begin to panic, but I don't see any blood. I look up to find her awake, smiling at me, even though the sirens grow louder still. Her mouth is moving but I can barely hear her over the screeching wails. I lean in close to her mouth, fearful I'm going to miss something important; fearful that she'll be gone any second, and I hear her softly say, "Everything will be okay. You're loved by so many. Just be you." I can feel her lips moving under my ear, but her words grow quieter underneath the siren's mounting blares. I start screaming. "Baby, I need you! Please don't leave me, baby. Come back!" She disappears.

My eyelids ripped open and I'm lying in the same spot I fell asleep, only this time my camera alarms were screaming throughout the house. I frantically patted my pants and the surrounding floor for my pistol in the dark of the night. My hands finally wrapped around the stock, and I leaped up, every sense fully awake. It was pitch black. I quickly grabbed my phone out of my pocket: five thirty in the morning. Turning on the flashlight, I kept it pointed close to the ground to just give myself enough light to see through the dark without alerting any intruder of my location. I knew I had the advantage if someone was here.

Backing into the master bedroom, facing the stairway, my back caught the side of the door frame as I passed into my bedroom and closed the door behind me. I crouched behind my bed—in a daze from the alarms—trying to unlock my phone before finally opening the camera app to watch the live video.

I hit play and watched as a white silhouette passed the camera located on the second story stairs before the video ended. Opening the next video from the front door camera, the same silhouette passes through the hallway then turns into the kitchen. What the hell am I seeing? I replayed the videos a few times and looked up to the top screen of my phone, and the time suddenly sank in. Five thirty. There's no way . . . could it be Shaina, waking up for her morning shift as she did every week over the last seven years and leaving for work? Meeting me in the kitchen for her iced coffee before exiting the kitchen door that leads into the garage and getting into her car—the one I woke up early to warm up for her.

Was I losing my mind? Is there an actual person here, who I should be calling the police on? I continued replaying the videos until sunrise came, when I finally had the gall to search the house. As I checked each room and shadowy corner, pistol in hand, I saw that nothing had been disturbed.

Chapter 8

SEVEN DAYS OF HAPPINESS

BEFORE THE NIGHTMARE – September 2018

Things in our relationship felt perfect.

Shaina and I took my boys to the state fair, and in true dad fashion, I bought everyone all-access passes and we watched my boys ride until they puked.

My eldest came up to me and announced, "Dad, come look at this huge corn pit!"

He led me over to a gigantic pit of corn kernels, about fifteen by twenty feet wide. I bent over to run my hand through it when my youngest son's body came barreling out from inside the corn pit. Startled, I jumped back then began cry-laughing. "I can't believe you buried your brother in this."

We all continued laughing as we made our way to the crash derby and watched as a brand new Dodge was hooked to the bumper of an older GMC, competing to see which could pull the other.

"That's so unfair," I whined, gesturing toward the cars. "We should hook my GMC Denali to that Dodge and *then* it'd be a fair fight." I gently nudged Shaina with my elbow as she rolled her eyes at me. It felt like we were finally calmed down; the late night partying had stopped, and I was seeing my kids more often.

Later that night we broke out the Monopoly game. Sitting around the kitchen table, my kids groaned, "Dad, you never let us win."

I almost always won, and the others threw playful jabs at me. We played until midnight ending the game when we all were half-asleep.

Although I was having fun, I'm not sure Shaina felt the same way. She would never say as much, but I always got the feeling that she wasn't too fond of having my kids around. She plastered on that charming waitress smile, but it never quite reached her eyes.

But I was infatuated with this woman, even to my detriment. My parents divorced when I was sixteen and as a teen, I had vowed to myself to never give up on a relationship because I believed communication and hard work was bound to make something last—something my parents hadn't done. With Shaina, that vow sometimes did more harm than good. I was innately stubborn, but my parents' divorce had also left me with blinders, incapable of looking at the red flags in relationships.

One night we were lying in bed when Shaina asked, "Do you think I'm a horrible person?"

I was a bit shocked by the question. I answered honestly, not knowing what she was getting at. "Absolutely not! Everyone who meets you loves you. Who would possibly think you're a bad person, baby?"

"It's nothing, really. I guess I just had some things happen in my life that make me question it."

Shaina wasn't exactly one for opening up, so I pushed her a bit. "Talk to me, you don't need to hold it in, Shaina."

Her eyes reached for the floor, not meeting my gaze. "I just experienced a lot of slut shaming when I was in high school," she admitted, then quickly looked at me. "Not that I was—a slut, I mean—but I just had a lot of bullies that didn't like me is all."

Grabbing her lower jaw gently with my hand I said, "I don't care what you did in high school, but those bullies were probably just a bunch of jealous bitches. To me, you're perfect."

She looked back down at the floor as if wondering whether to respond. I continued to stroke her cheek to coax her out of her shell She continued. "Sometimes I wonder if people would care if I was gone."

I immediately stopped caressing her, pulling my hand back in shock. Since I had known Shaina, she had been a bubbly, exuberant, burst of life, the outgoing type who made friends wherever she went because she was adventurous and kind. I'd never heard her talk like this before and it puzzled me as much as it concerned me.

"Shaina." I gently pulling her face to me so I could look into her eyes. "I would care if you were gone. Your family would care, and all your friends would care. I can *promise* you that." As I pulled her close to envelop her in my arms, she stayed quiet, so I asked, "What can I do to help you see you're amazing?" I felt her arms squeeze tighter around me.

"Just hold me tonight."

Pulling away from the hug, I searched her big hazel eyes, searching for the sadness I felt in her voice and willing it to disappear. "As you wish," I said, a line from *The Princess Bride* that I would often use with her. Attempting to shift the mood, I offered, "Should we eat edibles and be silly?"

That big smile stretched across her face. "Yes, please."

Early the next morning I decided I wanted to shower Shaina with love and appreciation to try and rid that beautiful brain of those toxic thoughts, and I set out on a mission to make her week amazing.

Day 1

"See you handsome."

She blows me a kiss as she gets into her car leaving for work into the pitch black of the morning. I spring into action and leave moments later picking up a couple packs of heart-shaped post-it notes from Walmart.

As we dozed off that night with her head propped on my chest and me kissing her forehead, whispering, "I love your brains baby," I had earlier set my phone alarm to four in the morning, a good while before she'd wake up for work.

I've found that setting alarms super early sends your body into a kind of trauma state, prepping your body to wake up; sure enough, I was up before my alarm even went off.

Shaina was still asleep and lying on my chest, so I slowly shifted away from her, then crept into the bathroom. I grabbed the sticky notes from the day before and started writing little love notes on each one, expressing how much I adored her.

Some would be slightly naughty like "I love your sexy butt" and some would just simply say "you're amazing." And, of course, I had "Beautiful" in there. I covered the entire bathroom mirror and used the sticky notes to spell out the words *I love you.* I took a picture to save the memory and went back to bed.

I woke up to a hundred kisses pecking my face.

"You are the cutest man ever! Babe, I want you to lie in bed. I've started my car this morning and made my coffee, so you rest. I got this today." She leaned in for a final kiss, but this time slipped in her tongue then whispered, "Tonight. *My* present." I fell back asleep looking like the Cheshire Cat.

Day 2

Now that I knew where she worked, I bought three dozen red roses and searched my house for the biggest vase I could find to hold them all. When I showed up at Village Inn, she was helping a customer and I admired from afar how incredible she was with people. A woman approached me and asked, "Can I help you?"

"I'd like to sit in her section," pointing to Shaina. It was at that very second she turned and saw me standing near the door, only I couldn't gauge her reaction. By now, a few of her coworkers had turned their attention to us, and Shaina plastered a smile on her face as she walked to greet me. She quickly grabbed the vase and groused through gritted teeth. "What are you doing here?"

"I came to get something to eat and to see the sexiest woman on this planet." Her face softened and her true, Shaina smile came out.

"Well, find a seat and sit down. I'll be right with you." She took the flowers to the back.

I observed how she worked with her customers: always a charming smile on her face, always happy to chat and lift others spirits around her. She was so happy and full of life; nothing like the Shaina I had seen a few nights before, worried that others didn't like her. She didn't have an ounce of makeup on, yet she looked so beautiful, and I sat back to bask in the glow of the wonderful woman I had fallen in love with.

Day 3

The next morning after Shaina left for work, I rushed to the computer to begin my project: One hundred moments I cherished. I planned to write them on a card for her, so she knew how much they meant to me. I figured it wasn't going to be easy to find so many moments for two people who had only been dating for a couple months, but the memories came surprisingly easy. I chalked it up to how active and adventurous our relationship had already been.

After I typed them, I rewrote them down on paper mainly because I didn't want to give her a printout—I wanted it to feel thoughtful. Then I arranged them on the bed for her to see when she got home.

When she returned home, she gushed over the surprise and graced me with another jump kiss.

That night we ate some edibles and laughed at all the silly memories we had made in such a short time, and I saw Shaina's spirit come back to life.

Getting high together was some of the happiest memories we had; it wasn't like when we drank. There weren't any fights or paranoia or resentment—just laughter and smiles and hope for a long future together.

Cuddled in bed, I made sure to hold her tight like she had told me she liked so much, never letting go of her throughout the night.

Day 4

Admittedly, I struggled with my creativity at this point. Hoping to switch things up, I booked a reservation at Ruth's Chris in Salt Lake City so I could treat her to some amazing food and wine. I bought her a sexy black dress that matched her hair perfectly. I laid it out on the bed next to a handwritten card that read: "Feel sexy tonight, Beautiful. And I know you don't anyway, but don't wear panties ."

After an intimate dinner, we talked more on the drive home about the coffee truck business as a side gig to her nursing. She also mentioned to me—with a little prompting on my behalf—that her dream vacation would be Thailand.

"So, would you rather go to the city of Bangkok or the beaches of Koi Samui?" I ask.

"I don't care, I just want go."

I was a little puzzled by the lack of knowledge of the country I didn't pursue the questions anymore.

Day 5

I had gone through the classics: handwritten notes, flowers, and a fancy dinner. This time, I wanted to do something unexpected.

As she walked in the door a new pair of ice skates awaited her in the bedroom. I had bought earlier in the day.

"I'm exhausted, all I want to do is lay in bed Cameron," she says as she heads upstairs.

But once she saw the skates, she ran to me and jumped on me, wrapping her long legs around my torso. As I held her legs in my arms—almost suffocating me as she wrapped her arms around my neck—she pulled away. "I've only been once . . . Are you going to help me?" Before I could even answer she added, "Cameron, I might be with you forever if you keep this up."

I pulled her close for a deep kiss.

"So," she said, hopping down to stand on her own two feet again, "we're ice skating tonight?"

"Whatever makes you happy. If you're tired, we can stay in."

"No way! I'll be ready in twenty," she gushed, bounding toward the closet to pick out some clothes.

We skated around the rink at Peaks Ice Arena holding hands, I pulled out my phone to record a selfie of us; later, we laughed when we saw that a photobomber had come up behind us. I tried teaching her how to skate backward toward the end of the rink, holding her hand every step of the way. As we got closer to the wall, she became increasingly worried.

"Cameron, I'm going to hit the wall."

Calmly, I responded, "Do you trust me?" Not saying a word, only nodding, I slowed us down as we approached the wall, then I smoothly pinned her against the glass barrier. My fingers traced her neck and moved past her ear before disappearing into black hair, her head pressed against the glass. "I love you, Shaina."

Her eyes fluttered to a close. "I love you, Cameron," she moaned before my lips reached hers, our mouths open as our tongues meet, oblivious to the people skating by.

Breathlessly, she broke the kiss and began to skate backwards, a twinkle in her eye. "Take me home, handsome."

Day 6

Saturday morning I got up early to make sure the UTV was all cleaned up and loaded for my surprise trip up to American Fork Canyon, about a half hour drive from my house.

When Shaina woke up, I led her out of the bedroom and downstairs, out the front door, and into the UTV. Shaina always said she wanted to drive it, and today, I handed her the keys. With a cooler full of drinks, we headed up the canyon.

The music was barely audible as the wind swept through the machine, making our way to Tibble Fork Reservoir and then up an old dirt road that led to the summit of Snowbird ski resort. Before we reached the summit, we stopped at an old mining cave that was open to the public and we took pictures. Then we got back on the trail and headed to the gate of the backside of Snowbird. We ditched the UTV and hiked the rest of the way to the restaurant at the summit.

"Are you having fun, baby?" I asked.

"Cameron, you're too good to me. Thank you for everything you've done this week." Smiling, she grabbed my hand as we continued our hike.

Day 7

It was Sunday, and all I wanted to do was serve her and wait on her like she did with all her restaurant customers. I woke up bright and early, sore from the day before, but focused. Growing up, Dad often cooked breakfast, and one of the family's favorites was "eggs on a golden rod," which consisted of hard boiled eggs with the cooked whites and yolks separated. The egg yolks are crumbled, and the white whites are chopped into little pieces; white gravy sauce that goes on top of the bread is mixed with the chopped egg whites, and the crumpled yolks sit on top of it all. It's a dish I'm still fond of, one that brings back memories of early weekday mornings before my parents got divorced. For Shaina's dish, I decided to switch up the gravy and made a hollandaise sauce instead.

She was still asleep when I entered the bedroom, so I woke her with a kiss.

"Baby, I made you breakfast."

After seven days of professing my love, I knew that the sad Shaina I had seen a week ago was gone. She grabbed my face and pulled me in—almost losing the plate of breakfast to the floor—and passionately kissed me.

"Cameron, I have never felt a love like this, and I love you!"

All seven days had been worth it. "I feel the same way, Beautiful." I placed the plate on the bedside table and sat at the edge of the bed next to her. "I'm not sure I've ever felt love like this."

Lifting the comforter, she commanded, "I need you in here," pointing into the covers next to her. We spent the rest of the day in bed making love, talking, kissing, and cuddling. Occasionally, she would send me to the fridge for snacks, and I had no problem serving her.

"Shaina, I love your brains, baby. And I could totally see myself with you for the rest of my life."

"Me too. I love you, you do need a wife." She reminded me again, nuzzling closer to my chest.

"I love you!" I responded, ensuring I didn't add a *too*.

We spent the rest of the day and night talking about our future together, with everything in the world ahead of us.

Together, we were unstoppable.

Chapter 9

IF YOU CAN'T BEAT THEM JOIN THEM

BEFORE THE NIGHTMARE – October 2018

Things felt right, I was on cloud nine. Pulling up to a work meeting I pull out my phone.

> **Cameron:** Hey babe, I want the world to know you're mine so I added you as my lover on Facebook.

I was giddy, actually, while I waited for her to accept—but it never happened. A few days went by, and I didn't bring it up, not wanting to disrupt our positive energy. A few nights later, though, we were lying in bed, and I glanced over at her to see she was on her phone scrolling through Facebook.

"Is there a reason you haven't accepted our relationship, but you're always on Facebook?" I couldn't hide the twinge of annoyance in my voice.

Without looking up from her phone, she coolly replied, "The people that know we are together are the important ones, like my family." She sighed. "I don't like to make this stuff public, Cameron."

Blindsided by this newfound desire for privacy, I was nearly at a loss for words. "If you're worried about losing likes or comments from your *fans*, maybe we shouldn't be together." It was a cheap shot, and I knew it. Shaina had every man in the world liking and commenting on her social media pictures, and I knew she reveled in the attention.

"Maybe." She was stone cold. I was shocked.

Everything had seemed so perfect. I had met her family, her friends. *But we couldn't make our relationship known to her acquaintances on Facebook and Instagram?* She was officially my girlfriend, or so she had claimed.

"Something to think about I guess." I got up and headed downstairs to make a drink and cool off.

Shaina would always drive over the instant she was off work, but the next night she texted me.

> **Shaina:** Hey, babe, going home to grab some things. I'll text
> or call when I'm on my way.

A few hours went by and no word, which wasn't typical behavior for her.

> **Cameron:** Hey, Beautiful. Just wondering if everything is OK,
> it's been a while since I've heard from you.

Still no response. My patience was being tested and my paranoia was heightened after our Facebook debacle, and I started texting some awful things out of frustration.

> **Cameron:** What the fuck are you doing? I thought you were just going home and grabbing a few things and coming straight here?

> **Cameron:** I told you I came home early to see you. I could still be at work or even with my friends if I knew you wouldn't be here.
> **Shaina:** Sorry, babe, just had to wash laundry and pack some things.
> **Cameron:** You know you can wash at my place, right?

She normally did laundry at my place anyway. If she went back to her mom's to spend time with her family, I had zero issue, the communication was all that was missing. What would normally take her just under an hour to get to my house had turned into five, and she wasn't giving me a valid reason as to why. An odd prickly sensation swept across my neck. That damn Facebook fight was looming in the back of my mind.

> **Cameron:** What in the fuck are you doing, Shaina? I'm so confused. Normally you'd have a weeks' worth of clothes at my place and now you're making daily stops at your moms. If things have changed, just let me know.
> **Shaina:** Cameron, I'm just going to stay at my mom's tonight if you're going to be rude.
> **Cameron:** Fine, be my guest. I'm going out with Brody tonight.
> **Shaina:** Going to go find bitches, huh?
> **Cameron:** Nope, I love you and just wish you'd stop playing games. Going to get some fresh air with the boys, talk to you

later.
Shaina: Tell her I said hi!

Brody was a friend of mine, a real bad boy, model type. He spent a lot of time at the gym and was always flocked by women. Shaina had met him at Reggae Rise Up where I'd dominated him in a game of pool. I knew that mentioning Brody would rile Shaina up; she'd assume that if I was with him, I was out on the town with some beautiful women as well.

This went on for weeks on and off. Shaina would claim she was coming over, she'd go quiet for an hour or so, then she'd eventually respond with an excuse. Many nights she would keep me on the hook leading me on to think she was coming and I would stay up waiting for hours.

She'd hit me with another "I'm leaving soon" and eventually I caught on that she was trying to sabotage my night—to keep me where she wanted me, which was at home by myself without the likes of Brody.

Meanwhile, I had no idea what she was doing while I was waiting around for her. Other times I would get, "Hey babe, I'm sorry, I want to come there but if you're going out with your friends, I'll stay home" even when I made it clear to her that I wanted to see her, not hang out with the guys.

"I didn't say I was going out with the guys" I would respond in frustration.

All I kept thinking was *games!* This younger generation had figured it out. I was nearly forty years old and knew absolutely nothing of these silly games of cat and mouse they played so well, of "ghosting" each other, or knowing how well to manipulate someone into using them for sex when you needed them. Shaina would come stay with me three nights and then be gone the fourth, with no explanation at home while anticipating her arrival.

After weeks of being played hot and cold, Courtney came into the picture. We live in a day and age when social media is all-consuming. You went to eat sushi, you posted it to Instagram or Facebook. You went on a short vacation, you posted it to Instagram or Facebook. Everybody was living for "likes," and Shaina was no exception.

Randomly, I had this hot blonde woman hearting my posts, and Shaina was quick to notice Courtney looked like your typical California bikini model.

Lying in bed one night, scrolling through Instagram, she snapped, "This Courtney bitch is annoying. Why is she hearting all your posts?"

"Probably because she sees I don't have a girlfriend, Shaina, don't you think?" I quipped.

Shaina just rolled her eyes, her eyebrows descending into a scowl. "Well, I don't like her and she's ugly."

I knew with that comment her insecurities were rising because Courtney was cute and probably someone I would date had Shaina not been around. It was illogical how her brain worked, though. I would watch as Shaina basked in the attention she would receive from social media—numerous guys would flirt with her and like her selfie posts—and it drove me batty, but I get some unsolicited attention from one woman and she's an "ugly bitch."

But if Shaina was set on playing these games, I might be able to use this situation to my advantage. So, I started liking Courtney's posts as well.

And just like that, I had become part of this new-age problem of manipulation and toxicity.

Shaina's and my fights started happening more and more often. One Friday night Shaina had led me on all day, stringing me along with her "leaving soon" texts, until finally I got sick of it. I got in my car and drove to her house around nine. It was nearly a forty-five minute drive to her mom's, and I kept in communication with her as I drove, not telling her I was in my car on my way over to her.

When I got close to her mom's house, I texted:

Cameron: Hey, babe, you still there?
Shaina: Yeah, so sorry, handsome. I got caught up talking to my mom and got in the bath. Guess what I shaved?

But as I pulled near her house, my heart may well have been ripped into shreds when I saw her car was nowhere to be found. I sent a text I'd later regret.

> **Cameron:** You're a liar! And a cheat! And if you need me, I'll be with Courtney.

I followed up with a Snapchat picture of the front of her mom's house—sans Shaina's car—and wrote *glad you shaved your pussy and cleaned it up cause it wasn't for me obviously* over the Snap picture.

I should've been the bigger person and drove back to my house and never talked to Shaina again. But I loved her and had never felt a love so strong and a connection so deep and genuine. Despite our problems, she was a drug to me. A habit I couldn't kick.

Then I made another dumb mistake on the drive home.

I fired up Facebook DM. I found in my single years, it was easy to use Messenger to build up a rapport with a woman online prior to meeting in person. In this case, she was already wanting to meet up, so it didn't take long to get a response.

> **Cameron:** Hey, gorgeous. Watcha doing tomorrow night? I see Yaegertown are playing at Scorez, wanna go?
> **Courtney:** Yes! Can I bring some friends?
> **Cameron:** Of course.

And down the path to emotional fuckery we go. I went home that night and drank myself into oblivion to keep my mind from wondering where or who Shaina could possibly be with.

Shaina and I had met a couple in Park City the week prior, and I could tell they took quite a liking to Shaina, which was unsurprising considering everyone liked Shaina. I suspected she went to see them the Friday night I showed up to her mom's house, but she never told me where she was.

Saturday morning, she texted me as if nothing had happened.

Shaina: Hey, babe, I went to the store for my mom when you came by and fell asleep when I came back.

It was a convenient excuse, but whether I believed it or not didn't matter because I had already invited Courtney out that night. *And, payback's a bitch, right?*

I led Shaina on all day like she had with me the day before, texting:

Cameron: grabbing a drink with Brody, be home later.
what are we going to do tonight?

and finally, as nightfall came:

Cameron: I have my kids tonight.

That was all it took to make her disappear.

I met up with Courtney that night with a few other couples at a local bar. We danced and had fun, then everyone came back to my place after for a few drinks. Courtney ended up getting a ride home with one of the other couples.

My plan had worked to perfection: Shaina ended up seeing pictures of me at the bar and learned Courtney had been there as well. I'm not sure if it was jealousy or wanting to keep what was hers, but Shaina didn't leave me alone at night for a while after that.

The horny goat weed had been working wonders and my time bringing her to climax became shorter and more frequent. She was teaching me, and

I was learning about her—our verbal, intimate communication could not have been better. I would buy her toys for her to use on her own, but she refused to use them without me.

Watching her climax had become a drug to me and my energy was channeled into achieving it.

But now, I had shown her a world she didn't know existed and she wanted more and more. We now had every sex toy you could imagine, and she would often criticize me for not using them more often.

Once when we were watching the *Fifty Shades of Grey* movies, Shaina commented, "Christian should be named Cameron." I laughed in approval.

Then she asked me to pull out more toys. "Cameron, you're turning me into a nympho." I wasn't going to complain.

One night after I had just finished, Shaina confessed, "I want to see you with another woman. I want to watch, and I might just start charging them for it." She peered up at me with those devilish eyes. As much fun as that sounded, I don't think I was willing to be shared. I just wanted to be Shaina's, and she mine.

"You sure about that? We're pretty early into the relationship."

"So, you'll do it for me?"

"Well, if you want to find someone, we'll see what happens."

The next weekend we got an invite to my friend Josh's place in downtown Salt Lake City, and we had planned on Ubering from his place to an underground club.

When we showed up to the club, there was a large group taking shots, including my friend Jack, who had previously seen me postcoital with Shaina while he lounged in the hot tub at Reggae Rise Up. They were getting ready to head out, which left little time to join the drinks before ridesharing to the next joint.

As we walked in the new club, the loud music overpowered any type of conversation you could possibly have, so we silently ordered drinks and listened to the DJ play his set. Shaina was growing bored and exclaimed, "Let's head up front and meet people!"

At the front was a group of four women talking in a circle and looking like the life of the party. Naturally, Shaina approached them and quickly made friends. "What are you guys doing tonight?" she yelled over the music.

"We aren't sure, just talking about it," one of them responded.

"We're having a party at my friend Josh's house if you want to come hang out with me and my hot boyfriend," Shaina chimed in, pointing to me.

Josh had a girlfriend but the other single guys in our group were quick to approve of Shaina's invite to the new women. Shaina leaned into my ear and suggested, "You want to talk to Josh about getting an Uber back to his place now?"

I nodded. "Consider it done."

There were about a dozen of us now, back at Josh's. We were all doing shots and having a good time listening to music when all of a sudden Josh's girlfriend pointed to me and hissed, "You need to go." Shaina quickly came to my defense, standing confidently beside me.

"Josh can tell him if he needs to go," Shaina retorted on my behalf. "What's your problem anyway?"

The girlfriend hiccupped. "I don't like his energy," she mumbled, before stumbling backward and knocking the shot glasses off the counter.

Josh joined in and tried to talk his girlfriend down, but by then I was feeling uncomfortable. I looked at Shaina and nodded toward the door. "Let's go, I don't even care to stay."

From behind Shaina, one of the women from the club walked up to us, clearly having observed the drunken girlfriend and not about to let it ruin our night. "My girlfriends are going back to that club, and I don't want to go with them. Can I come with you guys?" Her name was Evelyn and she had short blonde hair unlike Shaina and was much shorter.

I said, "Let's go to my house, Shaina," then looking to Evelyn added, "You can come along if you want." The three of us drove back to Cedar Hills.

As we pulled in the driveway, Evelyn had passed out in the back seat. When I opened the door for her, it was apparent she wasn't waking up anytime soon, so I threw her over my shoulder and carried her into the house while Shaina made a place for her to sleep on the couch.

I could sense that Shaina had hoped Evelyn would be the woman she would watch me sleep with, but I was relieved that Evelyn was too drunk for Shaina to proposition.

There was something about Evelyn that I just didn't like, so I had no interest in fulfilling Shaina's fantasy. Plus, the more I had thought about it, the more I had begun to think that opening up our physical relationship was playing with fire.

Shaina and I retreated up to bed.

Cuddled up, head on my chest as usual, I hesitantly said, "Babe, I need to ask something of you."

"Yes, babe?" she replied sleepily.

"We need to slow this down. I love you and we are going out of control. I mean, we're partying too hard and . . . and I've been rethinking this idea of bringing another woman to bed with us. If we don't slow down we'll implode and lose each other."

She looked up at me with a serious face for a moment. "As you wish, Cameron," she said, using my *The Princess Bride* quote. "I love you."

"I love your brains, babe." I kissed her forehead. "Can I ask you a question?"

"Of course."

"Do you like women too? I get this feeling you do."

She turned her head off my chest and looked at me. "Does that bother you?"

My hand tickled her skin, tracing a finger up her bare side. "Not at all."

My brain turned over the last couple turbulent weeks—the lies, the fighting, the silence. "Just please don't do anything in secret. If we can communicate, we can make it work.

One more thing, you need to know I won't tolerate cheating, not even once, if you cheat and I find out, I am gone." I pulled her in for a goodnight kiss, to reinforce how serious this was to me. "Do you understand?"

She lay back down on my chest. "I understand Cameron."

The week after the failed weekend at Josh's in Salt Lake City—and our deal to slow things down—Shaina and I decided we needed to stop drinking so much. A month or so went by on the wagon and things were good.

Toward the end of the month, Shaina came home from work one afternoon and said, "Evelyn invited me to a girls trip in Vegas. We'll be driving there, and I wanted to see how you felt about it."

We were doing so well with our sobriety that despite my reservations, I wanted to trust her. Besides, it was her choice to go and have fun. She was in her mid-twenties and deserved to have some fun now and then without me.

"If you want to go, then please go and have fun, babe. I trust you." That Shaina- smile swept across her face. She ran up to me, put her hands behind her back, and crouched down in preparation for her famous jump kiss, smacking me in the face. I started to flinch more often at those.

"Whoops," she said, wiping a small bit of my blood off her lip, "Guess I can't be perfect all the time."

"I'll take the blood if it means I can keep those kisses." I gazed at her in affection.

The work week flew by, and Friday came, and Shaina started texting me.

Shaina: I want you to come, babe.
Cameron: I can't, I have a big work appointment late this afternoon, so unless you want to leave late, you're going to have to go without me.
Shaina: OK bummer. I'm going to pick up Evelyn. I'm all packed so I guess I'll have to kiss you when I get back ☹
Cameron: No worries, babe. I'm going to miss you.
Shaina: What are you doing tonight? You better not be going out with Courtney! ☹
Cameron: If you're concerned, I'll give you access to my house cameras. I'm staying in tonight.
Shaina: OK, I love you, babe! Be a good boy for me <3
Cameron: As you wish

And then I went back to work. I didn't hear from her much that night as I lay in bed watching TV and sipping whiskey on the rocks.

I must have dozed off because I woke up to a call at two-thirty from Shaina. Concerned by the late hour, I picked up right away.

"Babe, are you okay?"

Shaina was heavily slurring her words on the other end. "Babe, Evelyn is being a bitch and she left me at the club. Will you get me a room and come down here and stay with me?"

My brain was finally waking up, realizing it wasn't exactly an emergency. "Shaina, you know I'm a five-hour drive from you and I can't get a flight until first thing in the morning and I'm sure I can't book you a room without me there. Where is Evelyn?"

"Babe, I just want you to be with me. Where will I stay tonight?"

I could barely understand her, and she was alone. "So, Evelyn left you?"

"No, she's trying to get an Uber." I heard her stumbling about, the honking of cars and muffled chatter in the background.

"So, she's with you?" I pressed.

"Okay, we got an Uber, but come down and save me from this bitch as soon as you can, okay?" She hung up.

Shaking my head, I jumped on Southwest's website and booked the first flight out to Vegas Saturday morning. I had bad vibes from Evelyn and her group of friends, and I wasn't convinced they hadn't left Shaina alone at that club.

We'd been doing so well together taking things slow and *sans* party life, and I didn't trust that Evelyn and her friends wouldn't send Shaina right back to square one.

After I landed, I checked into the MGM Grand at ten o'clock and upgraded to a suite. Now all I had to do was find Shaina, who was, unsurprisingly, not answering her phone.

Thoughts of the worst rushed through my head, and I remembered I had Evelyn's number saved and began furiously texting her. The responses were spotty and didn't make sense.

Cameron: Hi Evelyn, I'm in town. Shaina wanted me to come down. Where are you guys?

Silence for an hour.

Evelyn: Hey, you can come here.
Cameron: Come where? I have a nice room, I'd prefer Shaina come here.

Silence for another hour.

I must have texted Evelyn ten times but was only met with silence, and then finally, a single text came through with an address. It was forty-five minutes away and a hundred-dollar taxi. I was about to lose my mind. I grabbed my luggage and booked the taxi through the front desk, then checked out early. I just wanted to get Shaina home.

When I arrived, I tipped the driver then knocked on the door, having no idea where I was or who I was expecting to find. Two men answered the door.

"Uh, is Shaina here?" They glanced at each other and snickered.

"She's passed out in the bedroom. Evelyn will be back soon," one of them said, and he opened the door wider to let me in. I stepped into the bedroom and closed the door behind me so we could talk in private. I turned around to find Shaina peeking over the sheets, looking like a tornado hit her yet still somehow flawlessly beautiful.

"Baaaby! You came!" Putting her two hands together in front of her chest, she flashed me the shape of a heart. "I'm horny—come here." She seductively ripped the sheets off, exposing her fully naked body.

"Cameron, Evelyn was frustrated the men at the club were giving me attention and not her," she pouted. "That's when she started being a bitch to me, but I'm so happy you're here now. I promise nothing happened with any guys. I fell asleep here alone."

After convincing me to stay—or rather, knowing she wanted to stay, and I wasn't going to leave her alone again—we made plans to go to a club that night. Shaina stayed close to my side all night, and we ditched the group several times to go off alone and make out. I grabbed her hand and led her to the bar so I could buy us drinks, and she placed her phone face up on the bar when a drunken girl from the group came over to say hi. Her phone lit up with a text notification, and with her back turned, I leaned over to snoop. It read:

"Loved kissing you last night at the club. We're still at the same place."

Blinders up, I decided to ignore it, no matter how condemning the text was. She called me to come get her in Vegas instead of some random guy at a club. She loved me and we were doing better. The night would go better if I didn't rock the boat by accusing her of cheating while out with her friends. I rationalized it in my mind: it was a one-time kiss at the club, fueled by alcohol and lightheartedness. It was innocent enough. *Pick your battles, I thought.*

All night I dodged Evelyn throwing daggers at me from across the bar. She hadn't exactly been subtle about how pissed she was that I had shown up. I'd done nothing for her to dislike me; in fact, the last time I saw her, I carried her incoherent body from my car to the couch. Unless Shaina had said something nasty to her about me, I couldn't figure out why I was getting the shaft.

The next morning, we all drove back in Shaina's car and tensions were higher than ever. Evelyn barely spoke and when she did, it was only directed at Shaina. It was like I didn't exist. I closed my eyes to shut her and the suspicious text message out of my mind and tried to enjoy the drive.

In the end I had become her knight in shining armor coming all the way to Vegas to rescue her, so Evelyn daggers didn't bother me.

Back to happiness we go.

Chapter 10

CONFIRMATION

AFTER THE NIGHTMARE – Early August 2019

Adam: Hey we need to talk

Adam was an old friend and registered nurse.

We'd only communicated briefly over text since my release, so I was bewildered when my phone rang shortly afterward.

There was urgency in Adam's voice. "Cameron, I need to see you ASAP. I've got something you're gonna wanna see."

I immediately hung up and drove to see him. We arranged to discreetly meet up in the hospital parking lot, and I shot him a quick text when I pulled into a spot. As I sat waiting, I received an incoming call, but "Mom" was on the caller ID. When I picked up, I was greeted by an earful of shrieking—she had found out I came back from Vegas early and was worried about me.

"Cameron, can you please just move in with me? I hate the thought of you living in that house all alone."

"Mom, if I leave, then the people threatening me win. I have to stand up for myself, otherwise they'll *really* think I'm guilty."

Just then I glanced toward the hospital entrance just in time to see Adam emerge from the glass doors of the hospital wing. He worked as a nurse in the orthopedic department, and he jogged over my car, sporting his scrubs.

"Mom, I gotta go, we'll talk later."

Adam swung open the passenger side door and jumped in. "How're you doing, man?"

Truthfully, I was a mess—confused, paranoid, scared, angry—and I poured it all out to him. He nodded somberly and waited for me to finish before holding his cell phone in the air.

"I have something to show you, but I . . . uh—Well, let's just say I obtained these 'off the record.'"

"Okay, yeah, no problem. My lips are sealed." My hands shook in anticipation.

Adam leaned over to give me a clear view of his phone as he opened up his camera roll and started flipping through some images of X-rays. My blood ran cold.

"Holy shit, dude. Are these . . . these are Shaina's skull aren't they?"

"Ohhh yeah." Adam nodded as if he was showing me a map to the lost treasure of Atlantis. "I have access to the database of records at the hospital and I couldn't help but be curious. I snapped some pictures off the computer screen with my phone."

As he slowly slid through the images, I noticed that the X-rays of her skull clearly indicated the entrance wound on the right side, passing out the left side. My whole body quivered when I saw that the blast from the gun had cracked her head down the middle of her forehead. *Why had she done this ... holding my emotion in . . .*

I squinted at the photos in disbelief. "So, these X-rays show the gunshot wound direction clear as day—right to left. Right? Unless I'm missing something here, there is nothing showing up on the back of her head."

"I know." Adam was still nodding like a bobblehead. "That's what I don't understand, Cam. It doesn't make sense."

My brain went spinning into a fugue state, my reality shattering as the pieces became clearer. How could the news report it as back to front and right to left when there was unequivocal photo evidence disproving the widespread statement that she had been shot from behind. And then suddenly, the fog cleared, and my adrenaline rattled in my chest.

"I know you could get in a lot of trouble, but would you send these to me? I'd like to send them to my attorney . . . ya know, just in case he needs them."

Adam gave me a *are-you-fucking-kidding-me* look so I pressed him. "I promise I won't use them unless I need to."

He exhaled heavily and lay back in the seat, rubbing his hands over his eyes. "Fine, man. Do what you need to. You just didn't get them from me."

Relief flooded through me, and I felt levelheaded for the first time since I had been arrested. This was my ticket to freedom. This was the proof I needed to clear my name and win my friends and my boys back.

"There's one more thing, Cam," Adam hesitated. "I saw a post from one of Shaina's friends on Facebook today. She uploaded a video with some—what do you call them? Psychic mediums? The chick was saying that the medium told her Shaina wanted everyone to stop fighting with each other and start working together to convict you. I don't know, but my sister watched the video, and she says she has some of this voodoo shit capability, and says the medium interpreted the message wrong. She thinks Shaina was trying to tell everyone she wanted to stop the hatred toward you, against the suggestion of the mass idiots." He shrugged.

Three separate otherworldly encounters was enough for me that week. I was spooked, but I shook the feeling off, not knowing what to believe. Adam texted me the files and gave me a quick hug before exiting the car and jogging back through the glass doors.

I sent Glen the images and left for home.

My phone rang about ten minutes later, and this time it was Glen.

"I need you to go meet with the investigators we hired. They want to talk to you, and they have some information on the pictures you sent over."

Damn, already? Glen was on it, and I had a new spring in my step. Still in the car, I veered left and headed to the address Glen gave me for the investigator's house.

I walked up to the front door of an older home in a decent neighborhood, and the lady who greeted me introduced herself as Judy. Leading me inside, she motioned her hand toward a worn-out couch set in front of a wall-papered wall dotted with family photos. I was expecting an office full of private investigators, but Judy was clearly the one in charge. She took the chair across from the couch and leaned forward to brace her arms against her thighs.

"Cameron, I was a decorated officer and spent four decades with the police department." She held my gaze, still bracing herself. "First, you need to know that in my forty years on the force, I have never seen a suicide call turn into an arrest that same night. It just doesn't happen that way." She relaxed her arm muscles a bit, shaking her head and sitting back into the chair. I was relieved to see that Judy seemed to be in as much disbelief as I had been the last month.

"Thank you for confirming that . . . I thought I was going crazy there for a while. My life has been ruined by all of this."

"Well, as it turns out, I have another bombshell for you." She sat upright now, crossing her arms over her chest. "The radiologist screwed you." She declared it so matter-of-factly, but the confused look on my face kept her going. "Cameron, I don't know what the radiologist was thinking. Maybe he was drunk, in a hurry, or even persuaded to pin this on you—but his professional opinion was that the gun shot was back to front."

"But that doesn't make any sense. I sent Glen the images proving he was wrong." My mind immediately went back to that night in the police car when the officer questioned me for hours in the back of the cop car. "Conflicting reports of the gun shot" he had said.

"You're right. The radiologist was wrong. The medical examiner reported it as a gunshot wound from right to left only. I put in a request to review the original autopsy report the second your attorney sent me those X-rays."

Judy handed me the report. On June 25, 2019, the radiologist had erro-neously reported a back to front gunshot wound and on June 29, 2019, the medical examiner reported the gunshot wound being right to left clearly.

GENERAL OFFENSE HARDCOPY
REQUEST TO ACCESS PUBLIC RECORDS
(WEAP-FIRING WEAPON)

EXCEPTIONALLY
CLEARED

<u>Narrative Text</u>
　Type INVSTGTR F/U
　Subject SCENE RESPONSE
　Author
Related Date Jun-26-2019 17:02

On June 25, 2019, at approximately 2233 hours, I received a phone call from Sgt.　　to respond
on a suspicious shooting in Midvale. The preliminary information provided was a female was
transported ▇▇▇▇▇▇▇▇▇▇▇▇▇▇▇▇▇▇▇▇▇▇▇ after suffering a gunshot wound to
the head. Two females at the residence made suspicious spontaneous utterances upon police
contact.

<u>I contacted dispatch and was provided the following information:</u>

- Incident location:
- Call came in at 2209 hours
- Officer dispatch time was 2210 hours
- First officer arrival was 2214 hours (Officer　　　　　　　　')

I responded on scene and was briefed on the incident. The following information was relayed to me:
A 911 call came in as a self-inflicted gunshot wound to a female's head. Upon officer arrival, two
females identified as　　　　　and　　　　　　　were sitting in a Scion TC ▇▇▇▇
outside of the residence. When officers made contact with the listed females,　　　made
spontaneous utterance she was going to jail　　　stated she did not understand why they
were in handcuffs　　　　　　　　. Both
females were immediately separated and detained for further investigation on their possible
involvement in the case. A male, identified as Cameron Lundgren was located in the upstairs
landing area near the stair case applying pressure to a female, identified as Shaina　　who had
suffered a gunshot wound to the head. Shaina　　was lying on her back at the time of police
contact and a firearm was near her body. Cameron was detained and placed in a police vehicle for
further questioning regarding the gunshot. The firearm was cleared and rendered safe and placed
in the bathroom near the location of the shooting.

　　　　　　arrived on scene to assist with the investigation.　　　　I want to
▇▇▇▇▇▇ Hospital to make victim contact. The radiologist determined the entrance wound was
on the back of Shaina's head and exited the front, which is inconsistent with a report of a
self-inflicted gunshot wound. Based on that information and the spontaneous utterances of
and　　　　I contacted　　　　to get additional detectives to assist on the investigation.
I　　　　　　was assigned as the lead detective on the case which was now being
investigated as a homicide.

I did a walk through of the residence. The residence is north-facing. The front door to the residence
opens into a foyer/hall with an office to the direct right (west) of the door and a wall on the east
which is shared with the garage to the residence. The hall leads south with a staircase on the right
side after the office. If you proceed walking south in the hall there is a bathroom on the right after

Original Incorrect Radiologist report

"Listen," she continued, "I don't know what to say here, but if it were me,
I'd sue the police department for taking you into custody so quickly and I'd
sue the radiologist for doing such a sloppy job."

I really couldn't believe it. I went to jail based on a false report that was later rectified by the medical examiner's office, and no one had bothered to tell me. No one had apologized—least of all the radiologist who screwed me to begin with. Had the department checked their facts, I wouldn't have gone into that police car that night. I would've rushed to the emergency room with Shaina and held her hand until she passed. I would have mourned her properly, instead of hiding in my house with the curtains drawn like the town villain. I'd be able to seek solace in my children. I'd be free. My gut boiled with anger.

When I got home, I called Glen, who recommended that I hire a civil lawyer to sue the police department, per Judy's suggestion. I spent weeks calling attorneys, always to be told that the police and the radiologist were "in their professional opinion" allowed to make a mistake based on their inferences of the situation at the time. I was furious; I could see something so clearly that someone with a degree could not. But there was nothing I could do. *A mistake,* I thought, *someone that spent over eight years in school made such a dumb mistake to ruin my life!*

I woke up the next morning feeling utterly helpless and contemplated staying in bed for the foreseeable future. Up until the night of my arrest, I considered myself a lucky guy to have dozens of close friends and two dozen more acquaintances to depend on to talk with, or just to go out and have a good time with.

I chuckled to myself at the irony: I had been so desperate to find myself after the divorce, to revel in being "young again," to party. Now, I had neither my ex-wife, my kids, Shaina, or any friends to hang out with.

It was a rude awakening to find that friends I had known my entire life suddenly disappeared into thin air after I sent a text or a phone call. One friend, Cory, even admitted to not wanting to be seen in public with me. Of the few friends I had left, the one whose loyalty I never questioned was Chevy. I had spent the last month either holed up in my house or trying to escape the city so often that I hadn't seen him since he let me crash at his house when mine was being held by the state for "domestic violence concerns."

Even though I had asked most of my friends not to engage on social media in my defense, Chevy wouldn't have it. Chevy, who may be the single most popular guy in Utah due to his penchant for loyalty and what the ladies dubbed a "charming smile," had thousands of Facebook friends; the moment one of them posted something negative about me, he'd get on the phone to personally deliver the message that any shit talking wouldn't be tolerated. End of discussion. He never quite told me what he'd say, but sure enough, the post would be deleted by the time the call ended.

I was in dire need of some companionship, so I reached out to him. Before I could even say hello, his voice interrupted the ringing in my ear.

"Hey, buddy. Been thinking 'bout you." Chevy was a bighearted guy who always knew what to say. His salt-and-pepper beard and muscular build was menacing to an outsider, but anyone who met him considered him to be a teddy bear. The sincerity in his voice panged my heart, but I shoved the emotion down.

"I know, brother. I was wondering if I might be able to come stay at your place again for a week or two. I'm just—" I sighed, trying to rein in the tears for once — "I just need to be around friends. I'm slipping into a pretty dark place."

"Pack your stuff, bud, we're heading down to Maple Mountain Bar and Grill for paint night tonight."

The bar was opened a few years earlier by an old friend of mine when in my early twenties doing phone sales. It was new, and I wasn't sure if that meant I wouldn't see anyone I knew, or if I'd run into everyone I knew.

"You should come along with me and Gabby," Chevy said.

"Sounds good, man. I'm on my way to your place in thirty."

One thing that always made me feel good was buying new clothes, so I went to the mall and picked up a variation of my usual: a tight-fitted black shirt, Levi's, boots, and a baseball hat that matched the shirt. All of my clothes had been ruined anyway, and I hadn't felt comfortable enough to shop in public, but I didn't really have a choice. I was stoked to get out of the house and go to a bar with my friend—something I hadn't done since before Shaina's death.

As I walked into Buckle, a higher end clothing store for your average "metro male." I tried to lay low so that nobody would notice me keeping my eyes stuck on the floor in front of me to hide my face.

I was startled when a beautiful blonde employee came up to me "what are you looking for?" She asked flirtatiously hoping for a sale.

I quickly responded. "I just need something for a night out with friends and I'm in a hurry, please get me your most popular size 34 pants and collared shirt." I was short with her and just wanted to get the new outfit and get the hell out of there. I didn't even bother trying the outfit on as I checked out and hit the road to Chevy's house.

As I dressed to get ready for the party, I was feeling both apprehension and a bit of excitement.

When I arrived, before my knuckles could even make it to the door, it swung open to reveal a toothy-grinned Chevy, who immediately wrapped me up into a bear hug.

"Give me a hug, buddy." I couldn't help but beam trying to catch a breath. and my body warmed with the happy feeling, momentarily eclipsing the despair I had grown so used to. He led me to his kitchen where his girlfriend Gabby was sipping on a glass of wine. She smiled through a gulp and raised her glass toward me when she saw me.

"Dude, you know I love you, brother, right?" Chevy stared at me with a poignant look, making sure I knew how serious he was. It was just what I needed to hear.

I responded, "Of course, Chevy. You're one of my last few friends, man. Besides, you love—"

"I love my friends!" he finished for me, quoting his most famous motto. His cheesy grin returned, and he slammed his fist on the counter. "Let's get out and show you a good time, you've been cooped up and I won't tolerate your solidarity!"

As we neared the bar, I started to have doubts this was a good idea. I had just recently been afraid to leave my house in fear of people stalking me and a bar was definitely the place to draw further attention to myself.

I'd just tell Chevy and Gabby that I have to make a phone call real quick . . . stall a little. But then we pulled into park and the car came to a halt. I sucked in a deep breath through clenched teeth and exited the car, throwing a small smile at Chevy when he looked my way to reassure him I was all good.

We immediately ran into my old friend, Jason, who was the owner of the bar. I don't recall him ever not having a full red beard. He's also one of the smartest people I had ever met. We'd spent many a drunken night hamming it up before he'd lure the group into some political debate—not an easy thing to do as a liberal in a red state. He was a good dude; someone whose advice I respected.

He opened his arms to welcome me in and I gave him a hug, smiling again at having another friend who actually looked pleased to see me. As I went to pull away, he held me tight and whispered in my ear, "You don't need to tell me you didn't do it, Cameron. I know you didn't."

He released his tight embrace and slapped me on the back a few times before adding, "You can beat this, I know you can." I thanked him for his confidence before leaving him to greet some patrons who had just walked in.

Feeling a little looser, Chevy, Gabby, and I pulled up stools at the bar to order a drink before the painting began. I glanced around to survey the room when I saw an old childhood friend, Blake, sitting a few stools down. We'd grown apart over the years, but the last time we spoke we had been on good terms.

Making eye contact, he hopped off his stool to approach the three of us, never taking his eyes off me. "You're a piece of shit, you know that?" I'd been hoping to stay on a roll with my happy encounters, but clearly Blake had other plans for me.

Instantly, Chevy grew red and the muscles in his jaw clenched, but I knew Chevy. He wouldn't explode like that, here, especially not when he was trying to make my reintroduction into society as seamless as possible. Instead, Chevy relaxed his jaw and gave a weak smile. "Can we buy you a drink?" He offered to Blake.

It was clear that Blake had had too much to drink. "Why would you buy me a drink?" He wobbled a bit and leaned an arm on the bar.

"Well! Then we won't buy you a drink!" Chevy barked, before turning to me in an attempt to end the conversation and shield me from a drunken Blake. "Cam, what do you want?"

"I'll buy my own drinks," Blake muttered, then drifted back to his bar stool.

I could tell that Chevy wanted to knock his face off his body, but we both knew it wasn't worth it. Gabby, who had been sitting on a stool on the far side of the commotion, gently patted Chevy's hand, then signaled to the bartender— "Three whiskey cokes, please"—then we walked to the other side of the bar to set up our paint stations.

We chose three chairs along the wall, each equipped with an easel, and prepped our supplies while the bartender came around and took an order for another round of drinks.

The instructor, a middle-aged woman with short brown hair and wearing a paint-smeared smock, stood in front of the "class" and began painting strokes on her canvas. My attention was completely focused on her and my painting as I began to craft what I hoped would turn into a sunset.

It was nice actually. I'd never been one for crafts but focusing my brain on something other than Shaina felt calming.

Sitting on the other side of Gabby, Chevy muttered loud enough for both of us to hear. "If that motherfucker comes back over here, I'm going to say something."

I followed his gaze to some guy lurking behind the painting class, his eyes fixated on me. Gabby paused, brush raised, and assessed who Chevy was shooting daggers at. "Yeah, he's up to something," she murmured.

That sinking feeling in my gut took over, the kind where you just want to evaporate into thin air. The man turned to walk away, and I refocused my attention on my painting, trying to shake my discomfort.

"You're good, buddy," Chevy reassured me. "I'll handle this if it becomes a problem." He narrowed his eyes at the guy one last time before going back to painting.

Not more than a minute or two went by when Gabby interrupted the silence. "He's taking his phone out and I think he's taking pictures."

Sure enough, the guy had returned, only this time he had his cell phone unabashedly held out in front of him. Feeling incredibly uncomfortable,

I stood up to leave before Chevy beat me to it, placing his hand on my shoulder to push me back down in my chair.

"Here." He handed me his drink. "I got this, bud."

Seeing an angry Chevy beelining toward him, the guy quickly put his phone away and made for the front door, followed closely by Chevy who had disappeared behind the view of the easels.

I chugged the rest of his drink and went back to painting, only this time I could barely focus on what the instructor was saying. I looked up to see Chevy at the bar whispering to Jason, clearly scheming to get that guy kicked out. A few minutes later, he returned to his seat as if nothing had happened. He simply nodded in my direction and confirmed, "It's taken care of."

Miraculously, we all finished the session even though my sunset looked more like a pastel blob. We gathered at the bar and spent an hour talking to Jason, all the while checking over my shoulder to make sure no one else decided to take pictures of me. As much as I had been looking forward to this, and as much as I loved being back with friends, a voice in the back of my head told me that I still wasn't safe. Maybe I never would be.

Chapter 11

BIRTHDAY GIRL

BEFORE THE NIGHTMARE –
November 2018

Shaina's birthday was right around the corner, and I wanted to surprise her with as many special gifts as I could find, reminiscent of my seven-day challenge a few months back.

I went out and picked up all sorts of gifts from Victoria's Secret, including robes, lingerie, and perfume—all in, I had spent seven hundred bucks. Maintaining our recent current lovey-dovey status after Vegas Part 1, was a top priority; plus, I wanted to ensure that *Happy Shaina* was here to stay.

We had begun drinking again after Vegas, and I knew how easily she could spiral.

My friend Cory's grandpa owned a cabin at Lava Hot Springs in Idaho, about three hours north of Salt Lake City, and he offered to let us use it for the weekend. Cory was a young guy in his early twenties who I'd met at work. We weren't close friends in the way that Chevy and I were, but he was a colleague I had liked to party with before I met Shaina. I reached out to everyone I knew who was close to her, so that all her friends could be with us to celebrate. I couldn't wait to show Shaina the amazing hot springs and a birthday she'd always remember.

Using social media and friend's recommendations as my guide, I messaged all of her friends who I knew personally, and then a good number of people I had yet to meet. Even though Shaina was a social butterfly, I was still surprised by just how many people she knew. But my grand idea was too last minute, and most of her friends weren't able to come. My plan had already suffered a small dent, and I kicked myself for not planning sooner.

It ended up being a small group: Shaina, Evelyn, Cory and his girlfriend Becca, my friend Jack, and me. We arrived at the cabin late on Friday night—another dent—and I asked Shaina to wait in the car as I scurried inside to hang up all my decorations as best I could and lay out her presents from me—ten in all with confetti and strings of "Happy Birthday" on the wall.

Satisfied with my display, I called for the birthday girl to come inside, and we sang "Happy Birthday." As Shaina opened each present, her smile got wider and wider. I glanced over at Evelyn, who was scowling on the couch, clearly jealous that she hadn't gone above and beyond for her new best friend's birthday. After presents, we began drinking shot, after shot, after shot, and all the while Evelyn clung to Shaina's side and cornered her into private conversations.

I was losing time with my special birthday girl to a girl Shaina had just met, and it was eating at me, especially after all the effort I had put in. But there was something else weird about the situation, I just couldn't place it. *Why did it feel like a battle for Shaina's attention?*

Cory, Becca, and Jack ran into town to grab more booze, leaving Shaina, Evelyn, and me at the cabin. I was awkwardly loitering around the girls' conversation when Shaina looked at me and glowered. "Cameron, can you give us some time alone?"

Thrown off considering there was no one else for me to talk to and annoyed she didn't want to talk to me on her birthday, I nodded and grabbed a full bottle of Jägermeister off the counter and took it and our luggage to one of the second-story bedrooms.

I leaped into the bed, twisting the cap off the booze, feeling annoyed, upset, and even a bit jealous. Putting the bottle to my lips, I chugged every last drop, finishing just as Shaina walked in and gave me an odd look.

"Did you drink all of that?"

"Sure did." I grinned, wiping my mouth with the back of my hand. "You don't want to spend time with me after all I've done, then I guess I'll spend with my alcohol friend here."

"You're going to die, Cameron!" she squawked, rushing back downstairs to look for help.

Things went fuzzy after that. The next thing I remember was waking up the next morning to the most excruciating hangover I'd ever felt, and to top it off, I was still drunk. My eyes fanned open and I managed to force myself into a sitting position.

Cory was standing at the kitchen counter eating a bagel. "Big night eh, bud?"

I massaged my temples and winced in response.

"We stayed on watch last night to make sure you didn't die of alcohol poisoning in your sleep. Unfortunately, it looks like you stayed alive." He chuckled to himself.

"Where's Shaina? Where did she sleep last night?"

Cory merely shrugged his shoulders. "All I know is, it's almost noon and they left several hours ago for the hot springs, man."

Despite the throbbing ache in my brain, my anger lashed out. Nothing had gone as planned; I'd gotten drunk like an idiot and was too hungover to go to the hot springs, the one thing I was excited to show Shaina. And, she'd ignored me all night and then ditched me this morning after I planned this great weekend for her. I was losing.

I was pacing back and forth in front of a stunned Cory, each new jolt of rage only making my hangover worse. We didn't have reception at the cabin so there was no way of calling or texting her. *Did she even sleep with me last night, or was I moved to the couch?* My fury grew with every minute, but without a way to reach Shaina, I was helpless. The floor was beginning to move, so I laid back down on the couch and waited.

When their car eventually pulled up around noon, I had built up enough frustration to throw my still-drunken stupor to the wayside and I stomped out to their car.

"If you just want to hang out with your lesbian friend this whole fucking time, then she can pay for all this shit!" I thundered, glaring at Evelyn.

Clearly dismayed by my vulgar display of anger, Shaina responded, "Cameron, relax. We were worried about you all night—"

"No! Fuck this shit! I'm packing up and going home." I sneered at Evelyn then looked back at Shaina. "You two can have each other."

I stormed back inside and began packing my things. Shaina appeared in the doorway, her demeanor trepid and soft. "Baby, baby, listen to me." She strode into the room to grab my face and pulled me in. "You're mine and I'm sorry. I didn't know you were getting so frustrated with me." Her gentleness and the feel of her hands on my face started to dull the flames inside my chest.

"Shaina, I spent hours planning this and looking for those presents. I wanted to be the one to show you the hot springs, and I thought this would be a special time for us together. All you've done is ignore me since we got here." My face was still red with heat but cooling each second her hands held my cheeks.

"Baby, I'm so sorry, I really am. Please forgive me. I'll stay by your side the rest of the trip." She leaned in to rest her forehead against mine.

"Shaina, I don't want you to have to do that. I want you to *want* to do that," I pleaded right before she pulled me in for a kiss.

"I want to be with you. You're mine, got it?" I searched her face for a second, then gave a small sigh.

"Did you bring the toys?" she whispered, a smile playing on her lips. The pounding of blood in my head escaped my face and moved to another part of my body. She always knew how to win me over. It was that damn make-up sex.

"How am I supposed to give you a happy birthday without them, Beautiful?" She smiled and locked the door.

That night we had planned to go Blue Moon Bar and Grill downtown. Lava Hot Springs is a small, quaint touristy town, usually filled with kids coming for the bar scene. There probably isn't a building under 100 years old and it always seems there are a lot more people milling around than rooms to hold them all. We found a cozy bed and breakfast with a hot spring close by just a few blocks from the bar and picked up two rooms.

The place we chose was a packed house and the energy was palpable. I opened my tab to our group, wanting to give Shaina the best night after ruining it the night before. In normal fashion, we chose to take copious shots of Fireball, which went down fast and painlessly.

There was a final trick up my sleeve to add to her ten birthday presents: I planned to do a striptease for Shaina to a special song she loved. I approached the DJ and asked him if he could play Kygo's rendition of "Happy Birthday," and he agreed he would find it. Setting up a chair on the stage, I looked over to see that Shaina was already making lots of friends in the crowd, and the night was shaping up to be a good time.

The DJ got on his mic and called up Shaina to the stage and instructed her to sit in the chair. A few rowdy girls from the audience jumped on stage and tried to take over my dance routine for her, but I bounded up the stage and waved them off before ripping off my shirt. The girls shot me mean looks and hopped off stage, but I had no interest in befriending anyone that night—my sole attention was on Shaina.

I slowly danced my way up to her, shirtless, channeling my best *Magic Mike* impression. There were a few nearby tables of women cheering and whistling at me, but I didn't see the same intoxication in Shaina's face.

When the music ended and I walked her off stage, she hissed at me. "Cameron, you're embarrassing me."

I thought for sure a sexy dance from her boyfriend in a far-off city where no one knew either of us would have been just the thing she wanted, but it seemed like I couldn't do anything right by her.

"Are you even proud to be with me, Shaina?" I demanded, growing more upset.

"You need to calm down," she fired back.

I gave her some space and scanned the crowd until I found Cory at the bar, and we both ordered another shot.

"Dude, we're probably going to head back to the cabin. But, uh, my grandpa found out about your episode this morning . . . said a neighbor called him to complain about someone screaming, and he doesn't want you back . . . sorry, man." Nothing else could possibly go wrong this weekend.

"That's fine," I lied. "I'll grab a room in town tonight." He gave me a quick pat on the back, and I told him to be safe driving back as he walked away. Knowing I needed to tell Shaina about my change of plans, I plowed through the crowd for about half a song before finding her talking to one of the girls that tried to dance for her on stage.

"Shaina, where's Jack and Evelyn?"

She turned to me, making a show of crossing her arms. "I don't know, Cameron. Funny how you said you'd be by my side all night, yet you don't even seem to want to be near me," she replied coolly.

Confused, I said, "What are you talking about? You said you'd be by *my* side... Where are Jack and Evelyn?" I repeated, but she simply rolled her eyes as she grabbed my hand to shuttle me to the dance floor stage.

The Fireball shots had hit their peak, and both of us were drunk out of our minds. Shaina was swaying her head to the music in ecstasy when a man ten years older than me tapped me on the shoulder.

"This is my wife." He nodded his head toward the leggy blonde beside him. "I like your woman and I wanted to see if you wouldn't mind me dancing with her."

"Not at all," I slurred. Then we quickly swapped partners and started to dance. Nearly ten seconds later, two tall bouncers in black shirts came up to me, each grabbing an arm.

"Sir, you're eighty-sixed, and you have to leave. You're out of control," they boomed in their deep voices as they escorted me out the back. I didn't even have a chance to talk to Shaina before I was in the alley face-to-face with the closed, red-chipped door of the bar.

It was early November and freezing and I hadn't brought a coat—not that I would have been given time to snag it from inside before those big oafs carried me out. I yanked my cell from my pocket and began calling everyone from our group, but no one answered. Stumbling around the back entrance of the bar, one of the bouncers came back out, and yelled, "you can't be within 100 feet of the bar, you need to leave."

Without a house to go back to, I bumbled down the alley for about twenty yards when I heard the slam of the bar's back door echo down the alley as a group of about ten guys piled out, whooping and jeering. Then, toward the back of the group, I spotted Shaina. She was fuzzy, but it was her.

"Where are you going, Shaina?" I bellowed through my hands.

The same girl that tried to dance with her earlier had Shaina's arm in hers, and she looked back to me and laughed as they walked in the opposite direction down the alley "We're taking her with us, and you're not going to do anything about it!" she yelled, taunting me.

I broke out into a slight run after them and started screaming at Shaina.

"Shaina, you need to think this through! You should stay here!" I wanted to fight my way to her through the men, but it was hopeless—I was out-numbered by at least eight men—so I did the next best thing I could think of and called 911.

The group disappeared down the alley just as the operator picked up.

"911, what's your emergency?"

Fighting through the jumble of words in my head I managed to say, "I was with my girlfriend at the bar in downtown Lava and a bunch of guys just left with her. I'm worried about her safety." I managed slurring my words. I continued to follow the pack from a safe distance behind.

"You're a little ways away from my closest officer, but hang tight, sir."

I followed these guys and Shaina on foot to their hotel room. It was pretty cold being November, likely close to freezing, and it was about a half mile.

When the police showed up there to meet me, they said there was noth-ing they could do because she left with them on her free will, and went inside with them, even though she was heavily intoxicated. Defeated, I staggered about a block down from them to our hotel and sent a text to our group letting them know I was done for the night.

An hour or so went by when I got a knock on my hotel door. I opened it to find Jack standing there with a crumpled Shaina beside him, both of their long hair in disarray and matted to their faces.

"Cameron! Thank God I found your girl!" He waltzed right in, keeping Shaina upright. "How did you lose her? Evelyn and I were at the bar when we got your text and we were just about to drive back to the cabin when we found her walking around downtown, barely able to stand."

Jack used whatever muscle he had on his skinny body to bring her to the edge of the bed, and she immediately plunged onto the mattress. The room was spinning, and I knew if I didn't go to bed soon, I'd end up sleeping on the toilet.

"We'll talk in the morning, man. Thanks for bringing her here."

I plopped down on the bed next to Shaina with one arm around her.

That next morning, I woke up feeling ashamed, disappointed, and like a total dumbass. My attempts to give Shaina a memorable birthday had worked, but in the worst way. I had gotten too drunk, and I had let some skeevy local bouncers con me into thinking I was being kicked out, when really, they just wanted to get Shaina alone.

We drove back home to Utah in silence with Evelyn at the wheel and Shaina sitting passenger while I slumped in the backseat with Jack, sleeping off my hangover.

When Shaina and I got to my house, we both crawled straight into bed, barely speaking. I felt so ashamed of my behavior, and although I wanted to ask Shaina what happened in the hotel, I selfishly couldn't bring myself to face the truth. I wouldn't be able to live with the guilt.

Chapter 12

SURPRISING NEW FRIENDS

AFTER THE NIGHTMARE – Late August 2019

I had every news channel hitting me up to do an interview. They all wanted to know how I was getting away with murder covered as suicide as they all were reporting a gunshot "back to front, left to right."

But every time I approached Glen about it, he shut the idea down stating, "You'll have to find another attorney. An interview will jeopardize the ongoing investigation."

After discovering my arrest was a sham, I didn't really care about the ongoing investigation. I was innocent and others needed to know—I was already living in an emotional jail and the least I could do was try to clear my name and I also wanted to share the X-ray images I came across thinking maybe their story would be different after seeing them.

I paced back and forth around my room before picking up the phone and dialing Glen.

As soon as he picked up, I blurted out, "Glen, I've reached out to 'Get Gephardt' and they want to do an investigation into this. I know you've been advising against this, but you know I didn't do it and we have nothing to hide. I think hiding it shows we're afraid . . . I want to do this, and if I end up in jail because of it, so be it." I finally took a deep breath. "I can live with that."

There was silence for at least thirty seconds before Glen sighed on the other end. "If you want to do this, I'll allow it. But don't forget—if something happens, I told you so."

Permission granted, I immediately emailed the news team. "Get Gephardt" was a local investigative news segment of KUTV-Channel 2, similar to *Dateline.* I only had to wait a few minutes before I got a response, and they meant serious business; they wanted to meet at my home in a few hours.

My home and former crime scene was still left intact from the night of Shaina's death because I had been in so much turmoil, I had no time or desire to clean it and I wanted to leave it intact for this exact reason: I could walk someone through the scene, and they could see there was no way it could have happened back to front. I even threw a large rug over where she laid last because I couldn't bear the thought of cleaning up the bloodstained carpet.

I called Glen back and told him the news. "Glen, they want to meet at my house in two hours."

"Two hours!" he scoffed. "That gives us no time to prepare."

He was already cautious to hold the interview in the first place, and now we were facing a major time constraint. I'd never done an interview before, and I knew Glen would want to perfect my responses, but it was "go" time, whether we were ready or not.

"Remember, we don't have anything to hide," I reminded him.

Glen jumped in his car and drove over as fast as he could to take advantage of what little time we had to assess any damage control. Sitting on the living room couch, he nervously walked around in front of me, tossing out potential interview questions for me to practice.

"I know you like to talk but remember less is more. And if I feel like something is being said that shouldn't be, I'll stop the interview."

I didn't know whether to laugh or roll my eyes. Glen knew me too well.

I was starting to feel my life coming back soon, that everyone would see suicide, not murder. That I'd be able to walk the streets again without eyes watching over me.

A knock turned our attention to the door, and I could swear I saw Glen gulp. I stood up and shook out the nerves, then moved to the front door. A beautiful news anchor stood on my porch while four men behind her unloaded equipment from a van.

I could sense the anchor was nervous initially since I had been made out to be a monster, but as everyone settled into the kitchen and started making small talk, the tension in the air dissipated. "So," she started. "Tell me what happened."

Though I had recounted the story so many times, I still had difficulty holding back my emotions. Glen also eased up a little since he was worried that they wanted to try to pin the murder on me. I talked through how much I loved Shaina and all the reasons that pointed as to why she had committed suicide and I recounted how it happened. Glen was little more relived as they listened to my story later noting that the news crew seemed to better understand now what really took place instead of being intent on making me out to be guilty.

Then I presented my text conversations between Shaina and me, the ones where she had mentioned taking her life. I also talked about how we had often lain in bed at night, and she'd ask me things like "do you think people would show up to my funeral?"

I told the anchor that my response was always the same. "Baby, hundreds would show up at your funeral. I wouldn't miss it for the world. So many people love you, I love you. Please don't talk like that."

It turns out I had been right—hundreds of people had shown up, even people that never met her. All because she was murdered young by a "monster" in a tragic death.

The anchor followed up with a question I did not expect. "Cameron, why do you think Shaina shared these intimate thoughts with you, because people are saying she would never do that?"

I paused for a minute to consider the answer.

"Shaina and I had an emotional bond with each other I had never felt with any other partner before. There was very little we wouldn't talk about, and I believe she felt very comfortable with me. I also believe these thoughts had been going on a long time, way before me.

"She had a daughter when she was younger, but she gave her up for adoption. I'm not sure who else she told that to, but I know it caused her a lot of pain when I brought it up. She had wanted to give her daughter an opportunity at a better life."

I hesitated, but the anchor kept the microphone extended, waiting for me to elaborate.

"Shaina would often tell me she felt like she wasted her opportunity to be a mother, to party instead. I don't know . . . maybe those demons started to catch up with her."

The reporter moved on to the next preliminary question. "You mentioned she felt hopelessness. Can you explain?"

"Shaina was a waitress and she lived in her mother's basement. After we met, I helped her get a mattress and gave her my TV. Her prized possession was her car, which had just broken down two days prior to her death. It just needed a small fix, and I told her I'd help her. She made it seem so horrible and life shattering. I should've seen the writing on the wall then."

A cool chill slithered up my spine at the thought of our last conversation about that stupid car.

"Until she met me, all of her money went to partying and she lived paycheck to paycheck. Just before we went to Moab, she told me she didn't know how to set goals and achieve them. We talked about stuff like that a lot—the future, our goals. I printed off a yearly goal sheet from the Internet for us to fill out and we completed them together. But whenever it came down to actually, ya know, going through with anything, she'd just feel dejected. Stuck, I guess. I think it was too little too late."

While the reporter somberly nodded her head, I considered telling her what Claire had confided to me that night right before this all went down. If what Claire told me was true, yes it was devastating, and yes, I'd made a pretty heavy ultimatum early in our relationship. But we'd worked things out before.

But I pushed it down, I didn't want that to be the reason she killed herself and I didn't want anyone else to believe it either.

The reporter continued. "After seeing the text messages, you tried to build her up, but she was so sad. Cameron, what are you guilty of, if anything?"

This was the question I had been dreading and repressing. I wasn't guilty of pulling the trigger, but I still felt like somehow, I should have seen it coming. Maybe been able to change her mind or get her some help.

"If I'm guilty of anything, it's ignorance. In my forty years, I have never been close to anyone that talked about ending their life, and honestly, I just didn't know how to deal with it. I'm sure many people like me think that if you just love that person enough, they wouldn't do it.

"But I should have been asking questions and understanding her sickness, and even though she asked me not to share her feelings with anyone, I should have. If I'm guilty of anything, it's ignorance. Ignorant that someone so beautiful and so loved was capable of actually going through with it."

Satisfied with our pre-interview, the reporter signaled to the camera crew that they were ready to start recording.

Glen didn't interrupt once. After the news crew had left, he turned to me and admitted, "I think that went better than expected. Guess we'll have to see when it airs because I'm worried they'll twist it."

Glen went home and the interview aired a few hours later. I watched from my living room TV as Glen called to tell me he was pleased with the result. Sadly, it was old news—Shaina's death had been two months prior and there was little reaction to the piece.

I stand by everything in that interview, despite the lack of public interest. My only regret was a small lie I had told when the reporter had inquired if there was any physical violence in our relationship. I answered on my behalf that, no, there was not. But the truth was that there was violence, just not from me.

https://kutv.com/news/local/exclusive-boyfriend-of-shaina-bigby-claims-hes-innocent-shares-evidence-with-2news

With the "Get Gephardt" interview getting so little traction, and the possibility of suing the police department for negligence out the window, I had lost hope on a future. I lay in bed—my house still trashed—scrolling endlessly through social media, torturing myself with the slander that people were spewing my way. I threw my phone next to me and stared at the ceiling, contemplating my next move, or whether I had the energy to make a next move, when my phone buzzed on the bed.

I rolled over to grab it and saw a notification on Facebook Messenger with the name *Allison* under it. That was strange. She'd been one of Shaina's friends, though I'd never met her; I just knew she was one of the women Shaina went to Wendover, Utah, with for a girl's trip the weekend before she died. Funny enough, Allison was dating one of Shaina's exes, Jordan.

> **Allison:** I know you probably don't care to talk . . . but what
> the heck happened?

My brain immediately went to thinking this was a setup. The police had obviously asked her to get information from me, but I wanted so desperately for someone to hear my side that I responded anyway.

> **Cameron:** I'd love to tell you, but I won't do it over text.
> **Allison:** Sure, I get off at 3:30. Can you meet today?

It was already two o'clock. *But*, I thought, I *had all the time in the world now that I had been fired, my house destroyed, my kids forbidden from seeing me, and was otherwise unable to leave my house in fear of being beaten up or shot in the back.*

> **Cameron:** Yes, I'd love that. I want to tell someone because
> it's killing me how I'm being portrayed.

The hour went by quicker than expected and I began to grow nervous thinking this was a setup for people to jump me. At a quarter past three I panic-messaged her saying that something came up and asked to reschedule for the next day.

> **Allison:** I need to know . . . can I call you?
> **Allison:** Cameron!
> **Allison:** Hello . . . I don't believe you did it.
> **Cameron:** My attorney is advising me to not speak to anyone. Not to mention your boyfriend Jordan posted on Facebook saying he drove by my house last week to check if I was there. I don't trust anyone right now. Telling my side of the story isn't worth my life.

Minutes passed and I thought I had finally shaken her off, but instead I received a lengthy response.

> **Allison:** I completely understand where you're coming from, but I was with her the weekend before it happened. I knew of you but had no idea you guys were together and things just aren't adding up. I want to hear your side. My dad is in prison for a wrong conviction, and I just need to know the truth. I just want to hear your side. I'm just so confused . . . She was so secretive.

Huh. Maybe she was being sincere, and that she really was just seeking out the truth with no hidden agenda.

> **Cameron:** Ok, but what about your boyfriend? He's been driving by my house. What's he going to think about us meeting?

> **Allison:** Obviously Jordan wouldn't like it, you're the enemy. But I just want to hear the truth.

Fuck it, what did I have to lose at this point?

Cameron: Ok. Tomorrow at 3:30 at Arby's.

That night I barely slept wondering if I was willfully sending myself into the lion's den.

The next day, she texted me at three-thirty asking where I was, and I messaged her that I was in a city a few miles over. There was some back and forth, but I wanted to send her to a few fake locations before giving up my real one in an effort to confuse people if they were trying to find me. Eventually we met at a mall parking lot in Murray.

I made sure to park in an empty spot away from any cars. She walked up to the door, but I rolled down the window and first made her promise she wasn't wearing a wire. She said she wasn't, and I believed her. She climbed in and I got right to the story, tearing up once again as I relived the night I tried so hard to push out of my mind.

Allison reiterated that her dad was in prison on a wrongful conviction, and she was passionate about making sure I didn't end up in the same place. I told her if she wanted to come to my home, I'd explain the story piece by piece as we walked through the scene.

"But," I stipulated, "I want you to bring Jordan. Even though he's suspicious of me, I don't want him to think we met in secret—that's not going to help my case. And I want him to see everything too. Maybe make a believer out of him."

She agreed and we parted ways with a plan to meet at my house at seven-thirty that night. As I lay on my couch, I couldn't help but to think, *what if she was wearing a wire and the cops busted in for something I said wrong?* I had proof at this point that I didn't kill Shaina—the X-rays were evidence of that—but I was still paranoid of authorities twisting things.

Seven-thirty came and I received a message.

Allison: Jordan wasn't happy at all that I met you, but he wants to come. We're on our way and will be there in 30 minutes. Do you want us to bring beer?

Chumming it up with Shaina's vengeful ex was not what I had envisioned for the night but offering to bring beer seemed like a good sign. Cordial and casual, like two old friends. I hoped it wasn't a ruse.

Cameron: I've got some but bring what you want.

Making my way up to my room, I grabbed my pistol and checked that it was loaded before placing it in the back belt of my pants.

Allison: Here.
Cameron: I'll open the garage. You'll want to pull in and I'll close it behind you.

I stood at the kitchen door leading out to the garage and watched as they pulled up in his black Mercedes C300. My nerves were out of this world, my whole body abuzz with a soft tremor. Jordan eyed me suspiciously as they exited his car, so I offered a curt smile and welcomed them into the kitchen.

As Glen had so aptly observed, I wasn't one to shoot small talk. I looked Jordan in the eye and said, "I loved her, and I know you did too. I would never have killed her."

Half expecting him to draw back and punch me in the face, I was surprised to see his expression hadn't changed. In fact, he looked less suspicious than I had seen him a few moments ago.

"I knew Shaina well," he started, "and I have a good idea of what you were dealing with because I saw it too. I saw her mental health issues . . . she drove me crazy. She'd disappear on me for days and even though I never got the truth out of her, I knew what she was doing. To be honest, I now have serious trust issues because of her."

He looked down, then awkwardly glanced at Allison who was shifting uncomfortably from foot to foot. "She was sometimes, er, violent. And when things were bad, which they often were, she'd make strange comments, I thought she was just depressed at the time. I didn't know how real it was at the time, though. I thought it was just some sort of ploy to get me to stay or . . . I don't know."

I breathed the biggest sigh of relief, all of my nerves tumbling away with my former suspicions of Jordan and Allison's intentions.

"You're a good guy," he continued, "and I don't believe you did this. I brought this for my protection, but I don't feel like I need it." He pulled out a 9mm pistol and placed it on the kitchen table, removing the clip and taking a bullet out of the chamber. I smiled and reached behind me to pull mine out my brother had loaned me and place it on the table, mimicking his actions.

"Do you want to see where it all happened?" I offered. They nodded in agreement.

As we bounded up the stairs, I stopped just as we reached the landing. The spot of carpet was still stained deep in blood as it'd been the night I slept next to it, but I had since covered it with a large rug to avoid looking at it. Moving it, I then walked Allison and Jordan through each sequence of events as if I was an attorney in a courtroom reenacting the scene for the jury.

"See this"—I motioned them over to the hole in the wall across from my bedroom—"How could she have been shot in the back of the head? She locked herself in the room here"—I moved to stand in front of the door—"And I was in the bathroom."

I rushed to stand in front the bathroom doorframe. "And if I had been in the bedroom with her, and I shot her in the back of the head as she left, she would have fallen forward. The blood stain would be on the carpet six feet in front of the bedroom door, and instead it's in front of the bathroom door. If it didn't happen how I'm explaining it; there's no way the bullet could be on that wall."

To reinforce my explanation, I stood facing the bathroom door lifted my hand to my head. There was literally no way the scene showed a bullet to the back of the head, and I could see they saw that now.

To top it off I also shared the X-Rays with them.

I had been over the logistics of the scene with Glen more times than I'd care to count, and it was something that kept me up when I was alone late at night, wondering how the blood spatter analysis wouldn't have ruled out a "back to front" bullet, despite the word of a medical fraud.

Deep down, I knew the police knew the details of the scene didn't add up—even though they didn't bother to share their results with me or anyone else—and I knew this was one of many reasons they eventually released me.

Jordan and Allison stared at me with pained expressions as I talked holding in the tears as best as I could, and I wasn't sure whether they were going to throw up or cry. Feeling satisfied with my tour, I led them back downstairs to the kitchen. It was silent for a short while before Jordan stepped forward and wrapped his arms around me. Stunned, I hesitantly returned the gesture and realized how powerful that moment was—for both of us.

"Cameron," he started, stepping back and wiping a stray tear from his eye. "If I were you, there is no way I'd be able to live through this. I think I'd kill myself."

Instead of going home, the two of them spent hours at my house, sitting around the kitchen table drinking the beer they'd brought. The three of us talked about Shaina—the funny moments, the happy moments, the not-so-happy moments. When I usually talked about Shaina, I started out with a giant lump in my throat, threatening to choke me. Tonight, I was in the company of two other people who knew her and missed her, and it wasn't about me pouring out my heart as it was about sharing in our grief and reflecting on the memories we cherished. Eventually, Jordan and Allison wound up sleeping on my couch.

I took myself upstairs, walking past the covered carpet at the top of the stairs, and threw myself into bed, unable to feel sleepy after reflecting on the twists of the night. Jordan and Allison believed me. But Jordan's words circled around my head: *I think I'd kill myself.* Despite winning over two former enemies, I knew that the journey ahead would be grueling, and I still couldn't see a way out of my current predicament. *Was I doomed to live like this forever? Was I able to survive this?*

Chapter 13

I SHOULD BE ABLE TO TAKE IT AS A MAN

BEFORE THE NIGHTMARE – 2019

Early one January morning, I got the wrath of Shaina when she saw I had liked an Instagram post of a woman, Amanda, in her lingerie.

"Amanda is an ugly, fat bitch, and she looks like a man. If you want her, go get her—I won't be here."

I had never met Amanda; she was some random girl I had added a while back, but I knew I had made a mistake and was caught red-handed. Still, Shaina was guilty of doing the same, but she never heard me complain.

"This isn't a one-way street, Shaina. You don't get the privilege of liking other guys' photos and flirting with dudes on social media, but I can't do the same? If you don't like it, then we both need to stop."

I hated upsetting her, and she'd been particularly testy since her birthday night in Lava Hot Springs. She still wasn't willing to divulge anything about what had happened in the hotel room, and instead had become more withdrawn and quicker to anger. She left the room. I went after her and found her sulking on the couch. "Fine, I don't care. All I want is you anyway Shaina."

But she wasn't finished. "Well maybe you should hang out with Amanda this weekend since you like all her shit on Instagram."

I sighed and joined her on the couch, keeping a small distance between us. "Baby, I am so in love with you." Bringing my voice down a decibel I hoped it would calm her down. "It's just Instagram. I wake up every morning Monday through Friday and start your car and make you coffee hours way earlier than I need to get up. I give you back massages a couple times a week. I don't see how you're worried about another woman, when it's clear I'm so in love with you. But I'm sorry, I shouldn't have done that."

She stared across the room, avoiding eye contact, but I could see her expression had softened at my apology.

"Will you forgive me?" I reached over to grab her hand, but she pushed it away and stood up.

Her voice sharpened menacingly. "Well, I'm going to Moab with some friends this weekend so feel free to fuck Amanda while I'm gone."

I knew the friends she was talking about—Steve and Lisa, a married couple I'd only met once or twice who were dead set on getting Shaina to have a threesome with them. The first time I met them, Shaina and I had hung out with them at a local bar, but instead of being a fun double-date, I was basically shafted the entire conversation. Shaina told me afterward that Steve was courting her because Lisa was hoping to add a third to their relationship and wasn't sure if it was Steve or Lisa or maybe both that wanted this.

She was clearly threatening to hang out with them this weekend as punishment for liking Amanda's photo.

"If you want to go be a third wheel in a relationship, be my guest. Maybe I will hit up Amanda," I snapped back.

I stood up and went upstairs to the bedroom, followed by Shaina who was still hurling insults. I moved toward the closet, ignoring Shaina while texting Brody—my go-to friend when I wanted to make Shaina jealous—when my body was thrust forward into my wardrobe.

I whirled around in shock to stare at her. "You're going to push me? Really? Go to Moab with your friends, you've given me approval to hit up Amanda. Have fun this week."

Before I could dodge out of the way, Shaina cocked back and punched me in the face. Then she punched me again, and then again. I was raised by a man to be a man, and I kept my arms tucked at my sides while she got it out of her system, but by the seventh punch I had had enough, and I blocked her fist with my arm.

"Ugh!" She screeched, hurtling around the room like a madwoman to find her things and began packing them into her duffel.

"Shaina, I don't want Amanda, I want you! There's nothing more that I want than you!" Even though she'd hit me, I was growing desperate that she'd actually pack all of her stuff and leave for good.

She threw her bag over her shoulder and stomped out of my room while calling back, "We'll figure it out and we'll talk when I get back from Moab."

A few seconds later I watched her car pull out of the garage and she was gone.

I had my kids that weekend so there wasn't going to be any Amanda, nor did I want that. What I wanted was to figure out Shaina and how to capture her love for me again like we had found in Mirror Lake.

Friday night my sons and I broke out the Monopoly board before switching to Risk, a new game for us.

"Dad, you're such a bully." My oldest fake whined as I occupied Europe.

"I'd teach you nothing by letting you win," I said with a wink. As I moved all of my resources into Europe, my youngest son either struck lucky or had secretly been strategizing and occupied the surrounding countries, winning the game. He stood up and beat his fist into the air. "I won! I finally beat you, surrender!"

I lay back in my chair and laughed at his victorious display. "Yeah, yeah." I waved my hand. "I let you win."

"No, you didn't, Dad. I know you better than that," he pouted, earning a howl of laughter from his brother. We resigned to the couch to watch the latest *Avengers* movie and I nodded off within the first ten minutes.

I woke the boys up early on Saturday to take them for a hike in American Fork Canyon so I could take my mind off Shaina and what she had gotten into to last night. As we made our way to the small dam at the mouth of the canyon, my youngest huffed, "Dad, I'm tired."

"Stiffen up, soldier. We'll be there soon."

As soon as we made it to the top, the two of them began playing in the dirt, digging for bugs and rocks. Seeing an opportunity to check my phone, I pulled it out of my pocket and saw I had a new text.

Shaina: I miss you! I wish I had stayed with you.

Guess she wasn't mad at me anymore.

Cameron: Hope you're being a good girl. We're just out on a hike today.

I took a photo of myself, the boys playing in the background, and sent it to her.

Shaina: Of course, babe. I slept on the couch last night by myself, no need to worry.

But I was worried. Her behavior was becoming increasingly more aggressive and more erratic, and I wasn't thrilled about some of the people she was spending her time with. We'd been so good together the few weeks we'd removed ourselves from partying and drinking, and it seemed like Shaina had found herself in another spiral. But, she was stubborn—the more I tried to help, it seemed, the more she'd push me away.

Cameron: Love you babe! Have fun!

A few hours later, the three of us made it back home, the boys covered in dirt and dust. I made them stand out in the backyard while I hosed them from head to foot so their mother wouldn't kill me, chuckling as they squealed under the cold water.

As I lay in bed that night, thoughts of Shaina surrounded by strange men plagued me. I changed into my swimsuit and headed out back to my hot tub to pull my thoughts away. For a second, I had half a mind to hit up Courtney—Shaina was probably flirting and having fun, so I should enjoy myself too. But I corrected myself and let the heat of the water engulf my body as I laid my head back and dozed off.

My ex picked up the kids early that morning and Shaina returned a few hours later. I had asked her to come to my house straight after Moab, and she ran inside with her arms out, wrapping me almost to the point of suffocation.

"Cam, I'm so sorry! Moab was a mistake, and I spent the whole weekend sleeping on the couch. Nothing happened, I promise."

Happy she no longer seemed angry, all I could do was trust her and forgive her.

That night as we lay in bed, she snuggled in extra close. "I love you so much, Cameron," she cooed as I kissed her head. "I'm so tired of waitressing and don't know how to move ahead in life."

I'd been worried that her current behavior would lead to this again—Sad Shaina.

"Beautiful, what are you talking about? I've been trying to get you to meet with my nursing school client, I told you I'll help you. But waitressing is an honorable profession. As a matter of fact, you're basically doing the same thing as me with sales—working with people."

She rolled her eyes and pulled away while making the gun sign with her hand and pretended to pull the trigger as she slightly tilted her head.

"Don't you do that!" I scolded. "I think you're amazing, and the fact that you wake up every day at five-thirty and go to work and make all your customers smile makes me love you even more." I scooped her in close again, trying to devise a plan that she'd actually stick to. "We need to go see my client about nursing, can we do that tomorrow?" Thinking it would cheer her up, I was surprised my words had the opposite effect when I saw all signs of happiness leave her face.

"I just don't think people would care if I was dead."

"Shaina . . ." I was taken aback. I was offering a solution, yet she seemed fixated on the worst. "I told you not to talk like that. I love you and everyone that knows you loves you! Why would you think that?"

"I don't know . . . Will you just hold me?" Her voice was quiet. I wasn't quite sure what else to do so I did as she asked and held her as tight as I could, kissing her forehead over and over as she slept. I had a pretty sleepless night waking up every couple hours worried about her.

The next day, I called my client early to set up a meeting later with Shaina, then drove to downtown Salt Lake City to pick her up after her shift. As she got in the car, she mewled, "Baby, I'm tired. Can we just go home and take a nap?" Equally tired from my restless night, I selfishly wanted nothing more than to lie in bed and hold my queen in my arms, so I obliged.

Chapter 14

BACK TO BLACK

AFTER THE NIGHTMARE –
September 2019

Things seemed to be fairly quiet since my night out with Chevy and Gabby. There was a group on Facebook some people had set up a month prior, essentially a think tank on how to charge me. I checked it daily as people would try to form their own conclusions on the case, never in my favor, unsure why they allowed me, "the monster," in there anyway. Probably because they hoped I would slip somehow.

I was really losing my fight. Even with the results of my lie detector test and the corrected police report with the correct bullet trajectory, I was not going to convince a bunch of people of my innocence when they were looking to blame someone for her murder, rather than acknowledge that just maybe, Shaina had done this to herself—especially without a statement from the police department denouncing my involvement.

Glen mentioned the detectives had nothing on me and they speculated it was suicide. He simply suggested I needed to lay low and give it time but lying low was lulling me into a deep depression. I had no intention of going back to work, nor was I in the mindset to find a job anyway. I was now a murder suspect—who the hell was going to hire me?

I sat in my home—my fortress—and watched Netflix on my phone, slumping deeper and deeper into a void. The mess from the intruders still hadn't been cleaned up as I had zero motivation to do anything about it. My couches were still slashed, TVs still smashed, walls still spray painted. Each day that passed would take along with it any hope I had that my life would ever go back to normal.

At least I still had Shaina to talk to, or her spirit anyway. The numerous psychic encounters I had over the last few months had convinced me that she was still with me in this house watching over me. I spent my days talking to her and slept with her Crocs at night. As fate would have it, I was finding the same hopelessness Shaina had.

One morning I was still lying in bed when I heard a knock on the door. I trudged downstairs, my pistol on my side, and opened the door to find my mom standing there.

"Mom?" I said as she pushed her way inside.

"Cameron, you've been through so much and you can't do this on your own." Her eyes fell on all the damage and she sighed before turning to face me. "I want you to come live with me and your stepdad." The look on her face told me this was nonnegotiable.

"Where will I sleep?"

"We can move your bed and anything else you want to bring and set it up in the basement. I know it's unfinished, but I worry about you here by yourself."

She had a point. If I didn't do something now, I knew where this path was going to lead me.

"The entire family is on the way with trucks and trailers and we're going to move you out of this house, most of it obviously into storage."

As promised, my brothers, Joe and Logan, my sister, Noelle, and my dad each arrived to help with the move. We exchanged hugs and they each voiced their concerns and agreed that if I stayed in my home, I would find myself on the same path as Shaina.

The women boxed and the men carried the boxes, and with the large crew, it didn't take long to pack up.

I was the last one to leave for my mom's house when I realized I had a new Trager smoker that I had bought back in March in the back yard and had rarely used since; maybe I could consume my time and preoccupy my mind with cooking.

The problem was it was the biggest smoker they had, weighing in at over 200 pounds. My truck's suspension had been lifted six inches, and as I dragged the smoker out of my backyard, I wondered how in the hell I was supposed to hoist that bad boy into the back of my truck.

After lugging it to the driveway, I assessed my options. I tilted the smoker on its side, putting one side of the legs on my tailgate, and then in the most awkward fashion I picked it up and lifted it into the back of the truck. I felt a searing pain shoot down my back and cursed myself for trying to do this on my own but managed to finish the lift. I strapped it down and left for Mom's, the entire drive feeling like my back was going to give out.

We unloaded almost everything into a storage shed and set up my bed in her unfinished basement. I had my TV propped up on an empty cardboard box, powered by an extension cord leading from upstairs. Aside from that, the rest of my "room" included my phone charger and a portable heating unit since winter was around the corner.

That night my mom and I stayed up late and we talked about old memories, laughed, had a few shots, and I went to bed in good spirits. Lying in my new space, I couldn't help but feel that Mom likely just saved my life.

When I woke up, I tried to sit up but was stopped by the most excruciating pain that zipped through my whole body, rendering me paralyzed in a half sitting position. I very slowly laid back down hoping the pain would subside and tried to turn my head to look for my phone, but the pain was unbearable. I was stuck.

I started howling to get either my mom or stepdad's attention, but the minute I inhaled more jolts of pain shot down to my toes. My phone was on the floor and there was no way I could reach it, and I wasn't even sure that anyone upstairs was even home to hear me. Without moving my head, I frantically scanned the room and came upon an alarm clock my mom must've set up that was just in arm's distance. Gritting my teeth, I grabbed it as fast as possible while fighting through blurred vision, every movement the pain growing more intense. Like putting a horse out of its misery, if a gun was close, I would've gladly used it.

I managed to prop it against my chest, though I could barely look down to see it without risking another jolt of agony. Awkwardly, I set the alarm to go off in the next minute, hoping someone would hear it and grow concerned when I didn't shut it off. On cue, the alarm clock screamed for a few minutes before my mom eventually came down.

"Cameron, are you going to turn that off or—Why are you lying like that?"

"Call an ambulance" was all I managed, not even able to turn my head to look at her.

"Do what?"

"Mom! I can't move, please call an ambulance."

I'd had some bad injuries in my life, but this was pain I had never felt before—I knew something was terribly wrong.

When the paramedics and firefighters showed up, we soon found that the stretcher wouldn't fit down the curved stairway to the basement, so it was decided they would carry me out. Every bump and sway on our way to the ambulance felt like shards of glass piercing my back.

I was begging for pain meds by the time they wheeled me into the emergency room. A nurse assigned to me asked me to rate my pain on a scale of one to ten.

"Pain! Really! Pain? Please tell me you have something for me!" I shouted, uncaring how crazy I sounded. I would rather die than wait a second longer for relief.

Her stunned face disappeared out of the room as she went to find a doctor.

"Mom, please, get me something now!"

I heard the nurse in the hallway scream, "He needs something for the pain!" Almost immediately, a new nurse rushed in and quickly administered an IV. Within a few minutes I slipped into euphoria, and I couldn't control the blissful smile spreading across my face as my eyes fluttered shut.

The feeling was not only welcome, but I had known it before, long ago in 1999 when I had secured my first high-pressured sales job. I was only twenty at the time, selling high-ticket real estate development packages, surrounded by sales floors filled with other ambitious young dropouts. We were on the set of our very own *Boiler Room,* and success came with a price.

I'd recreationally used drugs in those years, mainly marijuana mixed with booze while out (frequently) partying. A colleague Jonathan came around one day and offered me an OxyContin tablet, told me I could make money I'd never dreamed of if I sniffed the "magic pill for sales echelon."

The thought of success seduced me into taking it, and looking around, it was clear to see that my colleagues were equally motivated by various pills to achieve success. As long as the drugs kept coming, the salesmen were motivated to sell, and any higher-ups turned a blind eye.

I took the tablets daily for a few months as my sales continued to sky-rocket. One day, I looked around to see that I had become the top producer at work, making anywhere from $4,000 to $8,000 a week—making more money in a year than my parents did in ten.

By month six, I realized I had developed a bad habit and quit cold turkey, hoping I could maintain my new cash flow without the help of a narcotic. And then I immediately felt sick—like, I needed to check into a hospital sick. I had surely succumbed to the worst strain of the flu I had yet experienced: unbearable aches and pains and profuse sweating I was curled up in the fetal position on my bed thinking I was going to die.

I called off work that day and thus, didn't buy my daily pills from my dealer a.k.a. my colleague. "Jonathan, I feel like I'm going to die, what in the hell is wrong with me!" Nearly screaming through the phone.

"Bro, you're in withdrawal, I'll be over in ten."

He left the call like it wasn't a big deal, that the gross feeling would just go away. So, I started up again, continuing to rake in thousands a week at work and setting aside around two grand each week for my OxyContin habit.

And then I met my ex-wife. Dating her only fueled my addiction as I'd spoil her filthy with gifts from the money I was earning; but as addiction often goes, my little habit was kept a secret from her. We had our first son in 2003 and we decided to get married. Shortly thereafter she uncovered my addiction. With a new baby in the house, she gave me an ultimatum: rehab or a divorce.

The next three years were a revolving door of getting clean and then relapsing. I was still working at the same sales job and the same drugs still ran rampant in the office, testing my sobriety daily. I knew the job was a trigger, but I also knew that I could provide so much for my little family if I continued on the same income trajectory.

But after so many broken promises, eventually my wife gave up on me and handed me divorce papers, took my son, and left Utah. What was already a rocky sobriety turned into a full-blown downward spiral and I got messy; so much so that my job found out about my drug abuse. In an attempt to clean up their sales floor, our bosses sent me and other high-earning performers to rehab and the not-so-high-earning performers got the boot.

By 2006, Rehab was a lost cause by this point. Even though our company had done a good job of trying to make drugs inaccessible in the office, I had resorted to finding drugs on the street. Like my wife, eventually my job had enough of me and I, too, got the boot.

I tried to stay afloat living off the money I had accumulated over the last six years, but so much money had already been spent on my addiction. Once my savings was dangerously close to empty, I tried to make money by selling my cars and boats, but that money just ended up back in my $2,000-a-week drug fund. Before I knew it, I was jobless, didn't have my wife or son, was broke, and was homeless. I learned quickly to numb out the pain of going from the top to the bottom so quick with the drugs.

And then I discovered heroin was way cheaper than OxyContin. It only took a week before another addict convinced me to shoot it up with a needle. A month in I was taken to the hospital by overdosing. It took only three months on the stuff to find myself wandering through the gun section of Cabela's with enough heroin coursing through my veins for the cops to be called when a worker found me shooting up in the restroom. I was convicted of multiple felony accounts for possession.

It was there in jail where I finally got sober. I'd only been there for a little more than a month and had written my ex-wife two letters a day with stamps provided by my family. Each letter was a variation of the same: I'm not a bad person, I still love you, I want to live a sober life with you forever. Though I wasn't expecting to, I finally received a letter back. My ex was willing to give me a second chance if I was truly focused on staying sober this time.

After a short few months in jail, I got out, got clean, and transferred my probation to Albuquerque where my ex and my son had been living. In January 2007, my ex and I rekindled our romance and remarried, our second son following that October. After the hell I had put my body and my family through, I knew that this time was different; this time I had the conviction to stay clean so I could support my wife and kids.

That was the last time I had touched an opiate. Thirteen years of sobriety, despite all the pain I'd been in since Shaina's death, and here I was in the hospital greeting the numbness of pain medicine like an old friend. God, I missed that feeling. Within moments, all of the pain and despair that had been bottling up inside me since June twenty-fifth seemed to float away, out of my body and down the hall. For the first night since Shaina's death, I quickly drifted off to sleep finding peace in the poison.

It wasn't a completely peaceful sleep, though—as I slept, I would be jostled by flits of pain and woke up every so often with discomfort. But the high would lull me back to sleep, a warm presence fighting both my physical and emotional pain.

At one point, some nurses wheeled in a stretcher and one of them informed me that the doctor had ordered an MRI. They gently maneuvered me on top of the cold mat and hauled me away, but I was hardly aware of my surroundings. My eyes rolled back, and I slept for what felt like hours until I awoke to hospital staff sliding me inside the tube.

I heard a low hum coming from somewhere above me and it grew louder as it slowly scanned across my body. The mix of pain and the drugs wearing off left my brain feeling like I was in another world. And then instantly, the ache in my back began to radiate and the tight quarters of the MRI sent me into a state of panic. "Get me the fuck out of this thing."

Before long I was back in my room with a fresh bag of morphine. I slept some more before a nurse woke me with an update.

"We're calling the on-call doctor to see if we need to perform surgery on your back, Mr. Lundgren. You have a compression fracture on your T12 spine.

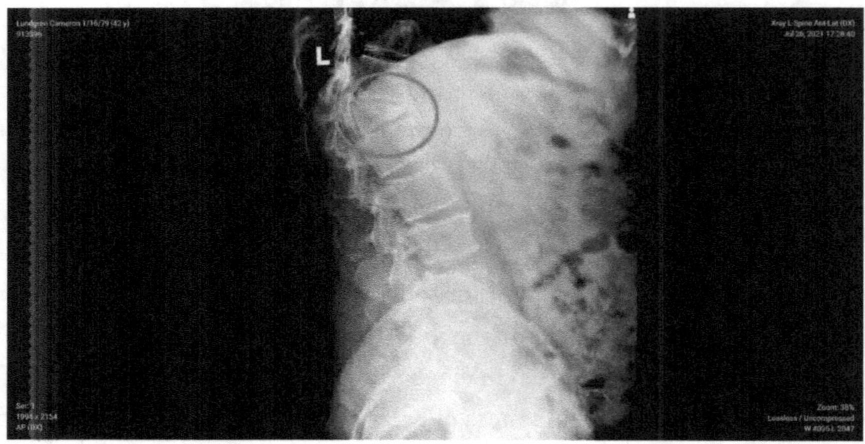

That definitely sounded like bad news. I hadn't been back to work in months—*did I still have insurance?* It seemed like I couldn't come up long enough for air; any minor progress was knocked down and I was trapped in this new hell that had become my life.

The nurse was in and out of my room for the next hour with no news except that the surgeon was still reviewing my X-rays and not sure what to do yet. I looked at the clock and it was around midnight. That lazy asshole probably just wanted to go back to bed.

The latest IV was running low and the pain was slowly making its way back. I was about to walk to the operating room myself when the nurse came back, and this time, had the results I'd been waiting for.

"The surgeon has decided not to do surgery."

Any sense of relaxation I had felt earlier from the pain medicine was snatched away in an instant. I could feel my face turn bright pink with rage as I clenched my jaw. "Are you kidding me?"

"No, sir. It's not a fracture that is approved for surgery." The nurse remained calm. I was impressed by all these professionals who were able to maintain their composure in dire situations, like being faced with the 911 call of a suicide or confronting an angry drugged-up ex-addict in excruciating pain. "And we need to let you know you've been in the emergency room for your maximum stay, and you need to elect to be transferred to a long-term care facility or leave."

I stared at her with a look that must have told her I wasn't happy with that option.

"But ..." She hesitated. "I would advise you to go home and follow up with your primary care physician. We'll send you home with some pain medication."

I got changed and headed back to my mom's, cursing under my breath the whole way home. At least they sent me home with Oxycodone—little did the doctors and nurses know they fed me the candy I had fought so hard to stay away from for thirteen years. By the time I made it to the basement and lay in bed, I didn't even care about the surgery. I had my old friend back, and I was looking forward to the blissful euphoric sleep ahead of me.

For several weeks I was not able to do a thing without the help of my mother. When we pulled up at the neurologist appointments, she would get out of the car and help me turn my feet out the passenger door, muscling through the pain with all the strength I had. Once she got me upright, I would put my hands on her tiny shoulders and slowly walk into the office, using her as crutches until we could find a wheelchair. Each visit produced the same result: they were not willing to operate on me, that it would heal, and I would just have to deal with the pain.

If I was feeling depressed before, it was nothing compared to now. In just three months, I had lost my girlfriend tragically, lost the respect of my oldest son, lost my job, lost my savings, lost my good name, lost some friends, lost my belongings, lost the right to live in my own house—and now I had a broken back, which caused me to lose my sobriety. Can't go much deeper than this I thought.

I was pretty much confined to my bed. When I had to use the bathroom, I would slowly turn on my side, hang my feet off the bed, and use my right arm to lift myself up until my feet touched the floor. I kept an office chair with wheels close by and cautiously transferred from the bed to the rolling chair. Then I'd slide on the concrete floors of my mother's basement until I reached the bathroom. It was a grueling process and I felt utterly useless and worthless. Mom helped as much as she could, but my stubbornness got in the way.

After accepting that no doctor would operate on me, I eventually found a doctor who assisted me with pain management, and he prescribed me the same medication I had been addicted to in my early twenties—OxyContin.

I was going through my pills like candy, checking out every chance I could. My mom just attributed it to the enormous pain I was in. Which was true, but I knew I was abusing the medication for other reasons too. I was checking out of life, wanting nothing but to spend the rest of my days in a fugue state blocking out all the terrible events that had led me to this dark place.

The more I took the Oxy, the more I craved something stronger. I missed the feeling of being able to remove myself from my thoughts by sticking a needle in my arm; that deep morbid love affair with a drug that promised silence. I hadn't put two thoughts into touching heroin in well over thirteen years until they threw me in jail the night Shaina died. It was all the inmates talked about, and I had felt so far removed from that life until their talk started to seduce me again. My cellmate had been in for heroin, and he made me feel like it was everywhere, and everyone was doing it.

One guy I befriended there, Gabe, gave me his girl's number after I shared with him my younger experience with drugs. "I'll be in here awhile," he said, "but if you get out, hit her up because she could use the money."

Carefully leaving the haven of my bed, I wheeled my way to the envelope I kept filled with all the letters I received in jail and fished around until I found a torn piece of paper. It had the name *Natalie* written in terrible cursive and a phone number scribbled beneath.

Staring at the name, a faint voice in the back of my head whispered, "Don't do it." I ignored the voice and grabbed my phone.

Cameron: Hey, I met Gabe in prison and he told me to hit you up.

Not even a few seconds passed before I got a response.

Natalie: Hey sweetie, watcha need?
Cameron: Black, darling.

I had met a lot of dealers in my day, and she was not like any of the others. Most were super paranoid about talking openly over phone or text; deals were usually done using key words and phrases, like *negra* for black tar heroin and *blanco* for coke.

Natalie: How much?
Cameron: Two ounces.

She went quiet for a solid hour. *Shit, she probably thinks I'm a narc.* Black tar heroin is usually dealt in grams, but I had coke money—I still had half of the hundred thousand I'd saved up for legal fees and bail, so buying $2,000 worth of heroin wasn't a big deal to my mind, despite the zero job prospects on my horizon. I was just focused on one thing only: getting as much heroin as I could to pass my life away, and not have the hassle of constantly needing to buy more.

Finally, my phone buzzed.

Natalie: Where did Gabe grow up?

I had to think for a minute, but it wasn't easy to forget a guy like Gabe. He was a real scrawny guy laced with tattoos and sporting a short-trimmed red mohawk. He'd told me a story about him running from the cops with his mom when he was eleven. I guess he and his mom had been living out of a motel in Vernal, Utah, with her dealer and had recruited Gabe to sell heroin on the nearby corner. Late one night he got tipped off that the cops were coming, but his mom was too strung out to move. By the time he heard the sirens, he was able to wrangle his mom out the back window, leaving the dealer asleep on the bed.

Cameron: Vernal.
Natalie: Lol alright boy you must be legit if he told you that story. You got cash?

I let out a long groan. Damnit, White Boy Rick doesn't buy drugs with checks.

> **Cameron:** No, but I can't move out of my bed at the moment, I broke my back.
> **Natalie:** If ya got Venmo, we can do it that way. Hell, for buying that much I'll even come to bed with ya and we can nod together.

Nodding referring to when you're so high your eyes roll back in your head while you're still standing so that your head continually drops like a bobblehead, going in and out of sleep.

I laughed at the idea that people bought drugs with Venmo nowadays. The means to buy drugs had changed, but the market for them was as strong as ever. I politely declined her pass at me, but I knew I had more to worry about than just payment. How was I going to meet this chick when I can't even walk?

> **Cameron:** Oh, by the way, if you can bring it to me I'll add another thousand to the deal.

She quickly agreed.

If I was going to shoot up, I also had to get some needles. I was somewhat mobile but still couldn't drive a car, so I'd have to somehow convince my mom of my plan without letting her read the fine print. She'd usually come down to check on me every now and then, so I double dipped my pain meds while I waited for her next visit. I wrapped the covers over me to get comfortable, squeezing on to Shaina's Crocs, only now I didn't cry anymore when I held them. The drugs had taken care of that.

The sound of the door opening woke me up and I blinked to hide from the natural light coming from upstairs. My mom shuffled down the steps and I instantly popped up at the sight of her.

"Mom, I spoke to my doctor, and he suggested continuing to take my testosterone to help my back repair, but I need the syringes from the box in your garage. I packed everything I need in there; can you get them for me?"

Shaina had been taking low levels of street steroids from a friend and I had previously been taking testosterone once we got back into our gym routine after we agreed to cool it with the drinking. Luckily, I had kept my supplies.

My mom frowned. "Cameron, is this prescribed by a doctor?"

"Of course, Mom, I was taking it for a while before all this happened. But the doctor says it will help. I have the prescribed bottle in my top drawer if you want to take a look." My innocent mother didn't need to know that I had bought the steroids off the streets, and I hoped she bought my bluff.

"Wouldn't your doctor call it in?"

"He said I needed to finish what I had before he'll prescribe me more."

I didn't exactly like lying to my mom, but manipulation comes easy to an addict. I was willing to say anything at this point to get what I wanted, even if it meant hurting the ones closest to me. The need to use—to escape reality and forget about your worries—becomes greater than any relationship. My ex-wife had been the victim of that.

My mom sighed but agreed, even though she still didn't look fully convinced. It didn't take her long to find my testosterone and needles, and it took Natalie even less time to show up at my house. She showed up at the door with a small bouquet of roses telling my mom she was only there to give me a kiss on the head to make my back feel better. I was partly impressed by her act, as she was clearly also a master manipulator—the addict's trademark.

My mom thought nothing of Natalie's surprise arrival and led her skin-and-bone frame downstairs to my lair. The first thing I saw come down the stairs was Natalie's pale, skinny legs draped in a miniskirt. She was cute, but years of drug use were marked on her petite frame, as if she hadn't eaten in months.

My mom closed the door leading down the stairs giving Natalie the opportunity to run over and jump on my bed. I squirmed in pain with a tight grimace.

"Oh sorry, sweetie, I forgot," she said with a giggle. All I could think was if Shaina really were here in spirit, Natalie was about to get her ass kicked.

Sitting on the side of my bed, she reached into her bra and pulled out what looked like a softball-sized black ball in a baggie.

"Here." She offered it in my direction. "Send the Venmo." I whipped out my phone to quickly pay her, then she handed me the baggie. "You're cute." She giggled again, grinning to reveal yellow-stained teeth.

I needed to dodge her passes at me before she thought this was anything more than a drug transaction. "Thanks for helping me, but my mom's going to start trippin' soon. You got to go." Trying to evoke some urgency, I motioned my head toward the stairs.

Without flinching, she jumped off the bed to head out, but turned back to wink at me before prancing up the stairs. "Call me soon, daddy."

I rolled my eyes once she was out of view.

Overdoses happen all the time, but like most users, I believed I was invincible. I was about to test a well thought out accident, proving to myself that I had a high tolerance to drugs, but also thinking in the back of my mind that I may be able to "accidentally" check out of this nightmare with Jordan's comment lingering about not being able to live through this.

Locked in the only finished room in the basement—the bathroom—I slowly peeled off the packaging for the single syringe. It wasn't your normal syringe used for dope or insulin; it was used to tranquilize a horse, to inject thick, gooey testosterone into your butt. The needle may have been as big as my vein, but it wasn't a deterrent in the least. Where there's a will, there's a way.

Earlier in the day I had been rummaging in my mom's kitchen drawers and found a small spoon that looked like something you'd use to feed a baby oatmeal or applesauce. I had grabbed it, feeling the weight of a thousand pounds on my chest as I thought about my kids. Looking at the spoon now, in the bathroom next to the syringe with my last dose of pills wearing off, I began to feel again. Feel the sharp stabbing in my back, feel the pain of missing my kids and what these drugs would do to me—to them.

Tears prickled at my eyes, a sensation I hadn't felt in a month, and it was all I needed to feel to focus myself back on the task at hand. I put a sizable amount of dope in the spoon, then used my water-filled syringe to douse the spoonful of black death.

"Be careful with this stuff, it's strong." I remembered Natalie warning me.

As the lighter warmed up the spoon, the concoction became milky brown, and as it bubbled, it looked like lava from hell. Putting the spoon down, I used a Q-tip to soak up the black milky mix. Finally sucking it all up into the syringe, I paused for half a second not sure what to expect. I hadn't done this for years—I was an adult now, with kids no less. I tried to talk myself out of it, but the need grew too deep and the pain of my kids and life crept in. I secured a shoelace around my arm, surprised to see that my once beaten-up veins had become strong again.

The thing about needles—I still squirm when a nurse draws blood —but there's something soothing, even satisfying and maybe even easy about pricking yourself. The act of using the needle becomes an addiction itself, an extension of the drug. I eased the needle into my arm and watched the black death disappear into my veins, the lights of the bathroom slowly going black as I sat hunched on the toilet seat, resting my head on the sink counter.

Weeks melted into what felt like days.

Chapter 15

BLOODY VALENTINES

BEFORE THE NIGHTMARE – Early 2019

After Shaina avoided her meeting with my client at the nursing school, I dropped the subject and looked for other ways to cheer her up.

Valentine's Day was coming up and this was my chance to bring out the big dogs. One morning after Shaina left for work, I got out my laptop to book two flights in July to Shanghai, then Shanghai to Phuket; then we'd finish off the trip by boat to the romantic island of Ko Samui.

A few weeks earlier I had purchased a framed star map picture, which captured the alignment of the stars above us that incredible night at Mirror Lake. The picture was outlined in the shape of a heart with these words at the bottom:

I had no idea, the day I drove to someone

I had never met,
the love I would find.
The stars on August 11, 2018.
The night we fell in love under the stars in
the back of my truck.

On the morning of Valentine's Day, I had the picture frame wrapped up and the trip reservations stuffed in a card and placed them both on my bed for her to find when she got home.

Then, besotted by my own romantic gesture, I made the brilliant decision to add our relationship—again—on Facebook with a cute post. I was absolutely giddy as I went about my day, waiting for her to finally accept my relationship request and to find my gifts. A few hours went by and I hadn't heard from her . . . I was growing frustrated as a sinking feeling began to set in my stomach.

She was pissed off; I just knew it.

My cell phone rang, and I fumbled to answer in my desperate attempt to hear what she had to say.

"What is wrong with you?" She was definitely pissed off. "I'll make it public when I'm ready, I've told you over and over again, the only people that matter already know about us."

Here we were fighting again because my girlfriend refused to publicly acknowledge our relationship, on Valentine's Day of all days, even though all of her close friends and her family already knew about us. My blood boiled.

"Who are you trying to hide us from, Shaina?" I countered.

"No one, Cam. There's lots of great guys out there—if I wanted one, I'd be with one, but I choose to be with you."

"Yeah." I couldn't help but scoff. "Choose to be with me in secret, huh? While we live together, nonetheless. Makes me feel so good."

"Then leave me, Cameron, and go be with someone else. I'll do it when I'm ready."

I hung up the phone in a fury, kicking myself for ruining the day. I should've waited until after dinner tonight, after she saw my gifts. Taking deep breaths in and out, I forced myself to calm down until she got home so I could try this again.

Like always, as she pulled up into the garage, I went out to help her carry the things she brought over from her mom's, then embraced her in the kitchen. "Baby, I'm so sorry. I know I should be more patient . . . I have a present for you upstairs and made us dinner reservations for tonight."

Shaina was never one to wait to open a present. She raced upstairs to find my gift and I followed suit so I could watch her reaction. When she got to the bed, I folded my arms and leaned in the door frame. "Open the long, tall one first."

She ripped off the wrapping paper with all the force of a five-year-old on Christmas morning, then held out the photo in front of her to admire it in full.

"Aw, babe, this is so cute! Where are we going to hang it?" Before I could even answer she was on to the next one. To her surprise, I had gotten her a remote car starter and I felt the mood change quickly. "Should I open the card now?"

I nodded. "As you wish."

After tearing off the seal, her face immediately lit up when the travel reservations dropped onto the floor. "What is this?" she asked excitedly, leaning down to pick it up.

"That's your dream trip to Thailand, babe. It's all booked up."

She stared at me in awe. "I'll tell you all about it over dinner. I bought you something to make you feel sexy when we get home." She rewarded me with her jump kiss.

Our reservation was at seven and we had about two hours to prepare. I always had Fireball in my kitchen, so Shaina and I took a few shots before leaving; then Shaina took a few more. Since we were going to an hibachi restaurant that only served sake, Shaina filled up a plastic blender bottle with Fireball to bring along. *How the hell were we going to drink all that?* I asked myself.

We sipped on her to-go Fireball on the drive to the restaurant, then both took a good-sized chug before heading into the restaurant, leaving the blender bottle in the truck's cup holder. Feeling buzzed and flirtatious, we checked in with the hostess, then followed her to our seats at the hibachi grill, touching each other's hands and smiling like two young lovers.

We ordered food and a couple orders of sake to top off the Fireball. We were seated next to another couple who were also clearly there to celebrate Valentine's Day. While Shaina and I held hands and watched our food being prepared, I felt emboldened by the liquor to strike up a conversation with the couple next to us.

"So how long have you two been together?" I asked the man seated next to me.

"Just a few weeks, but I asked her to be my Valentine today and she accepted." His girlfriend smiled next to him and squeezed his arm.

"Good for you two! So, is it official?" I was probing, trying to make a point to Shaina, and she knew it. She angrily squeezed my hand and her customer-smile was painfully displayed across her face.

"I asked him to be my boyfriend last week," the woman gushed.

Before I could respond, Shaina stood up and asked me for my keys. Feeling a little embarrassed, I fished for my keys, and handed them to her and she walked out the door.

"We'll take the food to go," I muttered to the waiter. Things got silent and very awkward with our neighbors while I quickly paid the bill.

When I got to my truck, it was already started, and Shaina was waiting for me in the passenger seat. Once I got in and shut the door, she unleashed.

"What the fuck is wrong with you!"

"Don't look at me, I'm not the one playing games!" I jabbed.

She huffed and turned to face out her window.

"Listen, we just need to get home. I shouldn't be driving in the first place at this point." As we pulled out of the parking lot and onto the road, I glanced down at the blender bottle and noticed Shaina had had more Fireball.

"Has it ever occurred to you that I've been in a public relationship before and after we broke up, I looked like a fool?" she said.

We drove down a small two-lane road with construction cones to our right, narrowly passing cars.

"I'm the one that looks like a fool, Shaina! I love someone that is afraid to show that love back. What is it about me you're so afraid of?"

"Maybe that you're old!"

Damn. I wasn't expecting a low blow. "Fuck you!"

We were both screaming as I tried to keep the truck in my lane, when out of nowhere I saw from my peripheral the blender bottle flying toward my face. It was a little more than halfway full of Fireball as it connected with my lips, then dropped into my lap. Dazed by the assault, I swerved into oncoming traffic then tried to correct my direction, but only ended up going off into the construction zone and hit an orange bin. I finally managed to straighten back out, seized by fear, when I felt something wet on my lip.

I touched it and looked down at my finger to see blood. "What the fuck is wrong with you, Shaina?"

I was *over-the-top* mad now. We could've been killed —or killed someone else— from that action, and she didn't seem to be at all bothered by it. Eyes still on the road, I searched for the shaker bottle in my lap and flung it at her. I swerved again at the sharp sound of Shaina bursting into tears, her hands covering her face. I quickly looked at her, trying to maintain vision on the road ahead, and was appalled to see that her hands were covered in blood.

"What the fuck just happened!" I yelled again, only this time the anger was directed at myself. Shaina was crying so violently she couldn't even talk. "Shaina, we need to get home or we're both going to jail." She continued to cry as she bled into her hands, so I pulled over at the first available parking lot to assess the damage.

I got out of the truck to grab a blanket out of my backseat and walked around to the passenger side to open her door and just then I saw a cop drive through the parking lot. Trying to act calm and casual, I handed the white blanket to Shaina and it quickly absorbed a *lot* of blood.

Fuck. "Are you okay? If we need to call the cops, we can."

She held the blanket over her nose, making sure not to look at me. "Let's just get home."

Fuck fuck fuck. I wanted to get her medical attention, but I also knew that would likely include jail with the amount of alcohol we'd been drinking, questions would be asked, and the answers would not be good. I knew with my bloody lip that wouldn't help Shaina either; she was already the angriest she'd ever been at me. As I walked back to climb in the truck, Shaina opened her Snapchat—I thought she was just using the camera to get a good look at her injury. But violence in a relationship was nothing new to Shaina. Her former one was plagued with domestic abuse charges, but I had no time to worry about documentation, I needed to get us home.

During the drive I felt like shit. I had no intention of making her feel like her relationship with Kyle when he choked her out on the street and neighbors had to come break it up with cops called.

She carried pictures of the bruises in her purse around with her as a reminder it wouldn't happen again. She told me he admitted to her later the only reason he stopped was because he felt her body go limp. *Had I become that guy, I worried?* It was an accident I told himself. I hadn't deliberately tried to hit her in the face. I tried to justify it with the blood on my cheek prior. But the fact is I threw it and it came from me.

When we got home, we bandaged our wounds and got in bed. I was about to fall asleep when Shaina finally broke the silence. "Cameron. I need a sober life or I'm going to end up dead."

I didn't really understand what she meant—was she blaming her drinking on the incident from earlier tonight?

"I couldn't agree more, Beautiful." I scooted over and pulled her in close before dozing off.

I'd barely slept more than an hour the night before, and I had convinced myself that I needed to make amends. That next morning as we made breakfast, I told Shaina, "I need to apologize to your parents."

Concern flashed across her face. "You don't need to do that. I'll tell them I fell down the stairs."

I wasn't taking no for an answer. "Shaina, I was raised better and even though it wasn't intended to hurt you, I should have never thrown that bottle back at you. I want—need—to meet with your parents and tell them what happened and apologize and promise them this will never happen again."

She threw her head back and exhaled. "Fine," she conceded. "It's kind of cute you want to go through all this trouble."

I had her text her dad and stepmom to coordinate lunch plans.

"By the way," she added, opening up Snapchat, "I sent this video to my stepmom yesterday."

It was the video from when we'd pulled over. God, this didn't look good . . . but at least I knew what I'd be walking into with her parents.

I showed up to the restaurant a little early and began rehearsing what I'd say in my head, my leg jumping up and down under the table.

Nothing like this had ever happened before.

Although it wasn't my intent to injure her, I should have had more self-control.

I can promise you it will never ever happen again.

I was nervous for their reaction, but depending on how the conversation went, I also had a question for Shaina's dad, Terry.

As he approached the table, I stood up to shake his hand.

"Hi, Cam. Just me today—Shaina's mom couldn't make it, she had plans with her husband."

I started in as soon as he was seated.

"Look, Terry, I want to tell you—" He put his hand up to stop me from going any further.

"Cameron, I saw the video, and we know our daughter. This isn't the first time something like this has happened. My wife and I have talked, and we don't blame you at all."

I stared at him for a few seconds, slack-jawed, then tried to hide my surprise. Well, that was better than best-case scenario. It was now or never.

"Well, that's good to hear . . . thank you." I cleared my throat before continuing. "Terry. I love your daughter and you can expect nothing like this will ever happen again. You have my word. Shaina and I talked last night and we're going to stop drinking. Together."

"I appreciate that."

I nodded, unsure how to proceed. "This may be bad timing, but we're going to Thailand in April. I uh, well I wanted to ask your permission to ask for her hand in marriage while we're there." I blurted it all out so fast I wasn't sure it had really happened.

Her dad fixed me with a stare, but I couldn't gauge his emotion. Then he leaned forward and rested his clasped hands on the table. "Cameron,

Shaina has her own problems. I don't know if I would do that just yet . . . Ultimately, it's up to you. You have my blessing."

In my car after lunch, I opened my phone and sent a message to Terry's wife and Shaina's stepmom, Miranda. Since I had known her, she was very open-minded.

> **Cameron:** Hi Miranda. Just wanted to tell you I love your husband, he's such a cool ass dude. Also sorry for the drama last night. I'm so embarrassed and hope you'll forgive me.

Not a minute went by when she returned confirming my meeting with Terry.

> **Miranda:** I don't blame you. I know my daughter very well and it's a hard thing being enamored with her, she's a bit fickle and I feel she hasn't quite figured out what makes her happy or better yet she hasn't made herself happy and is always looking outside of herself for it.

I felt a lot better about what happened despite still being disappointed in myself.

> **Cameron:** Ur very wise, thank you Miranda.
> **Miranda:** I've been through a lot in my life and Shaina is quite a bit like her father and mother and I've known them most of my life. They're a special breed lol.

I drove home and had Shaina meet me out front so I could take her to the hospital, like I should have done the day before. She had about an inch-long cut on her nose and a slight fracture, but I thanked God profusely it wasn't broken.

For a few weeks after, we seemed to hit our stride again, like the old days of Silly One and Silly Two. Shaina stuck to her promise of being sober and the two of us hit the gym together five days a week. Any yelling or fighting had stopped, and my heart fluttered at the possibility that I could really be marrying her, Shaina—Beautiful—the love of my life. Things were looking up.

Almost a month and a half later, we were still on our healthy-living kick in preparation for our Thailand trip. Our heads weren't clouded with alcohol and partying, we felt fresh and clear-headed. We spent every other week with my kids playing Monopoly, loving on each other, and laughing every chance we had.

Shaina came home from work one day and found me in the kitchen preparing our protein shakes for the gym. "Babe." I stopped to look at her—I didn't like the sound of that. "I need to ask you a question."

"Shoot, Beautiful. I'm here for you." I hoped the positivity in my voice masked my apprehension. She twiddled her fingers.

"So, Evelyn messaged me today and I guess it's her friend's birthday next week and they're going on a girl's trip to Vegas. She invited me to go."

Nothing could've stopped me from rolling my eyes. "Listen, Shaina, I support whatever you decide to do and trust you going." Her shoulders relaxed a little. "But," I added, "I would also warn you that I'm not sure she's the best friend for you right now."

I wasn't sure if she wanted me to think she didn't want to go or if she really didn't want to go, but she agreed. "Yeah, I think you're right. I'm going to find out more details and then make a decision. I love you, baby!" She kissed me before running up to the bedroom.

Over the next few days, Shaina kept me updated on the plans for Vegas. It all sounded fun and harmless on the surface, but I knew Evelyn was reckless and wouldn't support our newly committed lifestyle. She didn't like me, and I didn't like her, but I wanted to give Shaina the freedom to choose and to know that I trusted her if she decided to go.

The weekend prior, Shaina admitted, "Okay, I want to go. I'm not going to drink much and I'm going to be careful."

My stomach sank a little, but I didn't want to show her that I didn't think she could be okay on her own. "Baby, just *please* be careful."

My mind flashed back to the memory of a drunken Shaina in Lava Springs being hustled away by Evelyn and a large group of men.

"You know men take advantage of women out there. Do not accept any drinks from men and stay close to the girls."

She grinned at me, accepting my warning as approval to go to Vegas. "As you wish," she trilled before hitting me with a jump kiss.

Shaina left for the airport the following Friday and she was already mass texting me before she even got through security.

> **Shaina:** They're being bitches claiming I made them late and that we may miss their flight. They're ganging up on me, should I not go?

I couldn't help but feel vindicated in my correct assessment of Evelyn and the type of girls she'd be friends with. I knew this was a bad idea.

> **Cameron:** I don't think you should. If you're worried about losing the cost of the flight I'll reimburse you.
> **Shaina:** OK, we're at security, just checked our bags. I'll text you in a bit.

Thirty minutes or so went by and I kept texting her to check on her, suggesting she just come home.

> **Shaina:** I just got on the plane and I don't feel good about this. They're being so mean, they didn't even sit with me! I can hear them talking about me a couple seats up calling me a stupid bitch.

Jesus, what had I let her get into? I swear to God, the next time I saw Evelyn . . .

> **Cameron:** Shaina, get off the plane before it leaves. Baby, come home to me.
> **Shaina:** I can't get off now. Maybe I'll get a flight back when we land.

It was silent for an hour, so I sent a text while she was in the air.

Cameron: I'll get you a flight back when you land. If you're uncomfortable, you shouldn't be there.
Shaina: I'm just going to make the best of this. I'll text you when I get to the room.
Cameron: OK, be safe and I'm here for you.

I sighed. I should've told her how I really felt about her going to Vegas. Hours went by and I was a nervous wreck—so nervous that I quit my streak of no alcohol and drank to calm my anxiety while watching episodes of *Game of Thrones* until I fell asleep.

Then my phone rang jolting me up at two in the morning and the caller ID flashed *Shaina.*

I hurried to pick up but couldn't make out a word on the other end.

"Hello? Shaina? Shaina, hello? Babe, can you hear me?" The only response was mumbling, and then the line disconnected.

My heart sank. Fuck, something terrible happened and it's all my fault. I called her repeatedly only to get her voice mail. Frustrated, I hurried down to the kitchen and took a shot—my nerves couldn't take something bad happening to her again. I heard my phone faintly ringing from upstairs and bolted to my room; when I answered, the only feedback was more mumbling. It was clearly Shaina's voice, but I couldn't understand her. Our call disconnected again.

I tried calling back what felt like a hundred times when a voice I didn't recognize picked up. "Hello, do you know this woman?"

"Yes, she's my girlfriend. What's going on?" I demanded.

"Sir, I work with MGM security. We found her in a back alley passed out, and we're taking her to the emergency room now because she's unresponsive."

The security guard gave me the name of the hospital, then I rushed off the phone to dial Shaina's dad. Thankfully he answered and I filled him in on what little information I knew as I ran around my room like a cyclone, packing up random articles of clothing into my suitcase. "I'm driving to Vegas now to meet her," I told him. "I'll be there before a flight would."

I tossed my bag in the car and sped down the road, momentarily remembering that I had been drinking not too long ago. It didn't matter. I needed to get to her.

The road rushed past me in a blur, a kaleidoscope of car lights, buildings, and billboards. I was nearly halfway there—thanks to the fact I'd been driving about one hundred miles an hour—when my phone rang, and I was surprised to see it was Shaina's number again. Maybe the people who had helped her to the hospital had an update.

"Hello?"

A weak "Cameron" emerged from the other end followed by sobbing.

"Shaina! Baby! Tell me you're okay."

Clearly still delirious, she began to tell me the story, still mumbling, sounding drunk or drugged. "Cameron, I was doing good all night, I promise, babe." She sounded delirious and frail, probably still drunk. She started crying. "I wasn't even drinking until I took the shot."

"I know, baby, I trust you." I tried to sound soothing.

She continued to relay the night, barely able to talk over her weeping. "We were at the bar in the club, I hadn't drunk much, I promise—"

"I believe you."

"All I remember is these Australian guys coming up to buy all the girls shots, and one of them handed me one and then . . . I . . . I blacked out," she choked, crying even harder. "Please come get me, I don't want to be here anymore!"

There was nothing more I wanted than to magically appear at her bedside and hold her while she cried. I gripped the steering wheel tightly, trying not to cry. "I still have a three-hour drive, baby, but I'm driving as fast as I can, okay? Just . . . breathe, okay? If they release you from the hospital, call me."

I called Shaina's dad to give him an update.

"Terry, I'm driving as fast as I can. All I know is security found her passed out in a back alley after a few men gave her a shot and led her away."

"I had a bad feeling about her going to Vegas. This is—well shit, it's not good." Terry's voice was somber and suddenly my heart ached for him. I was a dad, too, and I couldn't imagine the feeling of total helplessness being in another state while my kid lay in a hospital bed.

"Cam, uh . . . Do you know if she was raped?" His voice tensed up at the same time my heart constricted. We'd both been thinking it, but I didn't want to deliver that news to a father.

"I can't confirm that, but the security guard who called me from her phone said she'd been found with her underwear down her legs." I wanted to vomit. I'm sure Terry did too. A moment of silence passed between us until Terry cleared his throat.

"Okay, keep us informed. And thanks for being there for her. Let us know if we can do anything."

I hung up and called Dave, a friend of Evelyn's I had met a couple months back. He and Evelyn were tight, and he lived in Vegas, so I assumed he'd been out with the girls that night. Dave seemed like a good dude, and I hoped he had more answers about what the fuck happened earlier.

Dave immediately seemed to know why I was calling.

He asked, "Do you know where Shaina is? She has our car keys."

I scoffed. "She's in the hospital! She said the last thing she remembers is a group of dudes buying them drinks and now she's in a hospital bed. She seems pretty fuckin' shaken up dude, what if she was raped? How was she just led away by strangers?" God, I couldn't bear to think of it. Not after what happened in Lava, when I wasn't there to protect her.

"*Shit*. Look, man—I wasn't there when we lost her, but I guess the girls were drinking and some guys came up to buy a shot for the birthday girl. Birthday girl gave it to Shaina, and last thing they remember is Shaina walking off with the guys."

Every cell in my body pounded in time with my heart; I couldn't remember the last time I had been this angry. "Tell Evelyn she's a *fucked up* friend to let her friend walk off with two strangers like that!"

"I know, man, I agree—Hey, Shaina had our car keys, hopefully we can come get those from you as soon as you get to her?"

I hung up before my rage got me into a car accident. These are the kind of people she's associating with. *Yeah, I'll get you your keys right after I punch you in the face.*

At 6:00 a.m. I got another call from Shaina. "Cameron, are you coming? I don't know what happened." I heard her choking back the tears, her voice raspy.

"I'm coming, baby"—I choked back tears of my own—"but I'm still an hour out."

"They're releasing me, and I need to find somewhere to go." I remembered my friend Jason had posted on Instagram the night before that he was on a guys' trip in Vegas that weekend. I couldn't imagine Vegas was really his scene, so he was probably in town for some business conference.

"I'll call you right back!"

I dialed Jason. "What's up, my man?" His jolly voice rang in my ear, completely oblivious to the meltdown I was having.

I swallowed so loud he had to have heard. "Hey, man, I saw you're in Vegas—my girl is in the hospital down there and I'm on my way, but do you have somewhere she can stay until I get there? The hospital has to release her. I'm only about an hour out, man."

Completely unperturbed, he responded, "Of course! Have her come to our hotel. Does she need a ride?"

"Nah, I'll send her an Uber, but maybe meet her in the lobby? She seems . . . out of it."

"Done deal."

I breathed a small sigh of relief knowing Shaina wouldn't be left on the side of the road while she waited for me. God, it was good to have such reliable friends. I owed Jason for this.

I called Shaina back, and she sounded like she hadn't stopped crying since our last conversation.

"Cameron, I don't know what happened and I'm so scared, are you here yet?"

"I'm so close! I just spoke to your dad. Your parents are so worried. I'm sending an Uber to the hospital now and it will take you to someone I trust."

"Okay," she blubbered. "I love you!"

"I'll see you so soon, baby, I promise!"

When I showed up to Jason's hotel, I was finally able to see the barrage of texts I'd received while driving. They were from Evelyn—Dave must have told her what happened and that I was coming to get Shaina.

Evelyn: Leave her alone, Cameron!
Evelyn: Where is Shaina?
Evelyn: Fuck you, loser, you're ruining our trip!

I couldn't begin to imagine the narcissistic reasons for Evelyn to think that I was the one ruining her trip, and not the fact that Shaina had been basically left for dead by Evelyn and her friends, so I sent one reply and left it at that.

Cameron: You're a piece of shit friend to let her walk off with two strangers.

When I got to the room Shaina was in the fetal position on a recliner. Her eyes never left the floor. I was happy to see that Jason and his friends had taken good care of Shaina, even giving her a change of clothes so she could slough off her hospital gown. I thanked them over and over before ushering Shaina into the safety of my truck.

I had booked a night at a nearby hotel for us so I could recover a little before hitting the road again. We checked in, keeping Shaina close to my side, and immediately Shaina started the shower. I plopped into the king bed and waited for her to join me. Eventually she climbed into bed and nuzzled into me.

"Shaina, do you remember—could anyone at the hospital tell you what happened?"

She stared at me stone faced. "I declined a rape kit if that's what you're asking." She readjusted her body as if trying to shake off the memory. "I just want to forget everything that happened, okay? Let's not talk about it." She pulled out her phone and angled the screen at me. "Look what Evelyn's been texting me."

Evelyn: You're just looking for attention, have fun with Cameron.

"I told her to fuck off and not talk to me again." I nodded, too exhausted to unleash my fury on how I really felt about that bitch.

"I think that was smart," I said simply. "She's not a good friend."

Chapter 16

THUGS

AFTER THE NIGHTMARE – November 2019

By November my back was feeling much better, probably due in large part to the opiates. I'd been sleeping all day and all night, high, until one day I woke up to my mom and stepdad arguing upstairs.

"He lays down there and sleeps all day!" my stepdad bellowed.

"I don't care! He's my son, and he's been through so much. If you don't like it, leave!"

I waited for the commotion to subside and just kept quiet in my basement "home." It was hard to say whether my mom knew what was really going on; I wasn't acting normal, that's for sure, but I think she considered me to be a fragile flower, unwilling to rock the boat and probably hoping I'd just snap out of it one day, which wasn't surprising since I'd left home to be on my own and been self-sufficient since I was 17. Either way I welcomed it.

My friends messaged me over the months to check in, but I was checked out. The drugs had full control of me, like they were puppeteering my limbs. I'd use, sleep, wake up, occasionally meet up with Natalie to rebuild my stash—rinse, wash, and repeat.

I didn't care if I was ruining my own life, but I sure as hell didn't want my mom and stepdad to be fighting over me. My stepdad was right—maybe I needed to get out of the house and give them some space.

The heroin was at least numbing the pain enough for me to move about a lot easier. One evening, as the night grew, I waited for them to go to sleep, crept around to pack a bag of clothes, and headed down to the local Best Western. At least there I could eat breakfast in the morning and not feel like I was imposing.

I inched out the front door, peered to the left and right, the paranoia still in high gear.

Over the last few weeks, I'd noticed a suspicious white Camry parked a few houses down from my mom's, and someone was always inside the car. I didn't know her neighbors well, and a lot of the drama after Shaina's death had settled down so I didn't think too much of it, but suspicious, nonetheless. I had been making trips every other day to my home in Midvale so it's possible someone could have followed me here, too.

As I eased the truck into the street, the Camry pulled out a few seconds later and began to follow me from a safe distance. *Okay, am I just paranoid? Or what?*

When I pulled up to the hotel parking, I scanned the area—no Camry to be found. I hopped out of my truck and grabbed my luggage and darted inside as was common in the rare event I left the house these days. I approached the front desk and immediately wondered whether the woman would recognize the name on my license. If she knew who I was, she didn't make it known.

Walking down the hallway to my first-floor room, I saw a group of five men enter from one of the side entrances, which happened to be in the direction I was headed. We locked eyes and I quickened my step to get to my room a few feet ahead, quickly inserting my key card and double locking the door behind me.

I shoved my eye to the peephole to see the group standing around my door, whispering.

"Well, that was good timing," one of them whispered.

What was that about?

The windows faced outward toward the parking lot, so I drew the blinds and prepared a shot of dope in the bathroom, periodically checking the peephole and peering outside the window.

As I injected the deadly black drug, my eyes started to become sleepy, my worries subsiding.

I sprawled out onto the bed and resumed my usual routine of talking to Shaina, her spirit the only company I kept lately with conversations like, "I miss you baby," "I hope you're in a better place," and "remember when we...."

I was deep in my black tar dreams when I heard knocking. *Wait, that's at the door. Someone's knocking at the door.* I squinted at the alarm clock and felt a pit in my stomach. It was 2:00 a.m.

"Hotel service," a young woman's voice sang.

Slinking over to the door, high as a kite, I checked the peephole. A young woman dressed in a white top stood in front of the door.

I'm peering through the peephole and there's now another voice—this one much deeper. "Go check the window outside," it whispered.

Fuck. Rushing to my bag, I realized I left my gun at home. *What the fuck were you thinking, Cameron!* My worst fear had come true: I was being hunted down, only this time I was unarmed and fighting through a haze of heroin while whoever outside my door plotted to attack me.

More knocking. I grabbed my phone off the bed and rushed to open the window, hoping I could make a quick getaway.

The window jammed on the safety latch, preventing it from opening.

Now the pounding on the door intensified. I knew I had to make a last-ditch effort—I grabbed the lamp off the nightstand and began beating it against the window latch until it finally released. I leaped out the window sharp pain pricking my back.

The group of guys I had seen earlier came rushing out the same side entrance to the hotel as before, one of them screaming, "Get him!"

I dove behind the closest car and crouched low.

"I got a gun, motherfuckers!" I shouted.

Peeping over the hood, I saw them duck behind a truck about six or seven cars away, then the muffled sound of shoes against the pavement as they moved through the cars toward me.

Goddammit, I couldn't even call the cops, not without them finding enough dope in my room to send me to prison.

I could hear them getting closer. Still crouched, I began moving in reverse behind car after car until I reached the street, which meant giving up anything to act as a shield.

Across the street, a gas station sat on the corner that led down a residential street. I didn't have much time to weigh my options.

I made a mad dash across the street, then booked it down the row of houses. I was an open target if they wanted to shoot me, so I wildly scanned for something to hide behind before landing on a parked van in someone's driveway.

I sat down against the van to catch my breath, then cautiously peered around the car, spotting the six men rushing across the street. I crawled toward the back of the driveway, which backed up to a gate to the backyard of the house across the street.

The backyard was fenced, but to my advantage—if I hopped it fast enough, there's no way these guys would catch me.

I took a few steps back and ran toward the eight-foot fence, jumping up to grab the top plank and using my upper-body strength to carry me over the top. I flung my body over and jumped down onto the ground. The sharp stabbing pain was shooting through my back. The drugs were thankfully holding up, but I knew I'd pay for that tomorrow.

The moonless night was on my side tonight. The adjacent backyard was unfenced and I raced through the next-door neighbor's backyard, around the side of the house, and out onto the new street. The men behind grew faint. I'm still moving at a quick speed reaching the front sidewalk. My foot catches the storm drain and I go flying, toppling over flat on my face.

Moaning, I turned my head to the side and came face-to face with an exhaust pipe; my back can't take anymore and I'm in agony. I had fallen right behind a parked car in the street, which coincidentally gave me a nice hiding spot—from the right angle.

The crunch of tires against asphalt alerted me to a car approaching around the corner. With every ounce of strength left, I pulled myself as far under the car as I could hoping I'm not causing permanent damage to my back. The car crept down the street, its headlights growing closer and closer until they illuminated the patch of ground below me. Slowing to a stop in front of the car I was hiding under, suddenly lights from inside some of the houses began to flicker on. Their residents probably heard me face-plant . . .

The intruding car picked up speed and drove off. Barely able to move, I rummaged around in my pockets until I found some dope and stuffed it in my mouth. The rancid taste burned my throat and I choked to keep it down. Then I reached in my other pocket for my phone.

"Cameron, why are you calling this early?" Glen's voice was drowsy and irritated.

Why the hell did I just call a lawyer of all people? "Glen, people are after me, chasing me. Can you come get me?" Every word that came out felt like a thousand bee stings in my back.

"Tell me where you're at."

I pinged him my location and continued to lie there for at least another thirty minutes. The feeling of a knife in my back subsided; the drugs were kicking in. It was enough to allow me to roll out from under the car and slouch behind it.

Glen pulled up shortly after and I jogged to the passenger door, then did a double take. His wife was in the passenger seat. "Sorry, my wife wanted to come along."

I felt like an idiot—I was high in front of my lawyer and his wife. I silently slid into the back seat and buckled up, feeling suddenly ashamed.

"I didn't see anyone suspicious coming down here," Glen said. "Are you okay?"

"Yeahhh . . . I'm fine. My things are still at the hotel, but I don't think it's a good idea to go back there."

Glen drove back to the hotel anyway. "Don't see that car you mentioned. You want to grab your stuff real quick while I wait by the door?"

Defeated, I obliged.

As we drove to my mom's, it was dead silent in the car and in the outside world; people had yet to wake up and begin their day. *How much longer could I continue this circus?*

If someone wanted me dead, was it just a matter of time? Should I just give up and stand in front of the firing range?

Chapter 17

SOMEWHERE ON A BEACH

BEFORE THE NIGHTMARE – March 2019

Shaina was never the same after that night in Vegas, and I felt like she lost a piece of her soul.

I tried to fix her, but I couldn't; I couldn't give back what those men took from her. The depressive episodes and talk of suicide increased after that—lots of "I just want to give up," and "I'm over life," and "I'll never accomplish anything."

She became quiet at home, her usual excitement replaced with coldness and despondence. She lost her Shaina Shine. I asked myself, *How much more could I keep trying to save her, how far could I keep trying to show her the way?*

Even her terms of endearment and displays of affection had stopped. Before, she'd come home from work and greet me with a silly jump kiss;

now, she'd come home, put her bag down, and immediately lie in bed to play on her phone.

"Why don't you say you love me anymore, babe?" I asked her one night.

"Sorry, I'll get better." That was all I got.

The drinking resumed; the fighting got worse than ever. I tried so desperately to fix this, but I didn't know how.

Was she depressed? I hadn't experienced a loved one with mental illness before. *Had she fallen out of love with me?* Maybe I could remind her about the good times. I did what I knew how to do. I threw money at the problem.

One early afternoon while Shaina was at work, I jumped online and booked a trip to Cancun, Mexico, at a Five Diamond adult all-inclusive resort. I had arranged airfare and all the vacation details; we were set to leave in four weeks. It was booked several months before our two-week Thailand trip, but I didn't care. Presenting Shaina with a new, fun event to look forward to is what mattered most, and I was confident it would turn her mood around.

When Shaina came home, I met her at the garage door; her eyes were sunken and she looked tired. Sad.

"Hey, you," she sighed as she got out of her car.

"Hey, Beautiful, I have a surprise for us." I grinned, hoping she'd match my mood.

"What, babe?" she asked excitedly. *Babe* was a good sign as I hadn't heard it for weeks.

I retrieved the reservations from my back pocket and handed them to her. "I know you haven't been to Mexico. You'll need to request a week off work in two weeks, you think you can do that?"

The old Shaina cheesy smile beamed before me and she jumped at my face, wrapping her hands around my neck to give me a long passionate kiss.

"I love you so much, Cameron," she said as she pulled away. "My first international trip!" She gleamed.

Without another moment, she walked into the house buzzing with activity. "Okay, I need to get two more bathing suits, I need more shoes, and—what else do you take to Mexico?" She continued to carry on a conversation with herself, talking animatedly and tossing smiles my way.

She'd come back to life.

Over the course of the month, we had gone shopping for all new clothes and new sex toys to bring. I scored a bag of mushrooms, which I stealthily placed in a baggie then hid inside a dildo that we purposefully spilled lube all over—in case anyone at TSA wanted to get curious and might want to change their minds.

We decided to go big, driving to spend a night gambling in Vegas before catching a flight from Vegas to Cancun the following morning. Shaina dressed in a sexy black mini skirt, a revealing white top, and high heels; I wore my standard tight-fitted shirt and black pants with a hat. I had no business being with someone so beautiful that night.

We shared a few drinks in the room, so my judgment was clouded, and I was never good at keeping secrets or holding onto surprises. I had a big surprise that was supposed to wait until we got to Cancun, but I wanted to start the celebrations early. There's just something about Vegas . . .

As we traveled down the MGM elevators, I told Shaina I wanted to get a picture by the lion statue up front. Shaina had already begun getting ready for a photo when I grabbed a couple passing by—out of Shaina's earshot—and asked if they wouldn't mind taking a video recording, and they agreed.

As I walked over to Shaina, I quickly bent down on one knee. I was planning to rehearse my speech for the Cancun proposal, but I was so excited that I just spoke from the heart.

"Shaina, baby, I love you so much. Will you marry me?"

"Yes!" She threw her arms out for me to come up and I kissed her.

We'd drawn quite the small crowd. I thanked the couple for the video, and they congratulated us — only Shaina had on her "customer-service" smile. As we walked away toward the casino, she tightly squeezed my hand and spoke sharply through a phony smile.

"Cameron," she scolded, "I wanted that to happen in front of my family. What is wrong with you?"

Taken aback, I got defensive. "Are you serious? Maybe we should just get in the car and drive home then."

She'd blown me off on Facebook twice and now she was making up some lame excuse about her family not being present when I proposed.

All I wanted was to move forward with our relationship—get married, have kids, start a business, attend concerts, travel . . . all of the things we dreamed of when we spoke in private. *Why was she so unwilling to take the next step? To make anything about us publicly official? Was I not seeing the writing on the wall?*

"Let's just try to make some money before our flight tomorrow. I need it for my time off work," she jeered as I rolled my eyes.

"Fine, whatever. Just glad you said yes."

———

We spent the first hour laughing and high fiving, winning big at the black-jack table until our drinks kicked in and we started making sloppy decisions. I had taught and funded Shaina's gambling experience and she caught on quickly, even far surpassing my winnings at the blackjack and craps tables. She was a natural.

Shaina doubled down on a Two of Spades and a Six of Hearts while the dealer had a nine. Her stack of winnings had started to diminish, and I could tell she was growing frustrated. The dealer turned over a Jack of Clubs.

"Do you want more?" I offered. "I know you wanted to try to win before we left."

"Nope, I'm done"—she threw up her hands—"I never win at life." She got up to leave and turned to me. "Are you coming or are you going to wait for the blonde over there that keeps eyeing you?"

I followed her gaze to the blonde woman in question and she quickly averted her eyes when she saw us looking.

"Wha—?" I looked at her dumbfounded. "Shaina, I asked you to marry me two hours ago. Stop being like this. Let's go."

We headed back to the room with the temporary good mood now oblivi-ated. The yelling began as soon as the door closed.

"I am so mad you proposed like that!"

"So sorry for ruining your big proposal. Maybe you should find another Prince Charming who will do it *exactly* the way you want!"

Before I knew it, she had her parents on the phone talking about scrapping the vacation and driving back home. We slept on the bed facing opposite directions that night.

We woke up to the alarm as drunk as we went to sleep. It was still dark out, and I wished for a few more hours of sleep. I slid behind Shaina under the covers and started kissing her neck. "I'm sorry. Let's leave for paradise and put these problems behind us."

She flipped over to face me and gently kissed my lips. "You're right. Let's go enjoy our trip. I'm sorry too." She kissed me again. "I love you."

When we landed in Cancun, we took a private shuttle to the resort and got checked in. Our room was small and facing into the jungle instead of the ocean; romantic, but hardly the best room available. That next morning, I went down to concierge and requested an upgrade; within a few hours we were placed in a bottom-level room in walking distance to the ocean.

Over the six days, we rode four wheelers in the jungle, took zip lines through the forest, snorkeled in the ocean, and went deep-sea fishing where I caught a mahi-mahi and a seven-foot marlin. But the real fireworks between us ignited on our last night.

I was packing my suitcase for our flight home the following day when I realized I'd completely forgotten I brought mushrooms.

"Hey," I called out to Shaina as I pulled out the baggie on full display. Shaina smiled and nodded from the bed, lying naked. I sat on the edge of the bed and fed her some before eating some of my own, then we started making out until they kicked in.

"Baby, did you bring the toys?" she teased as she got up and walked past me toward the glass-paned shower. I knew exactly what she had in mind.

"Of course, I did. Which ones did you want?"

She turned the water on. "All of them."

***

Our relationship returned to its gloomy state once we got back from Cancun. Shaina was back to being quiet and started spending the night less frequently, oftentimes getting off from work early and coming over before crashing at her mom's house for two or three nights at a time. Something was up, I could feel it in my gut. She became even more cold and distant than she had been before, and when I did see her, she'd ask me strange questions like "Do you think a relationship can last if money isn't there?"

"If I had a daughter, I'd encourage her to date someone older than her, someone more financially established, responsible, and mature. I'd want her to live a life without financial hardship," I'd confessed. Confusion settled into the crease between her brows, pondering a question she wouldn't let me in on.

"Maybe we should take a break," she blurted out.

"A break? Shaina, I just asked you to marry me."

"I just—I feel a little lost right now, Cam. Can we at least just take things slow? I still want to see you and I still want to have sex with you, I just need less stress over being in a relationship."

Gutted couldn't begin to describe my emotion. I wanted to be with her more than anything, would put up with all the bullshit just to have her be the one I come home to every night. If she needed to take things slow, I wanted to give her the space to do that. If I didn't . . . I couldn't bear the alternative.

A few nights later, she'd ghosted me again to stay at her mom's, so I lay in bed to watch some TV and hopped on Facebook to search her profile, curious what she had posted lately.

I scrolled to see a new event marked on her timeline. "In a relationship" it read. But it's not me. It's a guy named Travis, a large pudgy guy with red hair more her same age. I wasn't sure to be insulted or upset she left for someone so... far below her standards. I immediately shot out of bed and began pacing the room, digging deeper into her profile. My anger skyrocketed when I noticed we weren't "friends" anymore; ironically, I could still see her profile. Below the relationship event was a post on her wall from this Travis guy.

"I love you so much, baby, and so happy to have found you."

Judgment clouded by blind fury, I took to Facebook Messenger to chat Travis. Shaina's bizarre questions now made sense—she didn't want a break; she just didn't want to tell me she was seeing two men at once!

> **Cameron:** Hey man, just saw you and Shaina got into a relationship. Just so you know, she was with me last night, I took care of her. Thought you should know from man to man.

Less than an hour passed when I heard back.

> **Travis:** What are you talking about?
> **Cameron:** You weren't with her last night were you?
> **Travis:** No, she was with her girlfriends.

That sneaky little—

> **Cameron:** Sorry, man, but she was with me.
> **Travis:** You're kidding me, right?
> **Cameron:** Nah bro, I got all the proof to show you if you want. I don't play games, she was with me last night.

Moments later my phone rang. Speak of the devil herself.

"Cameron, what is wrong with you!" she shrieked. "We're not together!"

"Taking it slow doesn't mean not together, and if you're in a relationship with someone else I'm not going to be your dirty little secret!"

I hung up. My head was spinning, and my hands were shaking, reeling from the betrayal. My brain started to put all the odd pieces together from over the months.

Maybe she was a slut, maybe she had been playing me all this time, maybe it all makes sense now her efforts to keep me hidden from her social media, maybe all she needed from me was to be able to get off and that was her only attraction to me.

Didn't matter, it was time to remove myself from her emotionally, like she had me all this time. I felt duped and I was pissed!

I sat with myself for the rest of the day, replaying the discovery and my conversation with Shaina about our breakup. It seemed she still wanted to see me, just not be with me in the capacity I wanted her. Fine. I could play this game, I told myself, it's now time to remove my love for her and see her as one of my many toys.

But I wasn't going to be led on any longer.

Chapter 18

EXCEPTIONALLY CLEARED

AFTER THE NIGHTMARE – January 2020

After being hunted at the motel, I rarely left my mom's basement, continuing to sleep and get high all day. Natalie was coming over more and more to drop off the heroin. I checked social media constantly now, looking for any indication there were secret plans of more people coming after me. I was cornered with no way out.

Lying in my bed as I usually did, scrolling through Facebook, my curiosity got the better of me and I looked up John, the guy Shaina had seen in Wendover the week before she died. One of the many I found out about, but one of the more recent.

One post in particular caught my eye. A few weeks after she died, he had found one of the charms from Shaina's bracelet in his bed and posted a picture of it. When I zoomed in on the charm, it had the letter M in cursive;

I remembered when her stepmom gave her that charm on Christmas. She'd told Shaina the initial M was for Scorpio but also for her name, so that Shaina could always have a piece of her stepmom with her. I couldn't help but let out a laugh he had a charm that had more meaning for her stepmom than her. *Did that make me a bad guy?*

Nope fuck John, he'd been vocal about me throughout all of this, and he was another broke loser same as Travis, and hell I was joining them now. I no longer gave a shit about anyone and their negative feelings about me, after all their opinions of me on social media was far worse.

Still, I was a little frustrated at the thought of John thinking he had found something meaningful from her. I was jealous that he had been left a token of her memory. I scrolled through a few more posts, then rolled over to nap for a few hours.

When I woke up, I couldn't get Shaina's charm out of my head. I decided it was time to revisit some of my things. Pulling out my boxes of belongings from my mom's garage, I rummaged through to look for any reminders of Shaina. Nothing.

Fuckin' John. Whatever.

I stuffed the last box back onto its shelf and went back down to the basement when out of the corner of my eye I noticed the comforter from my old bed folded up in a box, I hadn't been able to sleep on it since it happened because I could still smell her scent on the blanket. Pulling it out thinking a spider jumped out at me as small metal piece falls barely clanking on the floor. Squatting down, I picked it up and couldn't believe what I was holding—another charm from her bracelet. Same shape and color as the one John had posted, but instead of an M was an engraving of a circle enveloping a ten-point star. A decagram.

Rushing back to the basement with the charm, I grabbed my phone and began searching the symbol. The first website I read stated it was a symbol of Jesus and his ten disciples, but as I kept digging, I came across an interesting post about conflicting positive and negative forces, the union of opposites. And there were ten points for the ten months we had dated. That. That was about us.

I had not experienced a higher love, a more beautiful love than my positive moments with Shaina; I'd also not experienced a lower low when our relationship was turbulent. It was either sizzling with passion or destruction. As much as I hated those lows, I was addicted to those highs, and it made the lows tolerable. Worth it, even.

Holding the charm in my hand, I closed my hand securely around it, protecting it. John could have his *M* charm. I had something better.

Then I began to think, how could we both have coincidentally found charms? Was her suicide premeditated or was this another spectral act? How could we both have received these gifts before she left? Guess I'll never know.

I checked in with Glen every so often to ask if there were any updates, but charges were still pending, nothing filed. It had been six months since Shaina's death, and I hadn't been rearrested—why wouldn't they just drop the charges?

Frustrated, I called a civil attorney for a second opinion. He suggested I request some information from the police department and gave me the link to their website. That night, I put in a document request for everything I was allowed to ask for and fell asleep. A few days later, I got an email stating the report was ready for pick up, so I jumped in my truck and headed back to where it all began.

As I walked through the metal detector, my paranoia got the best of me. *Maybe this was a setup, and the detectives were waiting to arrest me.* Walking up to the bulletproof windowpane, the receptionist asked for my name.

"Cameron Lundgren," I grumbled in a low voice, still embarrassed every time I had to ID myself in public. "I'm here to pick up the reports for the case on June twenty-fifth in the suspected homicide of Shaina Bigby."

Her long pink nails clacked against the keyboard for a few minutes before saying, "I'll be right back."

I nervously scanned the room while I waited. There was a middle-aged woman in the next line over. Maybe the case was old news by now. As Chevy said would happen, "before long people would forget."

The receptionist returned with a stack of papers and dropped them onto the metal counter. "That will be five dollars."

Files in hand, I walked back to my truck, debating with myself as to whether I even wanted to look at them. In the truck, I held the files in my lap; in all, there were about ninety pages.

I began to read. I started with the interviews the police had conducted with her friends and family. The fake stories Shaina had told about me went beyond what I had imagined. Some friends were telling stories of me physically abusing her which was confusing. I can't deny when she would punch me; I wanted to punch back but I proudly never did. *Was it to cover up what she had done, in case I came forward as a defense?* She was in an abusive relationship before me, and I knew there was some confusion there on Facebook with me and her ex. But now I could see why her friends had thought me guilty of violence. Thankfully there were two cases where her friends admitted to her hitting me at times and me not fighting back. Many of them even stated she was only with me for my money and didn't love me.

I started to cry. *No. No, I know she loved me!* If no one could believe it, fine, but I knew that our good moments were real.

Then I saw a statement from Brody. He was at my house for Taco Tuesday, the night Shaina turned the gun on herself. I broke down, my hands covering my face and tears flowing through my fingers as a read his statement.

Brody told the investigators that the night of the party, he had been on my back porch with Shaina smoking a cigarette and he'd asked her, "Do you love Cameron?"

"Yeah, I love him."

I had read so much gossip about her only being with me for financial reasons, but she did love me. She did.

I continued on through the reports and came to a page that read "Detectives arrived at the hospital and received information from the radiologist the bullet path was from back to front from right to left." The statement was from July 10, 2019, and went on to say the police department rectified the report to update the gunshot direction only right to left with the ME's observation, not the radiologist's.

POLICE DEPT·

GENERAL OFFENSE HARDCOPY
REQUEST TO ACCESS PUBLIC RECORDS
(WEAP-FIRING WEAPON)

EXCEPTIONALLY
CLEARED

Narrative Text
    Type INVSTGTR F/U
    Subject SAFE WARRANT
    Author
Related Date Jul-10-2019

On July 9, 2019, I authored a warrant on a safe that was removed by police from the home of Cameron Lundgren. After the warrant was reviewed by the Salt Lake District Attorney's office it was submitted and approved by the judge, for further see warrant #1966091. The warrant was served the same day, July 9, 2019.

After the warrant was served it was brought to my attention that a line in the warrant, taken from a previous warrant, warrant #1963301, was inaccurate after receiving further information from the medical examiner. The line in question is at the beginning of paragraph 4 on page 3 of the affidavit for warrant #1966091, where it states "Detectives arrived at the hospital and received information from the radiologist the bullet path was from back to front from right to left.". This statement is accurate in the fact that the radiologist did give this information to detectives, it is in inaccurate in that the information was later refuted by the medical examiner's office, where the medical examiner stated that it appeared to be a gunshot wound from right to left only, not back to front. I failed to make this clarification when I wrote, and submitted, the affidavit. This was brought to the attention of the Salt Lake District Attorney's office by me on July 10, 2019.

Corrected response to radiologist report

So, it was confirmed. Judy, the private investigator, had been right. They'd released me because the radiologist had been wrong in his report, and a part of me felt relieved to know it was written down somewhere, official, but by that time the damage had been done. I was already labeled as a murderer to anyone watching the news.

Continuing on, I read the report regarding the DNA findings on the weapon, but only Shaina's fingerprints had been identified on the gun—a single fingerprint on the trigger.

POLICE DEPT

GENERAL OFFENSE HARDCOPY
REQUEST TO ACCESS PUBLIC RECORDS
(WEAP-FIRING WEAPON)

EXCEPTIONALLY
CLEARED

<u>**Narrative Text**</u>
      Type INVSTGTR F/U
     Subject CRIME LAB REPORTS
      Author
Related Date Oct-02-2019

CRIME LAB REPORTS:

On the date of September 23, 2019, I received notification from   from the State Crime Lab that their evidentiary reports had been completed and uploaded to UCJIS. I then retrieved those reports and have added them to the case file.

SEROLOGY REPORT:

The State Crime Lab reported several visual indications of blood were detected on the firearm and several swabs were taken for DNA analysis from the weapon and the weapon's magazine.

FIREARM REPORT:

The weapon in this case, a CZ 75B semi-automatic pistol was examined at the State Crime Lab. The analysis determined that the projectile could not be eliminated or identified as having been fired from the CZ weapon, due to the deformation of the round, and the results were inconclusive. The expended cartridge was also analyzed and was determined to have been fired from the pistol.

DNA REPORT:

DNA profiles were obtained from the weapon barrel, magazine and several swabs. DNA was positively identified from the barrel of the weapon as Shaina   and no DNA from Cameron was located in the barrel swab.

All other tests were unable to form a conclusion of DNA profiles on the tested items.

Refer to the full reports for further details. No further action was taken. These reports were supplied to the District Attorney.

END OF REPORT.

I continued down the stack of papers, through the police reports from that night and other witness interviews. Then I got to the last page dated December 16, 2019, two weeks ago.

It was an internal police department declination letter. It read:

POLICE DEPT
GENERAL OFFENSE HARDCOPY
REQUEST TO ACCESS PUBLIC RECORDS
(WEAP-FIRING WEAPON)

EXCEPTIONALLY
CLEARED

<u>**Narrative Text**</u>
Type INVSTGTR F/U
Subject DECLINATION LETTER - LUNDGREN
Author 26M - CANNAVO, DANE
Related Date Dec-16-2019

DECLINATION LETTER - LUNDGREN:

On the date of December 16, 2019. I received a letter to decline charges against Cameron
Lundgren in the death of Shaina   . This letter was attached to the case file for further review.
No further action taken at this time. Refer to that letter for more information.

END OF REPORT.

Declination letter

In the top right hand corner were the words **EXCEPTIONALLY CLEARED**. I pulled up my phone browser to search *exceptionally cleared.* It meant the prosecution was declining to prosecute me due to lack of evidence, that there was no evidence that I had killed her.

Funny, I thought, thinking back to the Gephardt interview... the police department stating 'we don't clear anyone' ... yet here they are clearing me without a word. Like it never happened. Swept under the rug, conveniently "cleared" months later when no one cared anymore, as Chevy predicted. I guess I shouldn't have expected an apology, but perhaps a news release? Nothing.

I spent the next two hours sobbing in my truck, mostly tears of relief that it was over, and again talking to Shaina as if she were there with me. *But I knew she was gone.*

After I collected myself, I texted Glen to share my findings; he was just as surprised as I was that no one had contacted him. He asked me to scan all the pages and send them to him as soon as possible.

I wondered whether I should post these pages on social media. Should I call the news stations back? What should I do with this vital information that clears me? Nothing seemed like a good option—it was all too little, too late. No matter what I did or what I showed, no one would choose to believe me now, not when everyone thought that Shaina was a victim.

There were so many beautiful videos of her funeral, memories of her life posted to social media and memorialized in news articles, even balloon launches in her memory—all celebrating the narrative of the bubbly girl whose life had been taken too soon, not the bubbly girl who suffered in silence and chose to take her life when the pain became too much. *How could I destroy her memory with the truth?*

When I got home, I decided when my money ran out, when I could no longer buy the drugs that numbed my pain, I may just join her.

Chapter 19

MOAB

BEFORE THE NIGHTMARE – May 2019

Travis and Shaina didn't last more than a month.

He would often call or text me asking if I had seen Shaina, and I wasn't willing to lie so I'd often respond, "Sure have." Strangely it felt good to be on the knowing side of the deception. It didn't keep them from talking and seeing each other every so often but at least nothing was going on behind my back and I knew where I stood.

Shaina had moved back a lot of her clothes into my house. We were still seeing each other often, so I couldn't be bothered to care about Travis or Shaina's and my relationship status. Eventually, they stopped seeing each other altogether.

Despite not being an "official" couple anymore, we planned a trip to Moab for some romantic alone time. Even through the rockiness of the relationship, we both clung to the good bits—particularly the passionate physical moments of our relationship—and I think we both hoped Moab would reignite that spark we had our first night together at Mirror Lake.

It was a last-minute trip, but I had managed to secure a place to stay the morning we were set to leave. The plan was to take the truck and bring along the UTV so we could explore the red rock landscapes close-up. I spent the morning lazily packing, the repercussions of the previous night's cocktails from the local Thursday night concert hitting me hard. Shaina was probably having a rough day at work; God, I couldn't imagine serving people when my body felt like it had been hit by a truck.

Cameron: How's your morning? Ready to go to Moab?
Shaina: Eh, a little depressed again. I need to stop drinking, it messes with my mentality.
Cameron: Yeah, I agree. We need to show more self-control. I thought I had it yesterday, but it's kind of hard when you start taking shots. BTW I ended up getting a cozy Airbnb in Moab.
Shaina: Yeah, I need to get my life figured out or I might end up doing something stupid. OMG, really?!?!
Cameron: Really. Wait, what do you mean something stupid?
Shaina: . . . you don't want to know.

There it was again. Despite a wonderful time in Mexico, Shaina still didn't seem to be able to pull out of whatever funk she was in. It broke my heart. *What the hell was I supposed to do to make her happy?*

Cameron: Stop that! Don't be silly! Ur amazing, just need to act on things is all.

If vacations and presents had stopped working, the next best thing I could offer was encouragement.

Shaina: I kinda hit rock bottom and I don't know how to handle it. I literally have nothing.

Shaina: I have no motivation☹ I wish I could set goals and do
them.
Cameron: We'll put together a plan in Moab to help you get
on track. It's a lot easier than you think, I promise.

Putting my phone down, I went to my computer and started searching through my documents until I found my yearly goal sheet and printed off two copies.

Shaina was obviously hungover and fell asleep almost immediately once we got in the truck. Once she woke, we talked for a few hours about our relationship, our career goals, and what we wanted out of life. I told her I had a sheet we could work on together once we checked in to the Airbnb, and I began to have a little hope we could work this out.

It was dark when we arrived, the air quiet except for the whispering of wind rustling the brush. We were fairly isolated—the perfect spot for an intimate couple's vacation. Shaina walked in ahead of me to bring in our bags while I busied myself unloading the UTV. When I stepped through the back door, she had her back to me and was talking quietly on her phone. I came up behind her and touched her on the back of the arm to let her know I was there. "Travis, I assume?"

"I gotta go," she said to the caller while giving me a sidelong glance. She hung up the phone and turned to face me, looking incredibly uncomfortable. "He called and I had to answer."

I wasn't going to let the trip be wasted on an argument, so I nodded once then ventured over to the kitchen to cook dinner while she escaped up to the bedroom to take a bath. The entire time I cooked I couldn't help but wonder if Shaina was talking to Travis upstairs, and each time I pushed the thought out of my mind.

Sliding doors led out to a deck with a grill, and I walked outside to check on the steaks. I flipped them over just as I heard the screen door open; I spun around to find Shaina in the sexy lingerie I had picked out for her months ago that she hadn't yet worn.

"What are we going to eat, baby?" she cooed while walking toward me before wrapping her hands around my neck and giving me a kiss.

I reached down to hold her hips. "You are my world, Beautiful. You are everything I imagined in a woman and a partner, and tonight, I am going to make love to you." A smile spread across her face.

"When does that start?"

As our desires grew our hunger pains lessened and it was only 5pm, so I turned the grill down to low. The steaks could wait.

"My hands are going to massage every muscle in your body first." I pulled her back in for a kiss, but her impatience had other plans, grabbing my hand to pull me inside as we made our way upstairs to the bedroom.

The next morning before we loaded up to leave, I sat Shaina down at the kitchen table to help her set her goals. I pulled out my printed copies of my goal planner and explained that early in my sales career, a colleague told me to always have my goals printed and placed some where I could see them every morning. Although I hadn't done it myself in a few years, I had helped my boys create some a few years prior.

"Here," I said, pointing to the sheet. "Write your top ten goals on the left-hand side. The right side breaks up into three-month intervals, so as you reach each goal, you can adjust or add new ones every three months."

We sat in silence for an hour as we carefully thought out the goals we wanted to achieve. I finished some time before Shaina, so I began cleaning up the Airbnb, moving from room to room. When I got back to the kitchen, I noticed Shaina whimpering at the table. I walked up behind her to put my hands on her shoulders and asked, "Baby, are you okay?"

"I've never done anything like this in my life and it feels good to write it down." She was choking back tears and my heart swelled with pride. I pulled her up into my arms, which made her cry harder, weeping into my chest.

I felt her body calming down. She sniffed and wiped her nose, then gave me a smile. "Let's review our goals together so we can hold each other accountable," she suggested.

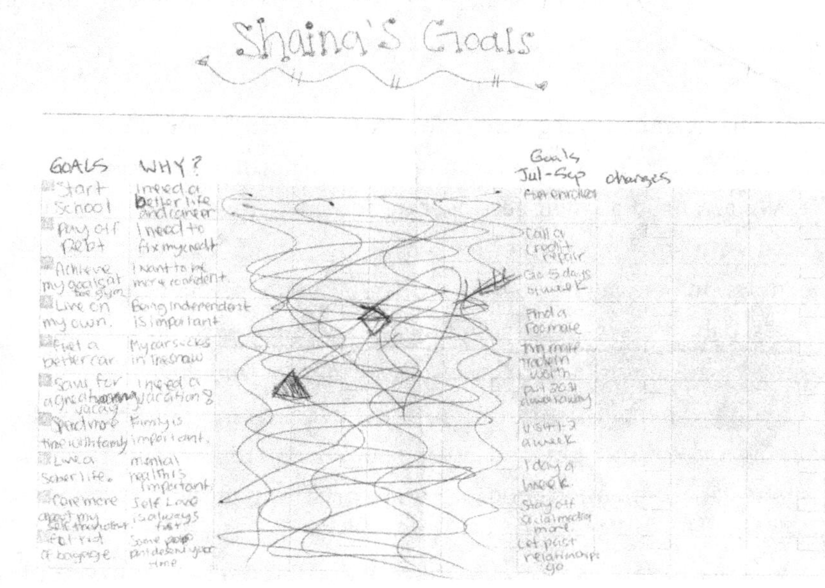

Shaina's Goals

Cameron's Goals

We worked on our goals in the weeks following Moab, both of our sheets taped to my bathroom mirror. We'd gotten back into a morning gym routine, which gave us time to talk about what we each were doing to achieve our goals as we prepared to leave the house.

On a Friday evening, I was making an after-school snack for my kids when Shaina called, suggesting we invite my friend Everett over to introduce him to her new friend Kristina since we needed more couples in our life. We arranged a small get-together for the following night, and I was tasked with smoking brisket for our dinner, which I started in the early morning. On her way home from work around noon, Shaina called.

"Hey, babe, I'm almost to your house but wanted to see if you wanted me to stop by the liquor store to grab some drinks for tonight."

I hadn't expected the question. We'd been keeping our heads down, working out, eating right, and cutting out booze. I didn't think through my response at all. "Sounds good. Nothing too strong though, I have my kids here."

When she got home, we spent the day playing Nintendo Switch with my boys, unlocking the new Mario Party levels, before moving on to some board games.

As night fell, my boys trudged to their rooms while Shaina and I cut the meat and set the table for our guests. Through the window I could see Everett pull up in the driveway in his new BMW, Kristina pulling up not far behind.

"Shaina's upstairs getting ready, she'll be down soon," I said as I led them inside to the kitchen.

Shaina had picked up Fireball earlier—despite my suggestion for something less crazy—but even I couldn't resist the temptation to drink after being sober for a few weeks. I offered everyone a shot, but Everett declined. Just as I poured the shots for me and Kristina, Shaina traipsed into the kitchen.

"Where's mine, babe?" She glared at me playfully.

"Coming right up," I said as I poured a third. Shaina and I took a step back from Everett and Kristina to let them get to know each other; the two of them talked and laughed in the living room while we snuck off to the kitchen to make out.

A few hours lapsed. Everett announced he was going to leave. We all walked outside to the driveway, and as he said his goodbyes to Kristina, Shaina took the opportunity to pull me aside.

"Cameron," she faltered. "Kristina and I are going out since Everett is leaving." Her voice was calm in anticipation of the firestorm she knew was about to erupt from me. She knew I couldn't join because my kids were home.

"Are you serious? We were supposed to hang out tonight and now you wanna go party?"

"We're just going to go downtown to see a local DJ. I might crash at Kristina's tonight if we're out late."

The alcohol didn't help my anger. "Fine! Go be a slut with Kristina. So much for our goals—"

Without warning, Shaina slugged me in the face. At this point, I wasn't surprised, but I wasn't going to allow this behavior to keep happening anymore. I cradled my cheek for a second before glancing over to Kristina and Everett chatting close by.

"Shaina, you just punched me!" That got their attention and would confirm what she was doing. I pulled my phone out of my pocket to dial the police. This time I couldn't let the violence slide.

"911, what's your emergency?"

"My girlfriend just punched me in the face."

"Do you want us to dispatch an officer?"

"Yes, please."

I stepped back into the brisk night. Everett was already in his car. He rolled down his window when he saw me come back out and said, "I'm out, man, this is too much."

I nodded as I waved him off—this was too much for most people. Shaina and Kristina were talking animatedly at the end of the driveway, Shaina clearly upset. She saw me and stopped mid-conversation, running over to me, and crying. "Cameron, please! Please, I'm sorry, tell the cops it was a miscommunication!" She was pleading loudly, and I looked up to see my boys in their bedroom window, looking down at the commotion on the driveway.

Damnit, Shaina!

Kristina, who had followed my gaze to the window, looked at me and insisted, "I'll take care of them" before dashing inside the house to perform some damage control.

Shaina was still inconsolable. "Cameron, please don't do this, I can't go to jail!"

I refocused my attention on her with a newfound authority. "Shaina, this can't fucking keep happening! You cannot hit me, especially not around my children!"

Just then a cop car pulled down the street. I'm sure they didn't even need my address—it was apparent from the pandemonium on the sidewalk who had called in the domestic dispute.

A middle-aged male officer with brown hair and a mustache to match exited his car and approached us. *What was the right thing to do here?* I wanted to prove a point to Shaina, to make it absolutely clear this type of aggression would not be tolerated, but I also didn't want to be responsible for putting her in jail.

The officer's stern look made the situation more real. I got cold feet. "Good evening, Officer, I'm sorry to bother you. It was all a misunderstanding. I don't want to press charges." He looked from me to Shaina—who was whimpering by my side and terrified as all hell—then back to me.

His eyes moved upward, and he nodded toward my Ariat hat. "I can respect a man wearing a hat like that. We'll log the incident and"—he fixed his gaze on Shaina—"you two try to work things out tonight. Ma'am, can I talk to you over here for a moment?"

I waited patiently as the two of them talked out of earshot before the officer returned solo. "Shaina is going to leave tonight, but she'll talk to you tomorrow. She says she's sorry."

"Thank you, Officer."

Since Kristina had had only a single shot and it had been hours, she drove as Shaina and the cops got into their respective cars. I went back inside to relieve Kristina from her duties. Quietly opening the door to the boys' room, I saw them sound asleep in their beds—or at least, they pretended to be. Closing the door, I took a deep breath and retreated to my own bed. Nothing good seemed to last forever, it seemed.

The next day, I woke up to the crashing reality of what had happened yesterday. I opened my phone and didn't have any texts from Shaina, so I started the conversation.

Cameron: We need to talk.

Shaina: About?

Shaina: How you tried to send me to jail?

Cameron: I have my children and we've been there before. After you punched me I couldn't let it go any further. It was a bad choice, and I fixed it by not saying anything to the cop. I was scared and confused.

No reply.

Cameron: Okay well I guess let me know if you're coming by today.

Shaina: Ugh. Why do we do this?

Cameron: Question of the century.

Shaina: Yeah ugh I wanna be sober

Her last text ended with the emoji of a water gun pointing at a sad face.

Shaina came over a few hours later once my ex had picked up my kids. We both made our apologies. In typical fashion, it took a blowout to get back to a good place. As we lay down for bed—Shaina in her normal pose with her head on my chest as we watched TV—she tilted her head up to me. "Do you think people would show up at my funeral?"

I had heard things like this from Shaina, but this one caught me off guard. "Baby, everyone loves you. Of course, lots of people would come." I leaned down to kiss her forehead. "I wouldn't miss it for the world."

She smiled up at me. "You wouldn't?"

"Of course not! I love your brains, Beautiful. You're not going anywhere anytime soon."

Her smile faded and she whispered, "Thanks, babe."

It was hard to keep up with her changing emotions, leaving me feeling more and more helpless with each sad comment she made. "Baby, talk to me, what's going on?" I insisted.

She pulled off my chest to situate herself on her own pillow but didn't reply. She didn't speak much about her feelings, choosing instead to keep them locked up inside her head, parading around with smiles and confidence until the emotions became so intense they burst from her in the form of screaming or hitting—usually after the coaxing of a little alcohol. The silence and the coldness were typically a prelude to the explosion.

"You know you can talk to me right, Beautiful?" I soothed as I pulled her chin up and toward me.

"I need to talk to you about something . . ."

"Anything, love."

"I have a gun in my room at my mom's." I squeezed her hand as she continued, "It was given to me by my ex, and now he's asking for it back because I owe him money. But he gave it to me as a Christmas present and I want to keep it for . . . I don't know, sentimental reasons I guess, but I don't feel safe with it. And he says if I give it back to him, I won't owe him anything."

I had known of this boyfriend for a while. Shaina would often talk about him as her best friend, citing that they broke up because she only liked him as a friend. He lived out of state now and she'd suggested many times we go visit him together. Whenever he was in town, I'd encourage her to see him. I didn't gauge him as a threat; in fact, I liked that Shaina had a close friend she could talk to, but she always elected to stay with me.

"Shaina, I think you should give the gun back. It's just a stupid present and if you don't feel safe with it, it's not a good idea to have it there." I gave her hand another squeeze. "Have I told you lately how much I love you?" I'd often use that line to get a smile out of her.

"No, you haven't told me lately," she said coyly.

"Shaina Bigby, I need to tell you something deep from my heart. I've never known a love like I have with you. Not only are you the most beautiful person on this planet, but you're also my best friend. I've never laughed so hard at nothing at all . . . if there's such thing as a soul mate, it's you, babe."

A small tear had formed in the corner of her eye, but it quickly disappeared beneath her growing smile. Pouncing on me, she leaned down and grabbed my face, kissing me like it was for the first time—a desperate hunger that never seemed to be satiated.

"You're right," she decided, pulling away. "It's just a stupid gun." She came in for one last peck. "I love you, Cameron. I'm going to leave it outside my mom's house so he can pick it up when he comes into town on Friday.

"I like that idea," I said, going in for another kiss.

Chapter 20

HOPING TO MOVE FORWARD

AFTER THE NIGHTMARE – March 2020

Seeing as how I didn't leave the house, I downloaded a game on my phone and instantly became obsessed. I played for hours, continuing to pass my life away. There was a social aspect to the app where you could interact with other players, and that's how I met Mia.

She lived in a different state, so we spent our days messaging each other through the app until she gave me her phone number. She was much shorter than what I was used to. Mia had beautiful olive skin—she told me she was part Italian, part Spanish. She had the face of a supermodel, with big chestnut eyes and long brown hair that glistened with caramel highlights. Her lips looked as if they were made to be kissed, sitting below the cutest little nose. Her curvy physique was the cherry on top.

We hit it off instantly. I shared my story with her, and she talked to me about her ongoing divorce—we were two adults in a bad place and looking for happiness.

Mia sparked new hope in me. I became motivated to start working again. I got my commercial driver's license and started driving my last remaining dump truck.

I spent every moment I could texting her and she was unknowingly pulling me out of my depression. I even tucked Shaina's Crocs underneath my bed, no longer needing to cuddle them to fall asleep. And, consequently, I stopped talking to her.

Mia made me want to move on and succeed, to start all over with a fresh outlook on life, and it felt good. I was still doing heroin, but I was really trying to scale back. *Could I possibly find love again?*

Mia had a naughty side to her, and her sexual prowess helped pull me away from my thoughts of losing Shaina. She'd often send provocative pictures of herself throughout the day while she worked to say she was thinking of me. I would reciprocate.

One weekend we agreed to meet on a whim. I made the nine-hour drive to meet her at a casino near her home. The first night she couldn't find a sitter for her kid, but we made up for it by video chatting the entire night, giddy at the prospect that we'd see each other soon.

The next night she made her way across the river ferry to the casino ... my anticipation levels were off the charts.

While I waited at the slip, she texted me how nervous she was—she had butterflies! For me, I couldn't remember the last time I had felt joy like this. As she climbed off the ferry and down the dock, my knees went weak. I couldn't even say hi. I just grabbed her face and kissed her before she could muster a word.

"You're hot, and I am nervous," she said, blushing as we pulled apart.

The sexual frustration between us was high; I hadn't slept with anyone since Shaina, and she hadn't slept with anyone since the start of her divorce. As we made our way to the room, my heart was pounding, and she kept side-eyeing me with a look that said *kiss me again.* We both nervously sat down on the bed before I jumped up to offer her a drink.

"I'll take two," she giggled. And she took two.

We made small talk for a few minutes, waiting for the other to make the first move before finally I couldn't take it anymore—I ripped her pants off and she greedily lifted off my shirt, the pair of us scrambling up the bed as our tongues entwined.

We had sex for hours into the night. After we were too tired for anything more, we lay sprawled next to each, panting heavily. Suddenly, I was hit with a sick feeling in my stomach: guilt. *Would Shaina be disappointed? Was I allowed to move on already?*

Mia snuggled up into my chest, just as Shaina used to, and I wrapped my arms around her as she fell asleep, while I stayed up a little while longer with my thoughts.

The next morning, Mia had to leave early to catch the ferry, but shyly asked me if I could drive her home instead—an hour around the lake—so we could draw out our time together. I agreed. I was ready to jump into this.

The next day I transferred to an Airbnb closer to her and I holed up there for a week. She came over when her parents could watch her kid, and those hours were spent ordering take-out sushi, cuddling, playing our phone game together, laughing, and having sex.

My reservations from our first night together had disappeared. This felt *good.* I couldn't give up on that. On the morning I departed back for Utah, I found a note she'd written and left on the kitchen counter. *I'll miss you. Hurry back soon.*

I spent a month back in Utah and things felt like shit again. I couldn't live a normal life here, not when I was being photographed by strangers when I left the house and threatened on social media. Although I was driving my dump truck, I was striking out finding a new job in sales—turns out employers don't want to hire people suspected of murder. No matter I was innocent. More and more, I began to think that a new life awaited me, but only if I moved out of the state. Mia and I talked about me moving closer to her.

Our next visit with each other was in Vegas, and I could not wait to see her again. I packed my best clothes and booked a penthouse suite, wanting to make the weekend perfect and going the extra step to get away from my life back home. I met her in the lobby, beaming with excitement, and I wanted to kiss her, but as soon as she saw me, she ran straight into my arms for a hug.

"What's that about?"

"Nothing, I've just been dealing with a lot."

What did that mean?

Trying to move past the awkwardness, I suggested we go for a walk, then stop for a drink. She agreed and I led her outside, but I could tell something was amiss. While we drank you could cut the tension with a knife, so I finished my beer quickly and invited her back up to my room.

As soon as we got inside and I closed the door, Mia spun around and blurted, "I can't stay the night, Cameron. I want to, but I just can't. It's . . . complicated." She looked at me with a pained expression before moving toward me and pulling me in for a kiss. I tried to protest, but her fingers covered my mouth and she whispered, "Ssshhh, let me handle this" as she began to unbutton my pants and then pushed me back on the bed.

Once we finished, she immediately sprung up to get dressed. "I have to tell you something," she said, clasping her bra.

Laying in bed unsure of what to do, hoping that maybe if I just stayed there, she'd change her mind about whatever she was about to say and come back to join me.

"My ex-husband found out about you and he did some digging ... He found out about your history with your ex. He kept calling me nearly my whole drive to see you and, well, he threatened me. He said his attorney told him if I keep seeing you, I could lose the right to see my boy."

She sat at the edge of the bed, struggling to wrangle on her shoes, then stood up to look at me with a sadness that said *this is the last time.*

"Cameron, I'm sorry. I really liked you." She walked over to pull me in for a final kiss before leaving out the door without another word.

I sat there, frozen, propped up on my elbow and staring at the door, doubting there really was any hope left for me after all.

When I got back home, I slipped into the deepest depression I had felt in my life, even more hopeless than before Mia. Now, I felt I had confirmation that nothing could ever be righted in my life; I was destined to be a leper—in Utah or anywhere else. People were bound to find out about me and my past. I had no energy and no motivation, except for one thing. My mind was racing.

Just after Mia had left me in Vegas, I started to formulate a plan. *I'd finish off the rest of my money, sleep the hours and days away in heroin-induced euphoria, and when that final day came, I'd join Shaina on the same date she'd left me.* A part of me conjured a scenario where someone would reach out to check on me, to make sure I was doing okay, or to say they missed me and loved me. But I was way too despondent. I really felt hopeless.

I would not leave the basement of my mom's house, wallowing in the darkness as she and my stepdad fought about me from the floor above.

Years before, when I was still married, I attended a seminar with Dave Ramsey to gain more insight on what to do with my money to ensure my family would always be okay, even when I was gone. He'd said, "The most selfless thing you can do in this lifetime is to get life insurance in case you die, for your loved ones when you pass." Immediately after hearing that, I purchased a million-dollar policy.

I remember when I got out of jail my mother told me that my former brother-in-law, who worked in the insurance business, had reviewed my life insurance policy, and that it covered suicide, but not for another six months. At the time, I wasn't quite sure why she was telling me that. I was distraught, no doubt, but the Cameron from eight months ago still held out a little hope that the police department would rectify the situation, that everyone would realize I was innocent. Never happened. I was just living in limbo.

But maybe Mom had foreseen the Cameron **now**—a mother's intuition—protecting her son as he navigated the pain and sadness that was to come. Now, I was glad she had told me about the suicide stipulation. I held onto that seed of news and planted it in my brain almost counting the days.

The Crocs had returned to my bed, and I cuddled them most of the day. Every so often when I would wake up from a drug stupor, I would have conversations with Shaina again. Lately, my question for her was: *why did you do it in front of me?*

Then I quietly muse in the silence of the room:

"Was it because I had just found out from Claire what you had done?"

"Was it because your car had broken down and you were behind on payments and the bank was about to take it?"

Was it because you could not live with the regret of giving up your daughter for adoption?"

Was it the partying and the drugs that fueled your depression?"

"Was it because you felt lost in life, living in your mom's basement, thinking you'll never achieve success because you were a waitress?"

"Was it that you hated me and wanted to send me a message I'd never forget?"

My mind had become an instant replay of the night she shot herself. I saw her hand gripping my nickel-plated CZ 9mm, the gun heavy. I saw her turning to face me through the doorway. I saw the pistol swing to her head and as it got close, she started to pull back from the momentum, her finger on the hair trigger. As it came to a stop next to her temple, the pistol went off—maybe by accident. It happened so fast. There wasn't a final plea or accusation, no words at all. The pistol swung up and went off the instant it got to her head.

If it had been an accident, and she'd had time to speak, what would she have said? Would she have said "I love you, but I can't do this anymore" and offer me the chance to talk her out of it?

Every day was spent thinking what I could have done differently, how I could have saved her. The pistol was locked in a personal safe under my bed, but the key was on my truck keys that were placed on the nightstand when I changed for the party. Could anyone have had the foresight to think, even being in a safe, it was still accessible by someone with motivation to get to it? But I also didn't believe she'd do it. I never really understood that possibility.

As high as I was on dope, the emotions overcame the high every time, and I consumed myself with these thoughts, crying so hard I would almost choke.

I also thought about my two amazing boys, who I still had not been allowed to see, and how leaving them would affect them, because I knew what Shaina's leaving had done to me. But even still, I couldn't talk myself out of it.

Suddenly, in a moment of clarity, I knew what had to be done.

Chapter 21

THE LAST STRAW

BEFORE THE NIGHTMARE – June 2019

One of our favorite things to do was to go to concerts, so I bought two tickets for us to see Brad Paisley at one of our favorite outdoor venues. Before leaving the house, I asked Shaina if we could talk. "Baby, can we please try to not drink liquor, especially Fireball, tonight?" I wasn't looking for a repeat of her punching me in the face.

"Of course, babe, we got this."

It was a reassurance, but one I never totally bought into. We headed over to Claire's, one of our mutual friends, to pick her up before heading to the concert, but when we strolled inside, Claire already had Fireball and shot glasses ready on the counter. Grabbing Shaina's hand, I gave it a tight squeeze to send a message, but she looked at me with puppy-dog eyes and asked, "We can have a few, can't we?"

Being a pushover, I agreed. One turned into two, then two turned into three, and three into four, which turned into us taking some to drink on the way.

As we checked in our tickets, I heard Shaina tell Claire under her breath, "Travis should be here, I don't want to see him."

That brought me a little bit of comfort. As soon as we passed the ID checkpoint for our wristbands we made our way to the Beer Gardens for a drink, and lo and behold, there stood Travis. And to my surprise, Shaina instantly left my side to go over and talk to him. A little bugged, I stood in line to order us beers, tossing glances back at the two. I carried over two beers to Shaina and noticed Travis seemed extra friendly with her, standing a little too close for comfort. I lost it.

"She's not yours anymore, bro!" I yelled as I approached them.

Travis smirked. "Doesn't look like she's yours either at the moment."

Shaina threw her head back with a laugh then turned to me with mocking eyes. "You're a piece of shit, fuck you!" She sneered.

What the fuck? She's taking *his* side, even though *we're* together? Was this some type of setup?

"Fuck you, Travis," I cursed. "I'll beat your fat ass!"

Just then a nearby group of strangers intervened, Travis and I both held back by two men.

"I'm good, I'm good!" I yelled, shaking off the dude's arms. *Let them be miserable with each other.* I walked off through the exit and called an Uber home. I was done with the games, with the lies, and with Shaina.

The second I was back inside my house I stormed straight to my liquor cabinet and began pounding whiskey. About an hour later, I received a text from Shaina.

Shaina: I'm so sorry, Cameron.
Cameron: Fuck you! I hate you!
Shaina: I'm really sorry, can we talk?

My thumbs were punching letters like they were boxing Travis's face.

> **Cameron:** Talk to Travis, Shaina. Fuck you!
> **Shaina:** I didn't stay at the concert and left Travis. Will you
> please come to where I'm at? I want to talk to you.

But I wasn't having it. I'd never been betrayed so viciously in my life and sent as many messages as I could in my attempt to hurt her as bad as she just hurt me.

> **Cameron:** Fuck you! Fuck you! Fuck you! You're a lying bitch
> and I hate you!

She kept trying to say she was sorry and wanted to see me, but I refused, instead falling asleep in bed.

That next morning, I messaged Travis, just to throw a few daggers his way.

> **Cameron:** You sleep in an empty bed last night, bitch?
> **Travis:** She made you look like a bitch.
> **Cameron:** Pretty sure the bitch was the guy she didn't stay
> with.

Pleased with my offense I started up my PC.

A few minutes later I got a call from a sobbing Shaina. "Cameron, stop talking to Travis! Please, I'm begging you!"

But I didn't have a care in the world. Months of manipulation and being gaslit had led to this moment.

"He's my buddy now," I bragged. "I'll talk to him all I want." *Fuck it,* I thought, *maybe I'll befriend Travis and as Shaina said, "we could go get bitches together."*

"I'm at work, I can't do this. Please stop," she begged one last time before hanging up.

> **Cameron:** She didn't sleep with you, motherfucker, so who
> do you think she ended up with?

Travis: I'm done with her, so I don't care. Get lost.

My phone rang again. "Cameron, I'm going to go to UNI, will you take me?" UNI was the mental health department at the local hospital it's where they'd check people in that were suicidal. "Please," she continued, sobbing in the bathroom at work. As pissed as I was, her statement was concerning. *Did she want to check herself in? Was she suicidal?*

"I'm on my way."

"Okay, give me a minute and I'll tell you when to come."

POLICE DEPT·

GENERAL OFFENSE HARDCOPY
REQUEST TO ACCESS PUBLIC RECORDS
(WEAP-FIRING WEAPON)

EXCEPTIONALLY
CLEARED

Narrative Text
       Type INVSTGTR F/U
      Subject PHONE RECORDINGS
      Author
Related Date Jul-29-2019 13:49

INVESTIGATOR FOLLOW UP:

On the date of July 29, 2019, I was reviewing the audio recorded files on Cameron's cellphone via Cellebrite when I came across two recordings that were conversations between Cameron and Shaina. During these two recordings, Shaina is noticeably upset regarding Cameron speaking with another unidentified male by the name of ____ . During the conversation, Shaina tells Cameron that she is thinking about checking herself into UNI because she's "in a bad place" and "needs help."

Shaina explains that she is in the bathroom at her work and plans to drive herself to UNI and check herself in. Cameron states he will respond and pick her up and take her to UNI instead of her driving herself. He expresses that he doesn't think she's in a position to drive herself due to her emotional state. These two recordings were found under the file name(s) if call_10_13_35_IN_.amr and call_10_30_49_OUT_.amr.

I waited all day for her to call until I got a message.

Shaina: I want to come to your house and sleep. I feel like shit
and I'll lose my job if I go to UNI.

I was furious from the night before, but Shaina talking about going on suicide watch washed away some of the anger. As much as I hated her right now, I'd never forgive myself if she did something drastic tonight.

Cameron: Come here, I'll have soup on the stove and a pot of coffee ready when you get here.

The minute she walked through my kitchen door she burst into tears. "I am so sorry, I don't even like Travis, and I don't know what I was thinking! I left him shortly after you left, and I felt so bad that I left too."

My anger had subsided a bit. "Shaina, I have not been more disrespected by a woman in my entire life, and I can't play these games anymore. If you want me in your life, it's not going to be casual dating anymore."

Tears streamed down her face. "I can't live like this anymore or I'm going to end up dead," she wailed as she draped her hands around my neck.

I held her and rubbed her back while whispering in her ear, "Everything is going to be okay."

Shaina had a trip planned in Wendover that weekend, a small town on the Utah–Nevada border that was full of casinos and restaurants. I conveyed my concerns to Shaina, but she assured me everything was fine, even showing me the texts between the girls regarding their low-key plans.

But at the last minute she told me she was hesitant to go because she was broke and didn't want to go if she couldn't spend the money to have fun with everyone. She'd been talking about her money struggles a lot in the past month or so, so earlier that day I took out a couple hundred dollars at an ATM to surprise her with.

After she walked in the door, I met her in the kitchen with the money in hand. "I want you to go to Wendover and have fun with your girlfriends."

She hesitantly reached for my outstretched hand. "Are you sure? I don't want to take your money."

"I want you to go have fun. Just check in every so often." A smile flitted across her face.

"Okay, babe, I promise I'll check in with you," she said, landing a kiss on me.

When she walked out the door to leave, I felt there was something off. After nearly a year of dating, I knew Shaina like the back of my hand. She was hiding something.

That night I had tickets to go to downtown Salt Lake City for a concert but as I pulled up, I couldn't shake the feeling that something wasn't right. As I walked toward the venue, halfway there, I stopped and turned around. Back in my truck, I headed home. *I'll just get a bottle of whiskey and watch some movies instead.*

When I pulled into my garage, I pulled my phone out of my pocket. There was a text from Shaina, a picture of her and the three other women I had known she was going with. Relief flooded through me, and I nearly laughed at myself for being so suspicious. I walked inside to open the whiskey bottle, filled a glass with ice, and took a sip, ready to enjoy my night in.

Shaina lived up to our promise; she texted me throughout the night, even calling before she went to bed. I could hear the drunk chatter of women in the background.

"Allison is being a drunk bitch in the hotel room," she said jokingly, and other women laughed. I fell asleep in peace knowing she was okay.

The next morning, I woke up to a text from her.

> **Shaina:** I lost all my money, but I miss you and can't wait to see you when I get home. I'm horny too, I need you to take care of me babe.

I couldn't help but smile at the thought she missed me. She was due to come today, and I wanted to see her, but Chevy had texted me to hang out.

> **Cameron:** That makes me happy. BTW Chevy is going out on his boat today and I think I'm going.
> **Shaina:** If you go out on the boat with Chevy, we are over!

And there was possessive Shaina again. Chevy often had a new girlfriend every couple months, which meant he was constantly around single women.

Cameron: Why, what's wrong?
Shaina: Because I know you'll be around bitches.

I'd nailed it on the head.

Cameron: I can wait for you to get home if you want?
Shaina: Good 'cause I'm horny and I want to see you. Please wait for me, babe.

It was a classic manipulative move from her, but I obliged anyway, not wanting to cause a fight.

Monday rolled around and we had not talked like we normally did on her way to work because I had fallen back asleep. I woke up to a text from her instead.

Shaina: I hate my life. Everything always goes wrong. My engine is leaking everywhere, I'm pretty sure it just blew. I don't have money to fix it. I'm over life.
Cameron: What color is the fluid?"
Shaina: Pink
Cameron: If it's pink, your engine isn't blown. Let me get ahold of Dave.

I immediately called Dave, a friend and certified mechanic, and relayed Shaina's information.

"It's probably a blown water pump," he explained. "I can fix that pretty easy if you want to get the parts, but don't drive the car."

I hung up messaged Shaina.

> **Cameron:** "Don't worry, babe, I'll order a wrecker to tow your car to my house and be on my way to pick you up. Dave said he'd fix it, we'll grab the parts on the way there."
>
> **Shaina:** "It's fine, Cameron. I don't have the money to pay for this—I'm behind on payments as it is. I'll just have it impounded and get a bus pass." Her tone was clearly frustrated.
>
> **Cameron:** "I'll cover the cost for Dave's time, he says the part is about a hundred dollars if you want to cover that."
>
> **Shaina:** "Money is always tight, Cam, I can't pay for this, I should have never gone to Wendover and gambled. I'll just have it impounded and you can keep your money."
>
> **Cameron:** "Did you lose more than the $200 I gave you?"
>
> **Shaina:** "I'm so DONE with life!!!"
>
> **Cameron:** "Shaina, if you need help I can cover it all, you just need to ask." I could feel her stress levels through the phone.
>
> **Shaina:** "You're being a jerk. Don't worry about this, I'll have my friends help me."

God, why did she always make things so impossible? Here I was offering help, only to be dubbed a *jerk*.

> **Cameron:** "Whatever you want. I'm sure you have plenty of groupies that'll come fix it for you."

Has she lost her damn mind? I'm clearly offering to fix it and I just thought she could have some skin in the game. *Why was she so erratic?*

I rushed out the house and drove to the restaurant to supervise the tow. I had arranged for the tow truck to show up before I got there and sure enough, when I pulled up her car was being pulled onto the trailer. Shaina was still on her shift, so I directed the tow truck driver to take it to my house. I sat in my car near the restaurant's entrance waiting for her to get off work.

I met her on the passenger side of my truck to open the door for her, so she knew I had her back. What happened next was totally unexpected.

She acted as if the world was ending. I was so confused and truly couldn't understand what was happening.

Slamming the passenger door with a huff, we drove to AutoZone, barely speaking to each other.

When we finally got back to my house, she went straight inside to the bedroom without a word and lay on the bed with her phone in hand furiously typing for, I'm sure, a knight in shining armor to come save her. Wasn't my helping her enough?

Downstairs, I was fixing lunch and scrolling through my phone when I saw Shaina had made a new Facebook post sometime before she got off work, before we'd just spent the afternoon dealing with all this, asking if anyone could fix her car.

How absurd was this? I had gotten her car towed, offered to help find someone to fix it, offered to cover the expenses, already driven her to get the parts, and even bought them. I put down the spatula I'd been holding and sent her a text.

Cameron: So when you pick out of the twenty guys that commented on your post about fixing your car, you can pack your stuff and find somewhere else to live. I'm over this too.

Not happy with her, I finished making lunch anyway, loading up the sandwiches and sweet potato fries onto a plate. As I reached the top of the stairs, I heard her sobbing in the bedroom. I slowly walked in, not wishing to startle her. She was lying on the bed with her hands covering her face, fingers drenched from the tears. Rarely did I see Shaina cry.

Feeling bad, I placed the plate on the end of the bed and approached her side, pulling her into my chest. Her hands left her face and she reached out to wrap around my midsection.

"I give up, I can't do this anymore," she choked out.

"Everything will be fine." I soothed. "I love you, I want to help you. Life isn't easy, Beautiful, and sometimes things like this prepare us to be stronger. I'm here for you, we'll get it fixed."

By now the tears were flowing freely as she tried to cough out her words. "I gave up my daughter for adoption when I was young to have an opportunity for a better life, and I've wasted it! I have nothing left now. I'm a waitress with no future, not even a car after all this. I'm behind on payments anyway, the bank can take it."

Hearing her talk about her daughter sank my heart into my belly. "Baby, we'll get this fixed, don't you worry. I'll have Dave come by tonight to take a look at it and we'll get it fixed. Maybe tomorrow we can invite some friends over for Taco Tuesday to forget about this, huh? Does that sound like fun?" Once I brought her eyes up to me, I continued. "After tomorrow, let's talk because I'm sure I can help get you caught up on payments too."

She looked up at me with a sadness so deep that I'd never seen before. "Cam, I love you. I'm sorry I'm such a horrible person to you."

"Beautiful, you are not a horrible person to me. You make me *so* happy, and I need you to know that." I assured her, moving onto the bed so she could lie on my chest. She continued to cry for a bit longer as I stroked her hair until we both fell asleep for a short nap. All I knew how to do was comfort with words.

Once we had woken up and Shaina's tears had dried, we sat around in the living room watching HBO waiting for Dave to get off work so he could come fix the car. Around five thirty, he sent me a text.

Dave: Hey, man, I've worked all day. Can we do this tomorrow?
Cameron: Of course.

"Dave needs to push to tomorrow . . ."

"My car, Cameron, I need my car!" She scolded.

"Shaina," I calmly began, "Dave's been working all day. He'll come over tomorrow for Taco Tuesday and he'll diagnose it, and if we still need to get parts, we'll get it fixed on Wednesday."

She turned to storm off upstairs shouting, "Whatever. It's all about what's convenient for you!"

Her anger didn't match the situation. I had two cars, and she knew she could drive one of mine if need be; plus, it was only an extra day of waiting. I shook my head in exasperation but stayed on the couch. She just needed to cool down, so I'd give her a break.

Early the next morning, Tuesday, I woke up before Shaina and snuck down to make her iced coffee. When I returned to the bedroom, Shaina was up, and she was packing up all her stuff.

What are you doing?"

"I have a shit life, and I'm sick of it." She emphasized this by angrily throwing a shoe into her bag. "Can I use your car today? I'll find a friend to come fix my car tonight."

My brow furrowed, utterly perplexed. This was now at least the third time we'd had a conversation about this damn car, and every time I thought we reached a solution, Shaina's mind went rogue. "What the fuck are you talking about, Shaina? Dave is coming tonight. We already bought the part. Why are you so adamant on doing this your own way, even when you say you can't?"

She finished grabbing the last of her things and then walked right past me out the door. "Okay, whatever you want!" I called after her. "Your coffee is ready downstairs, and the car is running!" A few moments later I heard the kitchen door slam shut.

The day went along as if we didn't even know each other, talking very little until just before she finished her shift.

> **Shaina:** Who are we inviting to Taco Tuesday?
> **Cameron:** I wasn't sure you still wanted to do it, but I know Brody and Claire said they would come when I talked to them about it yesterday. I'll confirm and see if they can bring a date, have a little couples party. I'm assuming you still want Dave to come by to look at the car?
> **Shaina:** Yes, please.
> **Cameron:** Okay, see ya home soon.

Chapter 22

THE MAN ABOVE ME

AFTER THE NIGHTMARE – June 25, 2020

I t's one year later, June twenty-fourth, the day before the anniversary of her suicide.

Although I wasn't entirely committed and hoped I'd talk myself out of it, thoughts of the pact I'd made with myself began to envelop me—that when I finally ran out of money, that would be my final day, the day that I would join Shaina.

I had fought hard but had given up hope:

Given up thinking I would get my kids back
Given up thinking I would get my career back
Given up thinking I would live anywhere but in my mom's base-

ment

Given up thinking I would ever be able to walk in public without
looking over my shoulder
Given up on ever finding love.

Dropping to my knees of my mother's basement tears fell and soaked in the hard cement.

Why had Shaina not seen another way out? I would have done anything to help her, but she was stubborn and would never accept my help. She captured the attention and adoration of everyone that knew her. And it finally hit me. After what Claire told me that night, maybe she felt all was lost, she had lost all hope of finding a way out of her situation, that once I learned of what she had done and my stance, I would be gone.

I really believe that Shaina did it, not because she wanted people at her funeral feeling sad for her, or because she wanted anyone to feel her pain, because if that had been the case, she'd opened up to more than just me. Shaina pulled the trigger because she felt she had no way out, no hope, no future, and no other option.

Still on my knees, tears streamed down my face and soaked into my shirt. God why, why, why, why? What was I supposed to learn? *Why had He allowed something so heartbreaking to happen to me? Why did I have to lose everything because Shaina took her life?*

I begged God, nearly screaming repeatedly to answer me. I was so confused, so lost, in so much hurt and pain. I now had no way out—Shaina had passed her hopelessness to me.

I had grown up in church learning that suicide was a terrible sin, one that always led you straight to hell. But, I was ready to join her; I just hoped to see her again. Still sobbing, I made one final request. "Dear God"—I spoke to the darkness of the room— "please forgive Shaina because I forgive her. I hold no resentment toward her, I just hope she's in a better place."

I continued. "Please watch over my boys. I hope someday they might understand the mistake I'm about to make. I surely never understood how someone could get to the point of giving up on life until all of this. There always seemed a way out before. Please forgive what I'm about to do, I just don't see another way out of this dark place, I'm sad, I'm lonely, I've lost everything, and I'm lost."

Feeling at peace with my final message, I wiped away the tears and got up. I was 70,000 words into the memoir that I was writing, and this was the final chapter. My last hope was that someone would read it and know what really happened, that it might save my name and my kids from living a life of shame. That some people would finally understand what really happened—my love for Shaina, the good and the bad, and the truth. The truth that, despite my best efforts to care for her, I couldn't save her from herself.

I had just enough to cover the last payment of my life insurance policy. I spent hours reading the fine print over and over, ensuring there was nothing about suicide that would nullify the policy. It had been well over the allotted six-month waiting period.

Hopefully, my boys would be taken care of in my absence.

I walked over to my heroin stash, enough to kill a city of first-time users, along with some cocaine I had bought off Natalie. Cocaine I learned multiplied the effects of heroin.

Mixing the two drugs was quite possibly the most dangerous way to shoot up, a sure death with a high enough dose. I went to the bathroom and closed the door. I knew friends that had accidentally killed themselves this way, shooting up way more than ever safe, thinking that their tolerance made them invincible.

The clock struck 2:00 a.m. I broke off the biggest piece I could fit into a spoon, then filled the spoon with water and cooked it. Using the syringe, I sucked it up before grabbing another piece, filling the spoon again with what I had cooked, and cooked the new charred black piece of death. Then I dumped as much coke into the spoon as I could and filled the spoon with my double concoction. I knew what I was doing and didn't want there to be any chance of failure.

When the syringe was full, the black liquid mixture was as dark and lustrous as an inkwell, beckoning me to its deep, toxic core. I tied off my arm and lay down on my bed. My veins were nearly gone from using so much over the months, and I prayed I'd be able to find one.

Suddenly, I felt a warmth on my forehead, like that night in my house when I'd fallen asleep in the spot Shaina lay bleeding.

She was here with me. It was time.

I poked around a few times before I found blood, and in one last breath I whispered, "Please forgive me, God, I'm broken." Then I injected the evil brew into my veins and released the tourniquet before everything went black.

I came to, in what felt like a dream my heart pounding so violently that it surely would explode. My surroundings were hazy and blurry, but I was able to determine I was still lying on my back in bed.

Dark silhouettes began to surround me and to the sides of me muttering words I couldn't understand.

I began screaming "why did you abandon me," screaming hoping God would hear me, the dark silhouettes chants began louder, my heart feeling like it was going to explode out of my chest.

I began to worry I would hold up and survive ... pressing on my chest, pumping it, hoping to help my heart explode ...this soon would be over when the shadows began reaching down towards me ... I knew I'd have to work harder and my pumping grew harder and more fierce ... when in an instant everything went calm like after a storm. A white shadow of a man came standing above me ... I couldn't see his face, the body looked like white smoke... he leaned over me and said, " I have not left you Cameron, we've been here the whole time."

I felt tears flowing down the sides of my face and all the sudden everything felt okay, and finally, "I'm not yet done with you, my son".

Then everything went black again.

Chapter 23

TACO TUESDAY

NIGHTMARE – June 25, 2019

Shaina came home in much higher spirits than she'd left that morning, seemingly less anxious now that Dave would be coming by tonight to try to fix her car. I'd confirmed with Claire and Brody that they were coming, and I asked them each to bring dates. About fifteen minutes before our four guests were due to arrive, I mustered up the courage to talk to Shaina.

"I don't think we should drink hard liquor babe, specifically Fireball, tonight. Let's have fun and enjoy tonight, no booze and no drama. Dave will diagnose your car, and if he can fix it with the part we bought then he'll do it tonight, otherwise we'll fix it as soon as we can."

"If he can't fix it tonight, then I'll just have the bank come pick it up," she said defeated. "I don't care anymore, I'm behind two payments anyway."

I was really beginning to have whiplash from her hot and cold behavior. "Shaina, I've told you before, if you need help getting current on payments, I can help you."

"But I'll have to pay you back!" She fumed, voice growing louder.

"Did I say that? We haven't even talked that far—"

She stood up and waved her hand at me. "I don't want to think about any of this right now, can we focus on the party?" Without awaiting a response, she stormed upstairs.

"What in the fuck is going on," I muttered under my breath. We could easily just fix the car tomorrow. I turned back to the kitchen counter to finish prepping the taco bar spread with bowls, plates, and all of the toppings I'd bought earlier, when I got a call from a client needing help with a software issue. I headed into my home office for some privacy.

"You can't just run the report until you've run a preprocess payroll," I'm telling the client, when without consideration I'm on the phone, Shaina calls out.

"Claire is on her way and she's asking if we need her to pick up anything?" As if we hadn't just had a tense conversation ten minutes ago.

Quickly covering the phone with my hand, I pinned her with narrowed eyes. "I'm on the phone with a client. Everything is out on the kitchen counter; you can go see if we're missing anything and let her know."

I'm only halfway concentrating on my business conversation now. *Ugh, I knew what she wanted Claire to pickup.* All I want is a drama-free night without liquor *for just one fucking night.*

Back downstairs in the kitchen, Shaina's leaning against the counter and texting. "Claire is bringing a guy she just met on a dating app and he looks cute," she said casually, back to her normal self.

"Good, I hope it works out for them. It would certainly help our relationship having a couple to go out with than single Claire around all the time. Oh, and I've set up the volleyball net out back. I have a playlist ready, and I brought out the Jenga set on the table. Anything we're missing?"

She sighed and looked around. "I don't think so." But I knew what she was missing. I walked up to her and pulled her into my arms. "Babe, listen, I know you want Fireball—"

"I know what you're going to say, and I agree, let's stick to just beer."

Relief flooding my body, I leaned in for a long kiss then picked her up and sat her on the counter to steal some more. I bounded up the stairs and in the bedroom I placed my wallet and keys on the nightstand before changing into something more comfortable.

Claire and Brody arrived at almost the exact same time, but both their dates were behind. The four of us were conversing in the kitchen when the doorbell rang and I jogged over to answer it.

Dave, still in his mechanic grease-stained overalls, stood on the porch and asked me to open the garage door. As I met him in there from the kitchen door, Dave was walking around the car, inspecting it.

"Should be the water pump," he confirmed, "but bad news is I don't have the parts I need to fix it today." Fuck. That was not going to go over well with Shaina.

"Okay, when do you think you'll be able to come back?"

"As long as I don't work too late tomorrow, I should be able to do it then."

Okay, not the worst news ever. I just had to tide Shaina over until tomorrow evening.

"Okay, buddy, thanks for stopping by to look at it," I said before Dave nodded and left.

As I walked into the kitchen, I pulled Shaina aside to deliver the news. "Dave feels it's the water pump, but he doesn't have all the tools to fix it tonight. I'm sorry, but he said he'd swing by tomorrow."

If looks could kill, Shaina would have killed me right then and there, but before she could yell at me Claire announced, "Tom is almost here, but he wants to know if we want anything from the liquor store?"

Shaina pivoted on her heels. "Have him pick up Fireball!"

My heart stopped. Before I could say a thing, she left the room. *Here we go. If you can't beat 'em, join 'em. I guess. Better strap in tonight, it may be a doozy,* I say to myself.

Tom, a tall guy in his late thirties with sandy-blond hair, arrives and proceeds to unpack the Fireball on the counter.

"Shots!" Shaina immediately screamed and ran to line up shot glasses for everyone.

We took our shots, and then a second round. By the third round, I had almost forgotten about Shaina's frustrations. Brody's date had not yet arrived, so I suggested we all go out back and play badminton until she got there. Hours later, his date, Avery, showed up—Ironically, it had meant to be a blind date, but the two quickly realized they'd met before. Perfect.

Finally. Let's get the party started. It appears things had taken a turn for the better.

"Who wants to play naughty Jenga?" I asked. All hands flew in the air except Claire's.

Naughty Jenga consisted of the same game play as regular Jenga, only the blocks had a truth or dare written on each one; the player who pulled the block had to comply with the instruction or they were out of the game.

I started a trial run to explain the rules and pulled a block that read, "Kiss either the person to the right or the left of you." Naturally, I kissed Shaina, pulling her in and French kissing her in front of the group.

Next, Shaina pulled a block that read, "Have you ever kissed someone of the same sex?"

Her pale skin tinged pink as she quietly said, "Yes."

I was feeling pretty buzzed from the fireball, so I nudged her and loudly cajoled. "Speak up! We didn't hear you, Shaina!" Her embarrassment faded and was replaced by a smile, throwing her hands in the air and exclaiming, "Yes!" gaining a round of laughter.

Tom went next. "Real or fake boobs?" He looked around—Claire and Shaina had fake boobs, and I knew he wasn't about to get himself in trouble. "Fake," he announced, but I didn't believe him.

Then Brody pulled a block that read, "Favorite sex position, and why?" The women in the room were fixated on his response. Brody could be a model, with toned muscles and tattoos.

"I like to lay the woman on her side and ride her leg as I enter her. I feel with that position I can go deepest."

The Fireball had gone straight to my head, leaving me without a filter. "That's funny," I smirked. "I had Shaina in that position last week." I started laughing but no one followed. Shaina gaped at me, her face growing redder by the second.

"What the fuck is wrong with you, Cameron? That's personal," she spat before striding into the kitchen, Tom following behind her.

I rolled my eyes and took another shot. The room was so silent you could hear a pin drop. I ushered to the group. "Let's keep playing," hoping to break the awkwardness.

We played a few more rounds, the four of us standing in a circle around the table while Shaina and Tom continued taking shots in the kitchen. I once turned to look at Shaina, who appeared to be leaning in for a kiss with Tom. I quickly approached to try to push them apart by placing a hand on each of their chests, but since Tom was a much bigger guy, all of my force went to Shaina, who fell down. I wasn't immediately aware of what I had done as Shaina started sobbing on the floor.

"Shit, Shaina, I'm sorry, I didn't mean to push you—"

Shaina rose to her feet, cocked her arm back, and landed a right hook in my jaw, followed by a left hook, then another right hook... I was so embarrassed about pushing her over that I stuck out my chin for her just as Claire grabbed Shaina and yelled, "OK, that's enough!" before handing Shaina over to Brody, who escorted Shaina out back.

Tom mumbled, "I'm out of here," walking out the front door, leaving Claire, Avery, and me in the living room. I walked into the kitchen, stopping to catch my breath for a moment, when Claire came up behind me.

"Cam, you were my friend before I knew Shaina and I . . . shit, I want you to know Shaina cheated on you last weekend in Wendover. She's planning on leaving you after her car is fixed." She looked like she was about to cry.

My face fell. "What the fuck did you just say?"

Shaina had been acting weird since the car problem, but this couldn't be true. I talked to her in Wendover, saw pictures of just her and the girls, heard the girls in the background when she called, and we must've exchanged a hundred text messages.

This was a lie. "I think it's time for you to go, Claire."

I looked to Avery, who had walked in at the same time Claire delivered her bombshell news, and I knew Avery hadn't been drinking much tonight. "Can you take Claire home?" Claire was just trying to cause trouble, which was the absolute last thing I needed after accidentally pushing Shaina. Avery nodded, and the two left out the front door.

Brody and Shaina emerged from outside and I told Brody that Avery left to drive home Claire. Brody ran out behind them, probably to say good-bye and apologize for the turbulent first date. Shaina came up behind me. "Cameron, I need to tell you something," she started, but I had tunnel vision from what Claire had just dropped on me.

I turned to face her. "Claire just told me you cheated on me in Wendover. Is that true?" Shaina immediately began crying again.

"She told you *what?*" she exclaimed, before running out the front door with everyone else. Sighing, wanting a few minutes of peace, I began to put away the food and do the dishes in a zombie-like state when Avery came back inside.

"I'm going to take Claire home, but I need to make sure you and Shaina are going to be okay. She said she's going to stay here tonight."

"Avery, I'm sorry this has been a total shit show, but I can assure you Shaina and I will be just fine. You have my word." It wasn't exactly anything new. Shaina and I had blowouts often, but we'd always make up. This was just a normal night in our twisted relationship.

Avery offered me a weak smile before hugging me and turning to leave out the door, almost crashing into Shaina who ran back inside and up the stairs while I stayed down to finish cleaning.

After loading in the last plate and running the dishwasher, I turned my head up to the ceiling and sighed. *Why couldn't we just have one normal night.*

After ensuring the front door was locked, I trudged up the stairs to the master bedroom. The door was closed. I tried it and it was locked. Twisting the handle a few times to make sure it wasn't stuck, I realized that Shaina had locked herself in. I pressed my ear against the door but heard nothing inside, not even the sound of her crying.

Frustrated, I banged on the door.
"Shaina, you can't lock me out of my house!"

Epilogue

When I came to, my only thought was how to stop the tremendous pounding in my chest. My eyes snapped open and I immediately recoiled under the bright lights, which were now stinging my teary eyes. Blinking hard from the impenetrable glare, I looked around at the familiar 2x4 barren walls of my mom's basement.

Was I alive?

I guardedly hoisted myself into a sitting position. I was still in bed, where I'd taken the lethal shot. My eyes darted toward my arm, covered in blood, the syringe laying by my side. The room was swaying a bit. Or maybe that was my heart causing the whole bed to shake.

Maybe I was hallucinating.

Maybe this was my purgatory.

A feminine giggle from the other side of the room ripped my head to the right.

"Cameron, catch," it declared, just as I turned to see a rubber ball flying toward me before smashing into my face.

My vision began to clear, as did the swirling fog in my brain—I recognized the voice. Victoria. One of my ex-girlfriends who I hadn't seen in a year. I staggered toward the office chair next to my bed, the one I had grown accustomed to over the last few months when my back pain was so agonizing I could barely walk. This time I only needed it to keep from falling over due to my haze. I stood still to gulp in air before finally making it to the chair and slid to the dark corner of the room where Victoria's voice came.

"Throw the ball back." Victoria's voice seemed to be materializing out of nowhere now back underneath my bed. The ball was magically in my hands again. I slightly sank forward and tossed the ball again. Mere seconds later, the ball rolled back toward the chair and I laughed. *I laughed! I* was playing catch with a disembodied voice and all I could do was laugh.

"Why are you in my mom's basement, Victoria?" I asked, full of bewildered curiosity.

"I'm just here to play."

Her voice was happy, casual, and matter-of-fact. We continued tossing the ball back and forth when nearby footsteps echoed down the stairs, breaking up our fun. The doorknob turned and my mom's head poked around the corner.

"What are you doing? It's three in the morning." Her quizzical eyes pinned me with uncertainty "Turn off the TV and go to bed Cameron".

"Mom, Victoria is here," I explained, as I sat in the chair holding an imaginary ball, a smile plastered on my face. "She's underneath my bed. We're throwing this ball back and forth." I reached out to show her the ball and frowned at my empty hand. The ball was gone.

Mom stared at me with sleepy eyes topped by hefted eyebrows. "Cam, Victoria isn't here. You need to go to bed." And with that, she turned off the lights and trudged back upstairs.

The emptiness that now filled the room kicked me out of my daze, and I was suddenly very aware that something weird was happening. The last thing I remembered was the needle in my arm and the conviction to leave this world.

Scooting the chair back over to my bed, I grabbed my phone off the nightstand, exposing the dried blood coating my left arm. *Had Mom not seen this? And where did Victoria go?*

A deep state of exhaustion began to cloud my mind again, no doubt the residual effects of the massive dose of heroin and cocaine I'd injected. Pulling myself back into bed, the delirium from the toxins began to grow faint as I fell into a deep sleep.

The sun was pricking at the darkness through the window, but it no longer burned my eyes. My heart had resumed its steady, normal drumbeat and I wasn't seeing the ghosts of girlfriends past. It was a miracle that I was alive, and I knew it. But even more, I knew there was a reason for it.

I think . . . maybe I was supposed to live. There had to be a purpose after all this pain and suffering; surely, God wouldn't let me live if I was supposed to be dead right now?

Yet, even with a tingling sensation of hope after cheating death, I still had one major question to resolve: *how am I supposed to rebuild from here?*

I was now forty years old living in my mom's basement; the woman I loved shot herself in front of me; my kids wanted nothing to do with me; I had either lost or sold most of my possessions; and my last dollar was spent on a life insurance policy that my kids would no longer be cashing in soon. To top it off, I had acquired a crippling drug addiction—how would my body tolerate a withdrawal?

It was Friday and I still had enough heroin to last me through Monday morning. But instead of using up my last stash, I lay in bed. Shaina and I had talked about our goals often, yet she never had the chance to achieve them. If I could make goals then, I could do it now. I would achieve them for both Shaina *and* me. After all, this wasn't the first time I'd fought my way out of a deep hole.

I lay there all day, strategizing the overhaul of my life. People at my old job used to call me "relentless": I was stubborn, and if I wanted something, there wasn't a thing in this world keeping me from it.

Twenty-four hours after attempting suicide, I had made up my mind. I was going to crawl, scratch, and kick my way back to happiness. The first step was getting off these drugs.

Monday morning I woke up in a cold sweat, my bones aching to the core. There are no words to explain an opiate withdrawal, and I can't explain it now. The drawer to my heroin stash called out to me, egging me on. I ignored it.

My mom was still asleep upstairs when I turned on the shower. I ran the water as hot as I could get it and soaked my bones until they were numb, trying to wash off the withdrawal, wash off any lingering thoughts of "you can't do this."

After throwing on my clothes, I walked out the door. I was three months behind on my truck payments and was near to losing it soon. *Coincidence?* But for now, it was still mine and it was going to serve me a purpose today.

The early morning sun accompanied me on my drive, the pastel pink and burnt orange hues gliding up behind the mountains. There was a different air today in Utah, one filled with something I hadn't felt in months: motivation. As I drove down the freeway, it was as if I could feel the small pressure of two people sitting on either shoulder: the angel and the devil. The angel told me to stay focused on my destination. The devil was telling me to find a quick cash grab to buy more heroin.

My leather seats were drenched in sweat by the time I pulled off I-15 and made my way to the parking lot. The truck's clock displayed 5:00 a.m.—just in time for the methadone clinic to open. The line to get in wrapped around the building, mostly filled with the city's homeless population. I shuddered to think joining that population wasn't far from my reality. As I walked past the front of the line to make my way to the back, a man wearing dirty white clothes grabbed my arm to stop me. *Shit, I didn't want any trouble.*

I sheepishly turned toward the man, ready for a fight, but my gaze was met with kind, piercing blue eyes. "You're among friends," he assured me, "and you're at the right place."

My jaw slackened momentarily before bursting into tears, and a woman a few people behind us ran over to envelop me in a hug. Before I knew it, two men grabbed my hands and led me inside. I was a mess and the old saying "takes one to know one" came to mind.

The counselor's office was sterile except for a picture frame on his desk, facing away from me. I sat in the metal chair across from his desk, exhaling everything that had happened to me, explaining my drug history, what had happened with Shaina, and my current drug use. His name was Gordon, and he promised he'd help me. It was a major step one in my grander scheme of rebuilding.

The next day I applied for a job and was shocked when I got a call back. I guess despite my history, they were impressed by my decade-long sales career. The position was 100 percent commission, but *still*, it was something.

Small traces of hope glimmered inside me, but I remained levelheaded. If I got too excited too quickly and then something fell through, I would undoubtedly unravel and spiral back to where I started. Instead, I opted for cautious optimism. After securing the position, I began setting up a more formal home office in my mom's basement. There was a gentle pep in my step.

My mom, of course, was ecstatic when I told her about the job. As much as I loved to see her so excited, her relief also fueled my guilt. I had put her through so much since moving in with her, delving into a nightmare world of drugs that altered my behavior leaving her confused and worried.

Now in the mornings, I'd be up early and say goodbye before "heading off to work," though at this time of day I was secretly meeting with Gordon at the methadone clinic. I wasn't quite ready to tell her about it yet, but she was a main force of motivation to stay sober. I owed it to her.

The methadone helped reduce my cravings and the severity of my withdrawal symptoms. I met with Gordon nearly daily for a month, steadily increasing my dosage to where I finally felt comfortable to be alone with my thoughts. I felt *good.* So good, in fact, that I already convinced myself that I could start reducing my dose and get off the methadone completely.

Walking into Gordon's office one morning I decided I'd tell him how good I was doing. He'd be so impressed by my fortitude he'd begin tapering me off. I had already rehearsed my acceptance speech the night before.

When he called me in, I sat down with all the confidence of someone on antidepressants who thought they were "happy" enough to stop the medication. I exhaled deeply and delivered my speech.

"Gordon, I don't want to be a lifetime member of the methadone clinic like some people I see here. I'm ready to get off once and for all."

He pierced me with a peculiar stare, then sighed incredulously. "Cameron," he began, shaking his head. "I see this a lot, and it's not a good idea. Methadone is to get you off the psychological idea that you need to use drugs and level you out. You need some time feeling normal before you get off. If you pull the plug too early, you'll likely relapse."

My shoulders sagged and I could tell he was gauging my reaction carefully.

"That being said, I'm not going to tell you 'no.' If you really, *really* want to stop now, I can call the doctor and see if he'll approve it."

Though I was disappointed in his response, my resolve to get better—paired with my unwavering stubbornness—was stronger than his advice. I had made my mind up. "Yes, I'd like you to ask the doctor, Gordon."

He shook his head once more and picked up his desk phone to call the on-site doctor. I watched intently as Gordon relayed my message, followed by a few *mhmm*s before hanging up. "The doctor won't approve it this early," he confirmed.

Fuck. Guess I'll need to form a Plan B.

Because of COVID's new social restrictions, the clinic was now closed for two days of the week—Saturday and Sunday—on those days, they'd send you home with two take-home doses. This was the answer to my problem. This was how I'd decrease my dosage myself.

My take-home doses went unused, and I'd grimace through the ensuing sickness until the following Monday when I'd go to the clinic in person. On the weekdays, I showed up and would wait in line until I reached the nurses station. They'd confirm your dosage before handing you a plastic cup in which you were expected to drink the cherry liquid right then and there in front of them. I'd swallow half and leave half in my mouth to spit out as I left the parking lot. Come hell or high water, I was doing this with or without the clinic's help.

At work, I introduced myself as CJ in an effort to disguise my real identity, though it was in vain. Anytime I sat across from a new prospect, my paranoia would tell me the prospect knew who I was—the monster the news portrayed me as. In a misguided effort to control the situation, I'd end up word vomiting my story to new prospects, only to never hear from the person ever again. I felt uncomfortably rocky in this new position when I compared it to how well I had been doing in my job before Shaina's death. My confidence in my career was faltering, but I still held on to my faith.

Six months passed and I had lowered my dose to literally nothing. But, I was still living in my mom's basement. My performance at work was incomparable to my previous sales job; where I'd once been making six figures a year, I now made only ten thousand so far.

If I was going to truly rebuild, I needed my independence back. I needed a place to call home – on my own.

I had to stomach the fact that fifteen years' worth of savings was gone. I had to start from the bottom up, just like I did when I was twenty—only this time I couldn't rely on drugs to turn me into a top earner.

One morning I decided to go to the DMV and take the CDL (commercial driver's license) test to see what would happen. I had previously owned dump trucks as a side business, which was whereas that side of the business was a total failure mainly because without my CDL, I was the blind leading the blind. This time would be different and maybe I could put all my efforts into something besides sales. I'd paid my own drivers around twenty-five dollars an hour, which was an amount I felt I could live on. To my shock, I completed the test just shy of passing. After going home to do a little brush-up on my knowledge, I went and took the test the next day and passed.

With my CDL in hand, the last step of my life-rebuilding plan was to officially taper off the methadone. I spent the next month taking as little as I possibly could, rationing off my take-home doses instead of going to the clinic for in-person doses. Underneath the months of heroin use was a mound of emotions I had buried away. They were coming to the forefront now and I didn't have drugs to numb the pain this time. I'd have to trudge through the dirt alone as I spent nearly every night for months crying until I fell asleep with nothing to now mask the pain I felt.

One day I was chugging along at work driving an old dusty dump truck when I paused and realized I hadn't taken the methadone in a few days and felt fine. The side effects had vanished into thin air. The finality of getting off the opiates was not like the times in my early twenties, hunched up in the fetal position in a pool of sweat, trembling through seconds that felt like hours. This time was different. The feeling of accomplishment was immeasurable and unexplainable, something I never thought was attainable six months prior. I could be normal again. I could actually get my life back.

My workday looked a lot different now than it had in the past, juggling both my payroll job and driving dump trucks. I'd set up a green screen behind the driver's seat in the dump truck so I could host virtual meetings with prospects from the payroll job. I was making twice the progress as usual.

I was working longer hours than I had in my previous sales job to make up for my insecurities during prospect meetings, but the long hours spent calling and driving became a main source of therapy for me, allowing me to process the years-long worth of thoughts I had banished.

I had been driving my friend's dump truck, starting with thirty-hour weeks that turned into more than fifty-hour weeks pretty quickly. I was maximizing my time while driving, which left me with personal time to work on this memoir.

I also sought out the support of a therapist who helped guide me through my trauma, allowing me to explore my emotions in a way that none of my friends or family members could help me with.

I finally moved out of my mom's basement and began renting a small three- bedroom house.

The first couple weeks in my new place were a tad unsettling; I often worried that I forced myself to be on my own too early.

Quickly settling into a new routine, I also found that having my own personal space was comforting. It was exhilarating to be self-reliant once again, capable of earning money, paying bills, keeping my truck, and having my own bedroom again. My family helped me move in with what furniture I still had left stored in mom's house. It wasn't much after many of my belongings were trashed, but it was enough.

After six months of getting clean, finding two new jobs, moving out, and seeing a therapist, I was finally able to mourn Shaina's death in the way my heart and body needed to.

Now in my new house, I sat down at my computer desk, opened up the draft of the memoir, and began to rewrite this story and fill in the gaps.

Two years later, my life looks a lot different. Working the two jobs allowed me to come up with a down payment for a dump truck. I was able to restart my trucking company. Today, I am a successful entrepreneur again.

After getting sober and working through my trauma, I was able to re-establish a relationship with my boys. By the time this is published we'll have been to Mexico twice, camping, driving go-karts, the nickel arcade, and playing board games. It's almost like it never happened. My oldest even moved in with me to make it more convenient for him to go to college. We talk about life and I'm proud to be able to guide them in both good and bad.

My life these days is a lot different than it was before Shaina died, but it's nothing like my life the year and a half after her death. Today, I'm happy. When I was making over a quarter million a year, I can't even say I was happy then. I assumed I was, but looking back it's clear to see the chaos that followed me.

My relationship with my boys had already begun to suffer when I was dating Shaina. I threw money at my problems instead of facing an issue head-on or reflecting internally. I was a middle-aged man obsessed with being young again instead of feeling blessed with the things already in my life.

I used to judge success on the amount of money you made and the materialistic things you owned. Gone now are my days of self-medicating with partying, women, alcohol, and drugs. Unfortunately, it took my attempting suicide to fix my way of thinking, which changed my addictive habits. Not the best way to handle things.

What kept me sober all those years between my first marriage and Shaina's death was a sense of mindfulness. Being sober means being careful with your choices, but most importantly it requires a good mental state of mind to be able to make good choices. I've learned that when my mental health breaks down, so do my choices, and I didn't have the tools I have now to repair my mental health in time before relapsing.

A big part of me believes that breaking my back was fate. The other day, someone on a radio talk show said, "heroin saved my life." At first, I scoffed.

How did drugs save my life?! But without the pain pills and the heroin, I can't be sure I'd be where I am today. I wholeheartedly believe breaking my back and the months that followed were an act of God. I can't be sure that the sober Cameron three months after Shaina's death would be alive right now if it weren't for the addiction masking those painful emotions, or at least in the mindset to believe he has a promising life to live.

Most everyone's disbelief of my recounting of events in this story stems from the idea that Shaina "wasn't the type" to take her own life because she was "always so happy." And sure, Shaina was great at masking her feelings and putting on a big smile for the outside world. But inside, she was drowning. As far as I know, I was the only person she confided in about her suicidal thoughts. I do feel we had a special connection when things were good and maybe that gave her comfort sharing her darkest fears with me.

That's the thing about depression and suicide that you hear over and over again—it's rarely from the person you expect. Despite a growing trend toward promoting mental health awareness, people who are depressed can still find that it's taboo to talk about their feelings or scared that admitting they see a therapist marks them with a big red CRAZY label on their forehead.

And treating depression at this stage is, lamentably, the most crucial time, because once someone has reached the point of deciding to take their own life, you'll never hear about it. It happened with Shaina and it happened with me; someone so deep in the depths of despair doesn't want to be talked out of their decision.

I've replayed that night in my mind thousands of times. It's bizarre—the entire night plays as a blur in my head, like the aftermath of an explosion, but the memory of Shaina standing in the doorway felt like it lasted ten minutes, as if time had slowed.

I want to believe Shaina didn't mean to pull the trigger, that it was an accident. I never kept my pistols loaded, let alone cocked, so she had the intent to do something, but I think it happened quicker than she expected.

The pistol had a hair trigger and was nickel plated a.k.a. *heavy*. I remember watching the gun in her hand with her finger on the trigger, sitting against her right thigh. She swung it backward a little, as if to get momentum to pull the heavy gun upward, before swaying it up and next to her head. It went off almost simultaneously as if the momentum of the pistol accidentally caught the trigger with her finger. Then again me and John finding a charm of hers in the exact same place makes it hard not to believe it wasn't premeditated. If it wasn't premediated, the only other explanation is an angel must've placed them there for us.

I play those final moments over and over in my head. I often wish she would've had the chance to say something: a simple explanation like, "I give up," or one final "I love you." Hell, I would've even taken "I hate you"—anything that would've given me precious moments to try to talk her out of it.

I'm still searching for my higher purpose, for why I was saved the night of my overdose. And now, I have the support of my family, friends, sons, and God to guide me. As I continue to rebuild my life, I think about how sharing my story of Shaina's death could have a lasting impact on someone, who may feel hopeless or without direction.

I recall our conversations lying in bed where she'd express her complete lack of motivation, and her need to cover up her sadness with drinking. Clear signs of depression that I recognize in hindsight—that I wish I would've known how to deal with before it was too late. I think about using my skills in sales and my love of working with people, and how I could transfer that to helping someone thinking about taking their own life.

I may set up a foundation at some point to do just that. Maybe my purpose was to write this memoir in the hopes it will touch one person, or someone who knows someone, who may be at the point of suicide, to read a first-hand account of how suicide affects all who love them. Or perhaps help someone recognize warning signs.

And maybe I have yet to find out what my purpose is. What I do know is today, and every day going forward, I choose life.

Not a day goes by where I don't think of Shaina—her smile, our laughter, the times we lay in bed and I'd tell her jokes, listening to music together, or even just holding her in my arms as we drifted to sleep. The memories are still clear, but the pain that accompanies them grows fainter.

Since meeting Shaina, I've felt a deeper connection to my spirituality, far stronger than I did before, to the point of being overwhelmed by it.

I've felt Shaina's spirit, as evidenced by anecdotes in this book. My reckless partying with Shaina put me on a crash course to death, but God had to intervene and remind me of who is in charge.

Miracles happen everyday even as simple as a breath. But miracles are not always what you think. It's not someone overcoming a deadly disease or being saved in a car accident by a matter of inches. Miracles are often disguised as a flat tire that just saved you from the person running the red light just ahead. Or the loss of a job you weren't meant to be in. I've come to see miracles much more clearly now. I embrace setbacks and hardships now because that's when I know angels are shaping my future.

Many people close to me know how big my ego is and how stubborn I am, but God has humbled me to my core. He removed everything good in my life. He stripped me naked of the woman I loved, the career I was so proud of, the kids I would do anything for, and all my silly possessions. And yet, now, today, after losing all of that, I have the strongest connection with God I've ever had.

I'm happy.

Since beginning this memoir, a National Suicide Hotline has been established.

Your life matters!! No matter how much we convince ourselves in those dark moments it doesn't, it matters to someone. I lost everything and had convinced myself I had nothing left to live for, yet look at me now.

Mental Health is a serious issue especially with how fast our world is evolving. My next step is to setup a foundation to help those in need, but in the meantime, should you find yourself with thoughts of suicide, ***PLEASE*** - I beg you - pick up the phone and call the **National Suicide Prevention and Mental Health Crisis Hotline and dial 988 to talk** to someone.

Our minds are our worst enemy in this state, but a friend will never convince you to do such a tragic horrible thing. People love you! You are loved! Choose 2 live! #C2L

Follow me on *https://www.instagram.com/beautiful_memoir/*

Acknowledgments

First, I'd like to thank Glen Thomas for believing in me and my innocence, although I'm sure he'd say belief wasn't needed. He knew just as I knew that he was the one to represent me. God led you to me as I'm sure you're led to all your clients in need of an honest and trustworthy attorney.

Second, I'd like to thank the hardworking detectives that worked on my case. Although mistakes were made, our law enforcement officers are tasked with the life changing decision to pull the trigger or not, just as they are when deciding whether to press charges. Had the detectives not been thorough and not spent countless hours processing evidence and statements, my life would be very different today. Likewise, I suspect if there was even a shred of evidence to suggest I was guilty, I'm sure they would have formally pressed charges. Thank you for doing a thankless job, and for taking great care of the people whose lives are in your hands.

Third, I'd like to thank my editor, Kitty. I came to her with a story to tell, but Kitty took that story and carefully crafted it into something I couldn't have done on my own. You are nothing short of amazing!

Fourth, I'd like to thank Gary S. James, jamesgangcreative.com It took two years to write this memoir and Gary polished it and help me perfect it both as a final editor and formatter. Thank you for your craftmanship.

Last but not least, I'd like to thank God for the miracle of life he continued to grant me after my attempted suicide. If it wasn't for Him saving me that fateful day, this memoir would not be possible, nor would my newfound relationship with my kids. Despite our occasional struggles and disagreements, He gave me the gift of life, sobriety, two sons, and the opportunity to experience the Beautiful love of Shaina. You are an amazing God.